The Keystone Library

THE KEYSTONE LIBRARY contains many of the notable works published during recent years. The subjects embrace:

Memoirs and Biography, Travel and Sport, History and Egyptology, Belles Lettres and Poetry.

Wherever possible production is identical with the original editions; illustrations are included; individuality is retained and not lost in the uniformity of a series.

5s. *net*, ILLUSTRATED

MEMOIRS AND BIOGRAPHY

My Early Life	WINSTON S. CHURCHILL
Frederick Edwin, Earl of Birkenhead: The First Phase	BY HIS SON
The Autobiography of Margot Asquith (2 vols.)	MARGOT ASQUITH
Nuda Veritas	CLARE SHERIDAN
Myself and My Friends. With an aside by G. B. S.	LILLAH McCARTHY
The Life of Horace Walpole	STEPHEN GWYNN
The Life and Friendships of Dean Swift	STEPHEN GWYNN
The Regent and his Daughter	DORMER CRESTON
Sarah, Duchess of Marlborough	KATHLEEN CAMPBELL
Florence Nightingale	I. B. O'MALLEY
A Very Gallant Gentleman	COMMANDER L. C. BERNACCHI
Anatole France Himself	JEAN JACQUES BROUSSON
The Wizard of Homburgh and Monte Carlo	COUNT CORTI
Men and Horses I have Known (3s. 6d. net)	GEORGE LAMBTON

HISTORY

The Life and Times of Akhnaton	ARTHUR WEIGALL
The Glory of the Pharoahs	ARTHUR WEIGALL
Alexander the Great	ARTHUR WEIGALL
The Life and Times of Cleopatra	ARTHUR WEIGALL
Marc Antony	ARTHUR WEIGALL
Nero	ARTHUR WEIGALL
John Hampden's England	JOHN DRINKWATER
Ghengis Khan: Emperor of all Men	HAROLD LAMB
The Crusades: Iron Men and Saints	HAROLD LAMB
The Crusades: The Flame of Islam	HAROLD LAMB
Baghdad: The City of Peace	RICHARD COKE

TRAVEL

East Again	WALTER B. HARRIS
The Conquest of the South Pole	J. GORDON HAYES
South America	KASIMIR EDSCHMID
Round the World with Rod and Rifle	MAJOR P. M. STEWART
The Wheels of Ind	JOHN W. MITCHELL

BELLES LETTRES, POETRY

Thoughts and Adventures	WINSTON S. CHURCHILL
Landmarks in French Literature	LYTTON STRACHEY
Selected Poems	SIR WILLIAM WATSON
Six Famous Living Poets	COULSON KERNAHAN
My Brother's Face	DHAN GOPAL MUKERJI
Egyptian Tales and Romances	

The Author, 1922

THE GLORY
OF THE PHARAOHS

BY

ARTHUR WEIGALL

KEYSTONE

LIBRARY

LONDON
Thornton Butterworth Ltd

First published . . . . *March* 1923
Second Impression . . . *March* 1923
First Impression in the Keystone Library . . 1936

CONTENTS

LIST OF ILLUSTRATIONS

PUBLISHER'S FOREWORD

In view of the fact that Mr. Arthur Weigall, while inclined to obscure himself owing to a distaste for public life, is widely known in several fields of activity, the Publisher has felt that a short foreword to this volume will be of interest to those who have wondered as to the author's identity.

The writer of these entertaining and scholarly essays was born in 1880, being the son of the late Major Arthur Weigall and grandson of the Rev. Edward Weigall, M.A., Vicar of Buxton, Derbyshire : a descendant of an officer of that name who came to England as Equerry to William of Orange in 1698.

Various members of the family of Weigall have attained distinction in England as scholars, painters, sculptors, authors, and diplomats ; but the writer of these essays was originally destined for the Army, and for that reason was educated at Wellington College. Later, however, he matriculated for New College, Oxford, causing some flutter in that academic circle by offering Egyptian hiero-glyphic texts as his special subject for the examination ; but he abandoned his 'Varsity career in 1900 in order to go out to Egypt as assistant excavator to Professor Flinders Petrie.

At the early age of twenty-four he was appointed Inspector General of Antiquities for Upper Egypt by his friend, Lord Cromer, a post for which his scholarship, his administrative ability, and his great energy eminently fitted him. This arduous position he held until 1914 ; and during his tenure of office he carried out the most important reforms with a view to the preservation and safeguarding of antiquities, the suppression of lawless excavation, and the advancement of the science of Egyptology. He was present at most of the great dis-coveries made during those years, and in particular he supervised the excavations in the Valley of the Tombs of

the Kings at Thebes, in which some of the famous royal
sepulchres were discovered.

Besides his administrative and archæological work he
found time to make several daring expeditions into the
unexplored regions of the Eastern Desert ; and in these
years he also wrote a number of Egyptological books,
including *A Guide to the Antiquities of Upper Egypt and
Lower Nubia : Travels in the Upper Egyptian Deserts :
The Life and Times of Akhnaton, Pharaoh of Egypt : The
Life and Times of Cleopatra*, etc.   He also made a considerable study of the political situation in the Near East ;
and his book *A History of Events in Egypt from* 1798 *to*
1914, and various papers in the *Fortnightly Review*, had
considerable influence on British policy.   For some
time, too, Mr. Weigall was a member of the Catalogue
Staff of the Cairo Museum, and in that connection wrote
an important work of a mathematical character on ancient
Weights and Balances.

These books, and his many papers in the *Nineteenth
Century, Fortnightly Review, Blackwood's Magazine*, etc.,
were received with a chorus of praise ; and he was soon
recognised as the foremost writer upon Egyptology, and
a master of felicitous expression and description.   His
friend the late President Roosevelt, writing in the *Outlook*,
spoke of him as having " that supreme quality of seeing
the living body through the dry bones and then making
others see it also ", and as being " not merely accurate,
but truthful with the truth that comes only from insight
and broadminded grasp of essential facts, added to
exhaustive study and wide learning."

" Mr. Weigall is one of the best living authorities on
Upper Egypt," said the *Athenæum*, " and his delightful
books are justly admired."   " He is a scholar," said the
Times, " deeply versed in Egyptian archæology and history and himself a partner in many discoveries . . . He
is an idealist gifted with insight and sympathy."   The
Observer described him as " a scholar who has let learning
quicken and not dull his wits ; " and the *Pall Mall*

Gazette spoke of him as " the key to one of the richest
storehouses the world contains." " He makes the sights,
the sounds, the very air of the Egyptian deserts visit the
senses of his readers with a keenness that is almost painful," wrote the *Westminister Gazette.* " He is the scholar-
sportsman," said the *Times* again, " gifted with a fine
sensitiveness to the mystery and romance of ancient
things."

In 1914, after receiving high honours from various
governments, and when his administrative work and his
writings had brought him to a position of eminence, he
suffered a breakdown in health, due to his exertions in
Egypt ; and he was obliged to resign and to return to
England. Here, during his convalescence, he occupied
his spare time by painting designs for stage scenery ; and
from 1915 to 1918 many of the leading spectacular pro-
ductions at the chief London theatres owed their success
to his art.

As in the case of his historical writings, so in that of
this hobby, his work was received with unanimous praise.
We read of a ballet of his at the Alhambra as being " one
of the most beautiful stage pictures ever seen "; of a scene
at the Palace Theatre " so exquisite as to make a success
of the production without anything else " (*Tatler*) ; of
another scene for which " there is no measure of praise
too high " (*Sunday Times*) ; and so on throughout the
entire Press.

Mr. Weigall, however, having deeply influenced the
whole art of stage decoration in this country by intro-
ducing bold simplicity of design and pure colour and
light effects, did not long continue to spend his time in
this manner ; and with the return of health he resumed
his archæological work and set himself to the long task
of preparing material for works on Egyptian art and
history, and on comparative ethics, which are not yet
completed. Meanwhile, and perhaps to some extent as
a means of livelihood, he wrote three novels : *Madeline
of the Desert* (1920), *The Dweller in the Desert* (1921), en-

titled *Burning Sands* in the United States, and *Bedouin Love* (1922). These books, again hailed with high tributes from the Press, have attained great popularity and have passed through many editions. From time to time he also wrote the lyrics for songs which have obtained wide appreciation, and he was the author of various little sketches, both dramatic and comic, which have been seen upon the London stage.

For some months in 1921 he came before the public in another guise. An article of his in the *Nineteenth Century*, in which he pointed out the influence being exercised by the Kinematograph on our national life, attracted the attention of the late Lord Northcliffe, who invited Mr. Weigall to write a long series of articles in the *Daily Mail* on the subject. This led to an intensive study of the whole subject of " films ", and the articles, of a fervently patriotic character, had the effect of removing some unpleasant features from the motion-picture theatres, while the general improvement in the tone of this form of entertainment is largely due to his influence.

At the time of writing (January, 1923) Mr. Weigall is once more in Egypt, and further archæological works from his pen may be expected. In November 1922, the present Publisher re-issued, and within a few weeks sold out, a revised (fourth) edition of *The Life and Times of Akhnaton*, perhaps the author's most popular historical work ; and it is hoped that this new volume will be found to be of equal interest and entertainment, The essays published herein were written between 1907 and the present year. Some of them appeared as part of a book many years ago ; others were printed in various leading journals ; and yet others have been specially written for this volume. In this regard the Publisher's thanks are due to the editors of the *Nineteenth Century*, the *Fortnightly Review*, the *Cornhill Magazine*, *Blackwood's Magazine*, the *New Statesman*, the *Century Magazine*, *Putnam's Magazine*, and the *Quarterly Review*.

THE GLORY
OF THE PHARAOHS

CHAPTER I

EGYPTOLOGY IN THE OPEN

In this first chapter I propose to extol the Egyptologist who works abroad in the field, in contrast to him who studies at home in the museum ; for, in reading over the papers collected into this volume, I see that there is a sort of *motif* which runs through them all, linking them together, namely, that the archæology of Egypt, to be properly appreciated, must be studied, so to speak, at the lips of the Sphinx itself.

It is an unfortunate fact that the archæologist is generally considered to be a kind of rag-and-bone man ; one who, sitting all his life in a dusty room, shuns the touch of the wind and takes no pleasure in the vanities under the sun. Actually, this is not so very often a true description of him. The ease with which long journeys are now undertaken, the immunity from insult or peril which the traveller usually enjoys, have made it possible for the archæologist to seek his information at its source in almost all the countries of the world ; and he is not obliged, as was his grandfather, to take it at second-hand from the volumes of mediæval scholars. Moreover, the necessary collections of books of reference are now to be found in very diverse places ; and thus it comes about that there are plenty of archæologists who are able to leave their own museums and studies for limited periods.

And as regards his supposed untidy habits, the phase of cleanliness which, like a purifying wind, descended suddenly upon the world in the second half of the nineteenth century, has penetrated even to libraries and museums, removing every speck of dust therefrom. The archæologist, when engaged in the sedentary side of his profession, lives nowadays in an atmosphere charged with the odours of furniture-polish and monkey-brand. A place less dusty than the Victoria and Albert Museum in London, or than the Metropolitan Museum in New York, could not easily be imagined. The disgusting antiquarian of a past generation, with his matted locks and stained clothing, could but be ill at ease in such surroundings, and could claim no brotherhood with the majority of the present-day archæologists. Cobwebs are now taboo; and the misguided old man who dwelt amongst them is seldom to be found outside of caricature, save in the more remote corners of the earth.

The archæologist in these days, then, is not often confined permanently to his museum, though in many cases he remains there as much as possible; and still less often is he a person of objectionable appearance. The science is generally represented by two classes of scholar; the man who sits in the museum or library for the greater part of his life, and lives as though he would be worthy of the furniture polish, and the man who works in the field for a part of the year and there lives as though he regarded the clean airs of heaven in even higher estimation. Thus, in arguing the case for the field-worker, as I propose here to do, there is no longer the easy target of the dusty antiquarian at which to hurl the javelin. One cannot merely urge a musty individual to come out into the open air. That would make an easy argument. One has to take aim at the less vulnerable person of the scholar who chooses to spend the greater part of his time in a smart gallery of exhibits or in a well-ordered and spotless library, and whose only fault is that he is too fond of those places. One may no longer tease him about his dusty surroundings ; but I think it is possible to accuse him of setting a very bad example by his affection for home comforts, and of causing indirectly no end of mischief. It is a fact that there are many Greek scholars who are so accustomed to read their texts in printed books that they could not make head nor tail of an original document written in a cursive Greek hand ; and there are not a few students of Egyptian archæology who do not know the conditions and phenomena of the country sufficiently to prevent the occurrence of occasional glaring errors in the exposition of their theories.

There are three main arguments which may be set forward to induce Egyptologists to go as often as possible to Egypt, and to urge their students to do so, instead of educating the mind to the habit of working at home.

Firstly, the study of archæology in the open helps to train up young men in the path of health in which they should go. Work in the Egyptian desert, for example, is one of the most healthy and inspiring pursuits that could be imagined ; and study in the shrines overlooking the Nile, where, as at Gebel Silsileh, one has to dive into the cool river and swim to the sun-scorched scene of one's work, is surely more invigorating than study in the atmosphere of the local museum. A gallop up to the Tombs of the Kings puts a man in a readier mood for a morning's work than does a ride in a street-car or an omnibus through crowded thoroughfares ; and he will feel a keenness as he pulls out his notebook that he can never have experienced in his western city. There is, moreover, a certain amount of what is called " roughing it " to be enjoyed by the archæologist in Egypt ; and thus the body becomes toughened and prepared for any necessary spurt of work. To rough it in the open is the best medicine for tired heads, as it is the finest tonic for brains in a normal condition.

In parenthesis an explanation must be given of what is meant here by that much misunderstood condition of life which is generally known as " roughing it ". A man who is accustomed to the services of two valets will believe that he is roughing it when he is left to put the diamond studs in his evening shirts with his own fingers ; and a man who has tramped the roads all his life will hardly consider that he is roughing it when he is outlawed upon the unsheltered moors in late autumn. The degree of hardship to which I refer lies between these two extremes. The science of Egyptology does not demand from its devotees a performance of many extreme acts of discomfort ; but, during the progress of active work, it does not afford many opportunities for luxurious self-indulgence, or for any slackness in the taking of exercise.

As a protest against the *dilettante* antiquarian (who is often as objectionable a character as the unwashed scholar) there are certain archæologists who wear the modern equivalent of a hair shirt, who walk abroad with pebbles in their shoes, and who speak of sitting upon an easy-chair as a moral set-back. The strained and posed life which such *savants* lead is not to be regarded as a rough one ; for there is constant luxury in the thought of their own toughness, and infinite comfort in the sense of superiority which they permit themselves to feel. It is not roughing it to feed from a packing-case when a table adds insignificantly to the impedimenta of the camp ; it is pretending to rough it. It is not roughing it to eat canned food out of the can when a plate might be used : it is either hypocrisy or slovenliness.

To rough it is to lead an exposed life under conditions precluding the possibility of indulging in certain comforts which, in their place and at the right time, are enjoyed and appreciated. A man may well be said to rough it when he camps in the open, and dispenses with the luxuries of civilisation ; when he pours a jug of water over himself instead of lying in ecstasy in an enamelled bath ; eats a meal of two undefined courses instead of one of five or six ; twangs a banjo to the moon instead of ravishing his ear with a sonata upon the grand piano ; rolls himself in a blanket instead of sitting over the library fire ; turns in at nine p.m. and rises ere the sun has topped the hills instead of keeping late hours and lying abed ; sleeps on the ground or upon a narrow camp-bed (which occasionally collapses) instead of sprawling at his ease in a four-poster.

A life of this kind cannot fail to be of benefit to the health ; and, after all, the work of a healthy man is likely to be of greater value than that of one who is anæmic or out of condition. It is the first duty of a scholar to give attention to his muscles, for he, more than other men, has the opportunity to become enfeebled by indoor work. Few students can give sufficient time to physical exercise ; but in Egypt the exercise is taken during the course of the work, and not an hour is wasted. The muscles harden and the health is ensured without the expending of a moment's thought upon the subject.

Archæology is too often considered to be the pursuit of weak-chested youths and eccentric old men ; it is seldom regarded as a possible vocation for normal persons of sound health and balanced mind. An athletic and robust young man, clothed in the ordinary costume of a gentleman, will tell a new acquaintance that he is an Egyptologist, whereupon the latter will exclaim in surprise : " Not really ?—you don't look like one." A kind of mystery surrounds the science. The layman supposes the antiquarian to be a very profound and erudite person, who has pored over his books since a baby, and has shunned those games and sports which generally make for a healthy constitution. The study of Egyptology is thought to require a depth of knowledge that places its students outside the limits of normal learning, and presupposes in them an unhealthy amount of schooling. This, of course, is absurd.

Nobody would expect an engineer who built bridges and dams, or a great military commander, to be a seedy individual with longish hair, pale face, and weak eye-sight ;

and yet probably he has twice the brain capacity of the average archæologist. It is because the life of the antiquarian is, or is generally thought to be, unhealthy and sluggish that he is so often regarded as a worm.

Some attempt should be made to rid the science of this forbidding aspect ; and for this end students ought to do their best to make it possible for them to be regarded as ordinary, normal, healthy men. Let them discourage the popular belief that they are prodigies, freaks of mental expansion. Let them shun pedantry and the affectations of the dons' commonroom as they would the plague. Let their first desire be to show themselves good, useful, hardy, serviceable citizens, and they will do much to remove the stigma from their profession. Let them be acquainted with the feeling of a bat or racket in the hands, or a saddle between the knees ; let them know the rough path over the mountains, or the diving-pool amongst the rocks, and their mentality will not be found to suffer. A winter's " roughing it " in the Theban necropolis or elsewhere would do much to banish the desire for perpetual residence at home in the west ; and a season in Egypt would alter the point of view of the student more considerably than he could imagine. Moreover, the appearance of the scholar prancing about on his fiery steed (even though it be but an Egyptian donkey) will help to dispel the current belief that he is incapable of physical exertion ; and his reddened face rising, like the morning sun, above the rocks on some steep pathway over the Theban hills will give the passer-by cause to alter his opinion of the students of antiquity.

As a second argument a subject must be introduced which will be distasteful to a large number of archæologists. I refer to the narrow-minded policy of certain European and American museums, whose desire it is at all costs to place Egyptian and other eastern antiquities actually before the eyes of western students, in order that they may have the comfort and entertainment of examining at home the wonders of lands which they make no effort to visit. I have no hesitation in saying that the craze for recklessly dragging away unique monuments from Egypt to be exhibited in western museums for the satisfaction of the untravelled man, is the most pernicious bit of folly to be found in the whole broad realm of Egyptological misbehaviour.

A museum has three main justifications for its existence. In the first place, like a home for lost dogs, it is a repository for stray objects. No curator should endeavour to procure for his museum any antiquity which could be safely exhibited on its original site and in its original position. He should receive chiefly those stray objects which otherwise would be lost to sight, or those which would be in danger of destruction. He should make it his first endeavour not so much to obtain objects direct from Egypt as to gather in those antiquities which are in the possession of dealers or private persons who cannot be expected to look after them with due care, or make them accessible to students.

In the second place, a museum is a storehouse for historical documents such as papyri and ostraca, and in this respect it is simply to be regarded as a kind of public library, capable of unlimited and perfectly legitimate expansion. Such objects are not often found by robbers in the tombs which they have violated, nor are they snatched from temples to which they belong. They are usually discovered accidentally, and in a manner which precludes any possibility of their actual position having much significance. The immediate purchase, for example, by museum agents of the Tell el Amarna tablets—the correspondence of a great Pharaoh—which had been discovered by accident, and would perhaps have been destroyed, was most wise.

In the third place, a museum is a permanent exhibition for the instruction of the public, and for the enlightenment of students desirous of obtaining comparative knowledge in any one branch of their work, and for this purpose it should be well supplied not so much with original antiquities as with casts, facsimiles, models, and reproductions of all sorts.

To be a serviceable exhibition both for the student and the public a museum does not need to possess only original antiquities. On the contrary, as a repository for stray objects, a museum is not to be expected to have a complete series of original antiquities in any class, nor is it the business of the curator to attempt to fill up the gaps without thought of the consequences. To do so is to encourage the straying of other objects. The curator so often labours under the delusion that it is his first business to collect together by fair means or foul as large a number as possible of valuable masterpieces. In reality that is a very secondary matter. His first business, if he be an Egyptologist, is to see that Egyptian masterpieces remain *in situ* so far as is practicable ; and his next is to save what has irrevocably strayed from straying farther. If the result of this policy be a poor collection, then he must devote so much the more time and money to obtaining facsimiles and reproductions.

But the curator generally has the insatiable appetite of the collector. The authorities of one museum bid vigorously against those of another at the auction which constantly goes on in the shops of the dealers in antiquities. They pay huge prices for original statues, reliefs, or sarcophagi ; prices which would procure for them the finest series of casts or facsimiles, or would give them valuable additions to their legitimate collection of papyri. And what is it all for ? It is certainly not for the benefit of the general public. It is almost solely for the benefit of the student and scholar who cannot, or will not, go to Egypt. Soon it comes to be the curator's pride to observe that *savants* are hastening to his museum to make their studies. His civic conceit is tickled by the spectacle of Egyptologists travelling long distances to take notes in his metropolitan museum.

All this is as wrong-headed as it can be. While he is filling his museum he does not seem to understand that he is denuding every necropolis in Egypt. I will give one or two instances of the destruction wrought by western museums. I take them at random from my memory.

In the year 1900 the then Inspector-General of Antiquities in Upper Egypt discovered a tomb at Thebes in which there was a beautiful relief sculptured on one of the walls, representing Queen Tiy. This he photographed, and the tomb was once more buried. In 1908 I chanced upon this monument, and proposed to open it up as a show place for visitors ; but alas !—the relief of the queen had disappeared, and only a gaping hole in the wall remained. It appears that robbers had entered the tomb at about the time of the change of inspectors ; and, realising that this relief would make a valuable exhibit for some western museum, they had cut out of the wall as much as they could conveniently carry away—namely, the head and upper part of the figure of Tiy. The hiero- glyphic inscription which was sculptured near the head was carefully erased, in case it should contain some reference to the name of the tomb from which they were taking the fragment ; and over the face some false in- scriptions were scribbled in Greek characters, so as to give the stone an unrecognisable appearance. In this condition it was conveyed to a dealer's shop, and it now forms one of the exhibits in the Royal Museum at Brussels.

In the same museum, and in others also, there are fragments of beautiful sculpture hacked out of the walls of the famous tomb of Khaemhet at Thebes. In the British Museum there are large pieces of wall-paintings broken out of Theban tombs. The famous inscription in the tomb of Anena at Thebes, which was one of the most important texts of the early Eighteenth Dynasty, was smashed to pieces several years ago to be sold in small sections to museums ; and a certain scholar was instru- mental in purchasing back for us eleven of the fragments, which have now been replaced in the tomb, and with certain fragments in Europe, form the sole remnant of the once imposing stela.

One of the most important scenes out of the famous reliefs of the Expedition to Pount, at Dêr el Bahri, found its way into the hands of the dealers, and was ultimately purchased by the museum in Cairo. The beautiful and important reliefs which decorated the tomb of Horemheb at Sakkâra, hacked out of the walls by robbers, are now exhibited in six different museums ; London, Leyden, Vienna, Bologna, Alexandria, and Cairo. Of the two hundred tombs of the nobles now to be seen at Thebes, I cannot, at the moment, recall a single one which has not suffered in this manner at some time previous to the organisation of the present strict supervision which was instituted by Mr. Carter and myself.

The curators of western museums will argue that had they not purchased these fragments they would have fallen into the hands of less desirable owners. This is quite true, and, indeed, it forms the nearest approach to justification that can be discovered. Nevertheless, it has to be remembered that this purchasing of antiquities is the best stimulus to the robber, who is well aware that a market is always to be found for his stolen goods. It may seem difficult to censure the purchaser, for certainly the fragments were " stray " when the bargain was struck, and it is the business of the curator to collect stray antiquities. But why were they stray ? Why were they ever cut from the walls of the Egyptian monuments ? Assuredly because the robbers knew that museums would purchase them.   If there had been no demand there would have been no supply.

To ask the curators to change their policy, and to purchase only those objects which are legitimately on sale, would, of course, be as futile as to ask the nations to disarm.   The rivalry between museum and museum would alone prevent a cessation of this indiscriminate traffic. I can see only one way in which a more sane and moral attitude can be introduced, and that is by the development of the habit of visiting Egypt and of working upon archæological subjects in the shadow of the actual

monuments. Only the person who is familiar with Egypt
can know the cost of supplying the stay-at-home scholar
with exhibits for his museums. Only one who has
resided in Egypt can understand the fact that Egypt
itself is the real place for Egyptian monuments. He
alone can appreciate the work of the Egyptian Government in preserving the remains of ancient days.

The resident in Egypt, interested in archæology, comes
to look with a kind of horror upon museums, and to feel
extraordinary hostility to what may be called the museum
spirit. He sees with his own eyes the half-destroyed
tombs, which to the museum curator are things far off
and not visualised. While the curator is blandly saying
to his visitor : " See, I will now show you a beautiful
fragment of sculpture from a distant and little-known
Theban tomb ", the white resident in Egypt, with black
murder in his heart, is saying : " See, I will show you
a beautiful tomb of which the best part of one wall is
utterly destroyed that a fragment might be hacked out
for a distant and little-known European or American
museum."

To a resident in Europe, Egypt seems to be a strange
and barbaric land, far, far away beyond the hills and
seas ; and her monuments are thought to be at the mercy
of wild Bedouin Arabs. In the less recent travel books
there is not a published drawing of a temple in the Nile
Valley but has its complement of Arab figures grouped in
picturesque attitudes. Here a fire is being lit at the base
of a column, and the black smoke curls upwards to destroy
the paintings thereon ; here a group of children sport
upon the lap of a colossal statue ; and here an Arab
tethers his camel at the steps of the high altar. It is felt,
thus, that the objects exhibited in European museums
have been *rescued* from Egypt and recovered from a
distant land. This is not so. They have been snatched
from Egypt and lost to the country of their origin.

He who is well acquainted with Egypt knows that
hundreds of watchmen, and a small army of inspectors

engineers, draughtsmen, surveyors, and other officials now guard these monuments, that strong iron gates bar the doorways against unauthorised visitors, that hourly patrols pass from monument to monument, and that any damage done is punished by long terms of imprisonment ; he knows that the Egyptian Government spends hundreds of thousands of pounds upon safeguarding the ancient remains ; he is aware that the organisation of the Department of Antiquities is an extremely important branch of the Ministry of Public Works. He has seen the temples swept and garnished, the tombs lit by electric light and the sanctuaries carefully rebuilt. He has spun out to the Pyramids in the electric tramcar or in a taxi-cab ; has strolled in evening dress through the halls of Karnak, after dinner at the hotel ; and has rung up the Theban Necropolis on the telephone.

A few seasons' residence in Egypt shifts the point of view in a startling manner. No longer is the country either distant or insecure ; and, realising this, the student becomes more balanced, and he sees both sides of the question with equal clearness. The archæologist may complain that it is too expensive a matter to travel to Egypt. But why, then, are not the expenses of such a journey met by the various museums ? Quite a small sum will pay for a student's winter in Egypt and his journey to and from that country. Such a sum is given readily enough for the purchase of an antiquity ; but surely right-minded students are a better investment than wrongly-acquired antiquities.

It must be now pointed out, as a third argument, that an Egyptologist cannot study his subject properly unless he be thoroughly familiar with Egypt and modern Egyptians.

A student who is accustomed to sit at home, working in his library or museum, and who has never resided in Egypt, or has but travelled for a short time in that country, may do extremely useful work in one way or another, but that work will not be faultless. It will be,

The Author standing upon the cliffs between the Temple of Dêr el Baḥri and the Valley of the Tombs of the Kings

as it were, lop-sided ; it will be coloured with hues of the
west, unknown to the land of the Pharaohs and anti-
thetical thereto. A London architect may design an
apparently charming villa for a client in Jerusalem, but
unless he know by actual and prolonged experience the
exigencies of the climate of Palestine, he will be liable to
make a sad mess of his job. By bitter experience the
military commanders learnt in the late war that a plan
of campaign prepared at home was of little use to them.
The cricketer may play a very good game upon the home
ground, but upon a foreign pitch the first straight ball
will send his bails flying into the clear blue sky.

An archæologist who attempts to record the material
relating to the manners and customs of the ancient
Egyptians cannot complete his task, or even assure himself of the accuracy of his statements, unless he has
studied the modern customs and made himself acquainted
with the permanent conditions of the country. The
modern Egyptians are the same people as those who
bowed the knee to Pharaoh, and many of their customs
still survive. A student can no more hope to understand
the story of Pharaonic times without an acquaintance with
Egypt as she now is than a modern statesman can hope to
understand his own times solely from a study of the past.

Nothing is more paralysing to a student of archæology
than continuous book-work. A collection of hard facts
is an extremely beneficial mental exercise, but the deduc-
tions drawn from such a collection should be regarded as
an integral part of the work. The road-maker must also
walk upon his road to the land whither it leads him ; the
ship-builder must ride the seas in his vessel, though they
be uncharted and unfathomed. Too often the professor
will set his students to a compilation which leads them no
farther than the final fair copy. They will be asked to
make for him, with infinite labour, a list of the High
Priests of Amon ; but unless he has encouraged them
to put such life into those figures that each one shall seem
to step from the page to confront his recorder, unless the

name of each shall call to mind the very scenes amidst which he worshipped, then is the work uninspired and deadening to the student.

A catalogue of ancient scarabs is required, let us suppose, and the students are set to work upon it. They examine hundreds of specimens, they record the variations in design, they note the differences in the glaze or material. But can they picture the man who wore the scarab ?—can they reconstruct in their minds the scene in the workshop wherein the scarab was made ?—can they hear the song of the workmen or their laughter when the overseer was not nigh ? In a word, does the scarab mean history to them, the history of a period, of a dynasty, of a craft ? Assuredly not, unless the students know Egypt and the Egyptians, have heard their songs and their laughter, have watched their modern arts and crafts. Only then are they in a position to reconstruct the picture.

The late Theodore Roosevelt, in his Romanes lecture at Oxford, gave it as his opinion that the industrious collector of facts occupied an honourable but not an exalted position ; and he added that the merely scientific historian must rest content with the honour, substantial, but not of the highest type, that belongs to him who gathers material which some time some master shall arise to use. Now every student should aim to be a master, to *use* the material which he has so laboriously collected ; and though at the beginning of his career, and indeed throughout his life, the gathering of material is a most important part of his work, he should never compile solely for the sake of compilation, unless he be content to serve simply as a clerk of archæology.

An archæologist must be a historian. He must conjure up the past ; he must play the Witch of Endor. His lists and indices, his catalogues and note-books, must be but the spells which he uses to invoke the dead. The spells have no potency until they are pronounced : the lists of Kings of Egypt have no more than an accidental value until they call before the curtain of the mind those monarchs themselves. It is the business of the archæologist to wake the dreaming dead : not to send the living to sleep. It is his business to make the stones tell their tale : not to petrify the listener. It is his business to put motion and commotion into the past that the present may see and hear : not to pin it down, spatchcocked, like a dead thing. In a word, the archæologist must be in command of that faculty which is known as the historic imagination, without which Dean Stanley was of opinion that the story of the past could not be told. "Trust Nature", said Dryden. "Do not labour to be dull!"

But how can that imagination be at once exerted and controlled as it needs must be, unless the archæologist be so well acquainted with the conditions of the country about which he writes that his pictures of it can be said to be accurate ? The student must allow himself to be saturated by the very waters of the Nile before he can permit himself to write of Egypt. He must know the modern Egyptians before he can construct his model of Pharaoh and his court.

When the mummy of Akhnaton was discovered and was proved to be that of a man of only thirty years of age, many persons doubted the identification on the grounds that the king was known to have been married at the time when he came to the throne, seventeen years before his death, and it was freely stated that a marriage at the age of eleven or twelve was impossible and out of the question. Thus it actually remained for the present writer to point out that the fact of the king's death occurring seventeen years after his marriage practically fixed his age at his decease at not much above twenty-nine years, so unlikely was it that his marriage would have been delayed beyond his twelfth year. Those who doubted the identification on such grounds were showing all too clearly that the manners and customs of the Egyptians of the nineteenth and twentieth centuries, so many of which have come down intact from olden times, were unknown to them.

Here we come to the root of the trouble. The Egyptologist who has not resided for some time in Egypt, is
inclined to allow his ideas regarding the ancient customs
of the land to be influenced by his unconsciously-acquired
knowledge of the habits of the west. But is he blind that
he sees not the great gulf fixed between the ways of the
east and those of his accustomed west ? It is of no value
to science to record the life of Thutmosis III with Napoleon as our model for it, nor to describe the daily life of
the Pharaoh with the person of an English king before
our mind's eye. Our western experience will not give us
material for the imagination to work upon in dealing with
Egypt. The setting for our Pharaonic pictures must be
derived from Egypt alone ; and no Egyptologist's work
that is more than a simple compilation is of value unless
the sunlight and the sandy glare of Egypt have burnt
into his eyes, and have been reflected on to the pages
under his pen.

The archæologist must possess the historic imagination,
but it must be confined to its proper channels. It is
impossible to exert this imagination without, as a consequence, a figure rising up before the mind partially
furnished with the details of a personality and fully endowed with the broad character of an individual. The
first lesson, thus, which we must learn is that of allowing
no incongruity to appear in our figures. In ancient
history there can seldom be sufficient data at the Egyptologist's disposal with which to build up a complete
figure ; and his puppets must come upon the stage sadly
deficient, as it were, in arms, legs, and apparel suitable to
them, unless he know from an experience of modern
Egyptians how to restore them and to clothe them in
good taste. The substance upon which the imagination
works must be no less than a collective knowledge of the
people of the nation in question. Rameses must be constructed from an acquaintance with many a Pasha of
modern Egypt, and his Chief Butler must reflect the
known characteristics of a hundred Beys and Effendis.

Without such " padding " the figures will remain but names, and with names Egyptology is already overstocked.

It is remarkable to notice how little is known regarding the great personalities in history. Taking three characters at random : we know extremely little that is authentic regarding King Arthur ; our knowledge of the actual history of Boadicea is extremely meagre ; and the precise historian would have to dismiss Pontius Pilate in a few paragraphs. But let the archæologist know so well the manners and customs of the period with which he is dealing that he will not, like the author of the stories of the Holy Grail, dress Arthur in the armour of the thirteenth century, nor fill the mind of Pilate with the thoughts of a modern Colonial Governor ; let him be so well trained in scientific cautiousness that he will not give unquestioned credence to the legends of the past ; let him have sufficient knowledge of the nation to which his hero or heroine belonged to be able to fill up the lacunæ with a kind of collective appreciation and estimate of the national characteristics, and I do not doubt that his interpretations will hold good till the end of all history.

The Egyptologist to whom Egypt is not a living reality is handicapped in his labours more unfairly than is realised by him. Avoid Egypt, and though your brains be of vast capacity, though your eyes be never raised from your books, you will yet remain in many ways an ignoramus, liable to be corrected by the merest tourist in the Nile valley. But come with me to a Theban garden that I know, where, on some still evening, the dark palms are reflected in the placid Nile, and the acacias are mellowed by the last light of the sunset ; where, in leafy bowers, the grapes cluster overhead, and the fig-tree is burdened with fruit. Beyond the broad sheet of the river rise those unchanging hills which encompass the Valley of the Tombs of the Kings ; and at their foot, dimly seen in the evening haze, sit the twin colossi, as they have sat since the days of Amenophis the Magnificent. The stars begin to be seen through the leaves now that the daylight dies, and presently the Milky Way becomes apparent, stretching across the vault of the night, as when it was believed to be the Nile of the Heavens.

The owls hoot to one another through the garden ; and at the edge of the alabaster tank wherein the dusk is mirrored, a frog croaks unseen amidst the lilies. Even so croaked he on this very ground in those days when, typifying eternity, he seemed to utter the endless refrain, " I am the resurrection, I am the resurrection," into the ears of men and maidens beneath these self-same stars.

And now a boat floats past, on its way to Karnak, silhouetted against the last-left light of the sky. There is music and song on board. The sound of the pipes is carried over the water and pulses to the ears, inflaming the imagination with the sorcery of its cadences and stirring the blood by its bold rhythm. The gentle breeze brings the scent of many flowers to the nostrils, and with these come drifting thoughts and undefined fancies, so that presently the busy considerations of the day are lulled and forgotten. The twilight seems to cloak the extent of the years, and in the gathering darkness the procession of the centuries is hidden. Yesterday and to-day are mingled together, and there is nothing to distinguish to the eye the one age from the other. An immortal, brought suddenly to the garden at this hour, could not say from direct observation whether he had descended from the clouds into the twentieth century before or the twentieth century after Christ ; and the sound of the festal pipes in the passing boat would but serve to confuse him the more.

In such a garden as this the student will learn more Egyptology than he could assimilate in many an hour's study at home ; for here his five senses play the student and Egypt herself is his teacher. While he may read in his books how this Pharaoh or that feasted o' nights in his palace beside the river, here, not in fallible imagination but in actual fact, he may see Nilus and the Lybian desert to which the royal eyes were turned, may smell the very perfume of the palace garden, and may hearken to the self-same sounds that lulled a king to sleep in Hundred-gated Thebes.

Not in the west, but only by the waters of the Nile will he learn how best to be an historian of ancient Egypt, and in what manner to make his studies of interest, as well as of technical value, to his readers, for he will here discover the great secret of his profession. Suddenly the veil will be lifted from his understanding, and he will become aware that Past and Present are so indissoluble as to be incapable of separate interpretation or single study. He will learn that there is no such thing as a distinct Past or a defined Present. " Yesterday this day's madness did prepare ", and the affairs of bygone times must be interpreted in the light of recent events. The Past is alive to-day and all the deeds of man in all the ages are living at this hour in offspring. There is no real death. The earthly grave will not hide, nor the mountain tomb imprison the actions of the men of old Egypt, so consequent and fruitful are all human affairs. This is the knowledge which will make the Egyptologist's work of lasting value ; and nowhere else save in Egypt can he acquire it. This, indeed, for him is the secret of the Sphinx ; and only at the lips of the Sphinx itself can he learn it.

CHAPTER II

THE NECESSITY OF ARCHAEOLOGY TO THE GAIETY OF THE WORLD

WHEN a great man puts a period to his existence upon earth by dying, he is carefully buried in a tomb, and a monument is set up to his glory in the neighbouring church. He may then be said to begin his second life, his life in the memory of the chronicler and historian. After the lapse of an aeon or two the works of the historian, and perhaps the tomb itself, are rediscovered; and the great man begins his third life, now as a subject of discussion and controversy amongst archæologists in the pages of a scientific journal. It may be supposed that the spirit of the great man, not a little pleased with his second life, has an extreme distaste for his third. There is a dead atmosphere about it which sets him yawning as only his grave yawned before. The charm has been taken from his deeds; there is no longer any spring in them. He must feel towards the archæologist much as a young man feels towards his cold-blooded parent by whom his love affair has just been found out. The public, too, if by chance it comes upon this archæological journal, finds the discussion nothing more than a mental gymnastic, which, as the reader drops off to sleep, gives him the impression that the writer is a man of profound brain capacity, but, like the remains of the great man of olden times, as dry as dust.

There is one thing, however, which has been overlooked. This scientific journal does not contain the ultimate results of the archæologist's researches. It contains the researches themselves. The public, so to speak, has been listening to the pianist playing his morning scales, has been watching the artist mixing his colours, has been examining the unshaped block of marble and the chisels in the sculptor's studio. It must be confessed, of course, that the archæologist has so enjoyed his researches that often the ultimate result has been overlooked by him. In the case of Egyptian archæology, for example, there are only two or three Egyptologists who have ever set themselves to write a readable history, whereas the number of books which record the facts of the science is legion.

The archæologist not infrequently lives, for a large part of his time, in a museum. However clean it may be, he is surrounded by rotting tapestries, decaying bones, crumbling stones, and rusted or corroded metal objects. His indoor work has paled his cheek, and his muscles are not like iron bands. He stands, often, in the contiguity to an ancient broadsword most fitted to demonstrate the fact that he could never use it. He would probably be dismissed his curatorship were he to tell of any dreams which might run in his head—dreams of the time when those tapestries hung upon the walls of barons' banquet-halls, or when those stones rose high above the streets of Camelot.

Moreover, those who make researches independently must needs contribute their results to scientific journals, written in the jargon of the learned. I came across a now forgotten journal, a short time ago, in which an English gentleman, believing that he had made a discovery in the province of Egyptian hieroglyphs, announced it in ancient Greek. There would be no supply of such pedantic swagger were there not a demand for it.

Small wonder, then, that the archæologist is often represented as partaking somewhat of the quality of the dust amidst which he works. It is not necessary here to discuss whether this estimate is just or not : I only wish to point out its paradoxical nature.

More than any other science, archæology might be expected to supply its exponents with stuff that, like old

c

wine, would fire the blood and stimulate the senses.   The
stirring events of the Past must often be reconstructed by
the archæologist with such precision that his prejudices
are aroused, and his sympathies are so enlisted as to set
him fighting with a will under this banner or under that.
The noise of the hardy strife of young nations is not yet
silenced for him, nor have the flags and the pennants
faded from sight.   He has knowledge of the state secrets
of kings, and, all along the line, is an intimate spectator
of the crowded pageant of history.   The caravan-masters
of the past, the admirals of the " great green sea ", the
captains of archers, have related their adventures to him ;
and he might repeat to you their stories.   Indeed, he has
such a tale to tell that, looking at it in this light, one
might expect his listeners all to be good sturdy men and
noble women.   It might be supposed that the archæologist would gather round him only men who have pleasure
in the road that leads over the hills, and women who have
known the delight of the open.   One has heard so often
of the " brave days of old " that the archæologist might
well be expected to have his head stuffed with brave tales
and little else.

His range, however, may be wider than this.   To him,
perhaps, it has been given to listen to the voice of the
ancient poet, heard as a far-off whisper ; to breathe in
forgotten gardens the perfume of long dead flowers ; to
contemplate the love of women whose beauty is perished
in the dust ; to hearken to the sound of the harp and the
sistrum ; to be the possessor of the riches of historical
romance.   Dim armies have battled around him for the
love of Helen ; shadowy captains of sea-going ships have
sung to him through the storm the song of the sweet-
hearts left behind them ; he has feasted with sultans, and
kings' goblets have been held to his lips ; he has watched
Uriah the Hittite sent to the forefront of the battle.

Thus, were he to offer a story, one might now suppose
that there would gather around him, not the men of
muscle, but a throng of sallow listeners, as improperly

expectant as were those who hearkened under the moon to the narrations of Boccaccio, or, in old Baghdad, gave ear to the tales of the Thousand and One Nights. One might suppose that his audience would be drawn from those classes most fondly addicted to pleasure, or most nearly representative, in their land and in their time, of the light-hearted and not unwanton races of whom he had to tell.

Who could better arrest the attention of the coxcomb than the archæologist who has knowledge of silks and scents now lost to the living world ? To the *gourmet* who could more appeal than the archæologist who has made abundant acquaintance with the forgotten dishes of the East ? Who could more surely thrill the senses of the courtesan than the archæologist who can relate that which was whispered by Antony in the ear of Cleopatra ? To the gambler who could be more enticing than the archæologist who has seen kings play at dice for their kingdoms ? The imaginative, truly, might well collect the most highly disreputable audience to listen to the tales of the archæologist.

But no, these are not the people who are anxious to catch the pearls which drop from his mouth. Do statesmen and diplomatists, then, listen to him who can unravel for them the policies of the Past ? Do business men hasten from Threadneedle Street and Wall Street to sit at his feet, that they may have instilled into them a little of the romance of ancient money ? I fear not.

Come with me to some provincial town, where this day Professor Blank is to deliver one of his archæological lectures at the Town Hall. We are met at the door by the secretary of the local archæological society : a melancholy lady in green plush, who suffers from St. Vitus's dance. Gloomily we enter the hall and silently accept the seats which are indicated to us by an unfortunate gentleman with a club-foot. In front of us an elderly female with short hair is chatting to a very plain young woman draped like a lay figure. On the right an emaciated man with a very bad cough shuffles on his chair ; on the left two old grey-beards grumble to one another about the weather, a subject which leads up to the familiar " Mine catches me in the small of the back " ; while behind us the inevitable curate, of whose appearance it would be trite to speak, describes to an astonished old lady the recent discovery of the pelvis of a mastodon.

The professor and the aged chairman step on to the platform ; and, amidst the profoundest gloom, the latter rises to pronounce the prefatory rigmarole. " Archæology," he says, in a voice of brass, " is a science which bars its doors to all but the most erudite ; for, to the layman who has not been vouchsafed the opportunity of studying the dusty volumes of the learned, the bones of the dead will not reveal their secrets, nor will the crumbling pediments of naos and cenotaph, the obliterated tombstones, or the worm-eaten parchments, tell us their story. To-night, however, we are privileged ; for Professor Blank will open the doors for us that we may gaze for a moment upon that solemn charnel-house of the Past in which he has sat for so many long hours of inductive meditation."

And the professor by his side, whose head, perhaps, was filled with the martial music of the long-lost hosts of the Lord, or before whose eyes there swayed the entrancing forms of the dancing-girls of Babylon, stares horrified from chairman to audience. He sees crabbed old men and barren old women before him, afflicted youths and fatuous maidens ; and he realises at once that the golden keys which he possesses to the gates of the treasury of the jewelled Past will not open the doors of that charnel-house which they desire to be shown. The scent of the king's roses fades from his nostrils, the Egyptian music which throbbed in his ears is hushed, the glorious illumination of the Palace of a Thousand Columns is extinguished ; and in the gathering gloom we leave him fumbling with a rusty key at the mildewed door of the Place of Bones.

Why is it, one asks, that archæology is a thing so misunderstood ? Can it be that both lecturer and audience have crushed down that which was in reality uppermost in their minds : that a shy search for romance has led these people to the Town Hall ? Or perchance archæology has become to them something not unlike a vice, and to listen to an archæological lecture is their remaining chance of being naughty. It may be that, having one foot in the grave, they take pleasure in kicking the moss from the surrounding tombstones with the other ; or that, being denied, for one reason or another, the jovial society of the living, like Robert Southey's *Scholar*, their hopes are with the dead.

Be the explanation what it may, the fact is indisputable that archæology is patronised by those who know not its real meaning. A man has no more right to think of the people of old as dust and dead bones than he has to think of his contemporaries as lumps of meat. The true archæologist does not take pleasure in skeletons as skeletons, for his whole effort is to cover them decently with flesh and skin once more, and to put some thoughts back into the empty skulls. Nor does he delight in ruined buildings : rather he deplores that they are ruined. Coleridge wrote like the true archæologist when he composed that most magical poem *Khubla Khan*—

> " In Xanadu did Khubla Khan
> A stately pleasure-dome decree :
> Where Alph, the sacred river, ran
> Through caverns measureless to man
>   Down to a sunless sea."

And those who would have the pleasure-domes of the gorgeous Past reconstructed for them must turn to the archæologist ; those who would see the damsel with the dulcimer in the gardens of Xanadu must ask of him the secret, and of none other. It is true that, before he can refashion the dome or the damsel, he will have to grub his way through old refuse heaps till he shall lay bare the ruins of the walls and expose the bones of the lady. But this is the " dirty work " ; and the mistake which is made lies here—that this preliminary dirty work is confused with the final clean result. An artist will sometimes build up his picture of Venus from a skeleton bought from an old Jew round the corner ; and the smooth white paper which he uses will have been made from putrid rags and bones. Amongst painters themselves these facts are not hidden, but by the public they are most carefully obscured. In the case of archæology, however, the tedious details of construction are so placed in the foreground that the final picture is hardly noticed at all. As well might one go to an aerodrome to see men fly, and be shown nothing else but screws and nuts, steel rods and woodwork. Originally the fault, perhaps, lay with the archæologist ; now it lies both with him and with the public. The public has learnt to ask to be shown the works, and the archæologist is often so proud of them that he forgets to mention the purpose of the machine.

A Roman statue of bronze, let us suppose, is discovered in the Thames valley. It is so corroded and eaten away that only an expert could recognise that it represents a reclining goddess. In this condition it is placed in the museum, and a photograph of it is published in the daily paper. Those who come to look at it in its glass case think it is a bunch of grapes, or possibly a monkey ; those who see its photograph say that it is more probably an irregular catapult-stone or a fish in convulsions.

The archæologist alone holds its secret, and only he can see it as it was. He alone can know the mind of the artist who made it, or interpret the full meaning of the conception. It might have been expected, then, that the public would demand, and the archæologist delightedly furnish, a model of the figure as near to the original as possible ; or, failing that, a restoration in drawing, or even a worded description of its original beauty. But no : the public, if it wants anything, wants to see the shapeless object in all its corrosion ; and the archæologist forgets that it is blind to aught else but that corrosion. One of the main duties of the archæologist is thus lost sight of : his duty as Interpreter and Remembrancer of the Past.

All the riches of olden times, all the majesty, all the power, are the inheritance of the present day ; and the archæologist is the recorder of this fortune. He must deal in dead bones only so far as the keeper of a financial fortune must deal in dry documents. Behind those documents glitters the gold, and behind those bones shines the wonder of the things that were. And when an object once beautiful has by age become unsightly one might suppose that he would wish to show it to none save his colleagues or the reasonably curious layman. When a man makes a statement that his grandmother, now in her ninety-ninth year, was once a beautiful woman, he does not go and find her to prove his words and bring her tottering into the room : he shows a picture of her as she was ; or, if he cannot find one, he describes what good evidence tells him was her probable appearance. In allowing his controlled and sober imagination thus to perform its natural functions, though it would never do to tell his grandmother so, he becomes an archæologist, a remembrancer of the Past.

In the case of archæology, however, the public does not permit itself to be convinced. In the Ashmolean Museum at Oxford excellent facsimile electrotypes of early Greek weapons are exhibited ; and these have far more value in bringing the Past before us than the actual weapons of that period, corroded and broken, would have. But the visitor says " These are shams ", and passes on.

It will be seen, then, that the business of archæology is often misunderstood both by archæologists and by the public ; and that there is really no reason to believe, with Thomas Earle, that the real antiquarian loves a thing the better for that it is rotten and stinketh. That the impression has gone about is his own fault, for he has exposed too much to view the mechanism of his work ;

but it is also the fault of the public for not asking of him a picture of things as they were.

Man is by nature a creature of the present. It is only by an effort that he can consider the future, and it is often quite impossible for him to give any heed at all to the past. The days of old are so blurred and remote that it seems right to him that any relic from them should, by the maltreatment of Time, be unrecognisable. The finding of an old sword, half-eaten by rust, will only please him in so far as it shows him once more by its sad condition the great gap between those days and these, and convinces him again of the sole importance of the present. The archæologist, he will tell you, is a fool if he expects him to be interested in a wretched old bit of scrap-iron. He is right. It would be as rash to suppose that he would find interest in an ancient sword in its rusted condition as it would be to expect the spectator at the aerodrome to find fascination in the nuts and screws. The true archæologist would hide that corroded weapon in his work-shop, where his fellow-workers alone could see it. For he recognises that it is only the sword which is as good as new that impresses the public; it is only the Present that counts. That is the real reason why he is an archæologist. He has turned to the Past because he is in love with the Present. He, more than any man, worships at the altar of the goddess of To-day; and he is so desirous of extending her dominion that he has adventured, like a crusader, into the lands of the Past, in order to subject them to her. Adoring the Now, he would resent the publicity of anything which so obviously suggested the Then as a rust-eaten old blade. His whole business is to hide the gap between Yesterday and To-day; and, unless a man be initiate, he would have him either see the perfect sword as it was when it sought the foeman's bowels, or see nothing. The Present is too small for him; and it is therefore that he calls so insistently to the Past to come forth from the darkness to augment it. The ordinary man lives in the Present, and he will tell one that the archæologist lives in the Past. This is not so. The layman, in the manner of the little Nationalist, lives in a small and confined Present ; but the archæologist, like a true Imperialist, ranges through all time, and calls it not the Past but the Greater Present.

The archæologist is not, or ought not to be, lacking in vivacity. One might say that he is so sensible to the charms of society that, finding his companions too few in number, he has drawn the olden times to him to search them for jovial men and agreeable women. It might be added that he has so laughed at jest and joke that, fearing lest the funds of humour run dry, he has gathered the laughter of all the years to his enrichment. Certainly he has so delighted in noble adventure and stirring action that he finds his newspaper insufficient to his needs, and fetches to his aid the tales of old heroes. In fact, the archæologist is so enamoured of life that he would raise all the dead from their graves. He will not have it that the men of old are dust : he would bring them forth to share with him the sunlight which he finds so precious. He is so much an enemy of Death and Decay that he would rob them of their harvest ; and, for every life that the foe has claimed, he would raise up, if he could, a memory that would continue to live.

The meaning of the heading which has been given to this chapter is now becoming clear, and the direction of the argument is already apparent. So far it has been my purpose to show that the archæologist is not a rag-and-bone man, though the public generally thinks he is, and he often thinks he is himself. The attempt has been made to suggest that archæology ought not to consist in sitting in a charnel-house amongst the dead, but rather in ignoring that place and taking the bones into the light of day, decently clad in flesh and finery. It has now to be shown in what manner this parading of the Past is needful to the gaiety of the Present.

Amongst cultured people whose social position makes it difficult for them to dance in circles on the grass in order to express or to stimulate their gaiety, and whose school of deportment will not permit them to sing a merry song of sixpence as they trip down the streets, there is some danger of the fire of merriment dying for want of fuel.   Vivacity in printed books, therefore, has been encouraged, so that the mind at least, if not the body, may skip about and clap its hands.   A portly gentleman with a solemn face, reading his *Punch* or his *Life* in the club, is, after all, giving play to precisely those same humours which in ancient days might have led him, like Georgy Porgy, to kiss the girls or to perform any other merry joke.   It is necessary, therefore, ever to enlarge the stock of things humorous, vivacious, or rousing, if the thoughts are to be kept young and eyes bright in this age of restraint.   What would Yuletide be without the olden times to bolster it up ?   What would the Christmas numbers do without the pictures of our great-grand-parents' coaches snowbound, of huntsmen of the eighteenth century, of jesters at the courts of the barons ?   What should we do without the *Vicar of Wakefield*, the *Compleat Angler*, *Pepys' Diary*, and all the rest of the ancient books ?   And, going back a few centuries, what an amount we should miss had we not *Æsop's Fables*, the *Odyssey*, the tales of the Trojan War, and so on.   It is from the archæologist that one must expect the augmentation of this supply ; and just in that degree in which the existing supply is really a necessary part of our equipment, so archæology, which looks for more, is necessary to our gaiety.

In order to keep his intellect undulled by the routine of his dreary work, Matthew Arnold was wont to write a few lines of poetry each day.   Poetry, like music and song, is an effective dispeller of care ; and those who find Omar Khayyam or *In Memoriam* incapable of removing the burden of their woes, will no doubt appreciate the *Owl and the Pussy-cat*, or the *Bab Ballads*.   In some form or other verse and song are closely linked with happiness ; and a ditty from any age has its interest and its charm.

> " She gazes at the stars above :
>   I would I were the skies,
> That I might gaze upon my love
>   With such a thousand eyes ! "

That is from the Greek of a writer who is not much read by the public at large, and whose works are the legitimate property of the antiquarian. It suffices to show that it is not only to the moderns that we have to look for dainty verse that is conducive to a light heart. The following lines are from the ancient Egyptian :—

> " While in my room I lie all day
> In pain that will not pass away,
>   The neighbours come and go.
> Ah, if with them my darling came
> The doctors would be put to shame :
>   *She* understands my woe."

Such examples might be multiplied indefinitely ; and the reader will admit that there is as much of a lilt about those which are here quoted as there is about the majority of the ditties which he has hummed to himself in his hour of contentment. Here is Philodemus' description of his mistress's charms :—

> " My lady-love is small and brown ;
> My lady's skin is soft as down ;
> Her hair like parsley twists and turns ;
> Her voice with magic passion burns..."

And here is an ancient Egyptian's description of not very dissimilar phenomena :—

> " A damsel sweet unto the sight,
>   A maid of whom no like there is ;
> Black are her tresses as the night,
>   And blacker than the blackberries."

Does not the archæologist perform a service to his contemporaries by searching out such rhymes and delving for more ? They bring with them, moreover, so subtle a suggestion of bygone romance, they are backed by so fair a scene of Athenian luxury or Theban splendour, that they possess a charm not often felt in modern verse.   If it is argued that there is no need to increase the present supply of such ditties, since they are really quite unessential to our gaiety, the answer may be given that no nation and no period has ever found them unessential; and a light heart has been expressed in this manner since man came down from the trees.

Let us turn now to another consideration.   For a man to be light of heart he must have confidence in humanity. He cannot greet the morn with a smiling countenance if he believe that he and his fellows are slipping down the broad path which leads to destruction.   The archæologist never despairs of mankind; for he has seen nations rise and fall till he is almost giddy, but he knows that there has never been a general deterioration.   He realises that though a great nation may suffer defeat and annihilation, it is possible for it to go down in such a thunder that the talk of it stimulates other nations for all time.   He sees, if any man can, that all things work together for happiness.   He has observed the cycle of events, the good years and the bad; and in an evil time he is comforted by the knowledge that the good will presently roll round again.   Thus the lesson which he can teach is a very real necessity to that contentment of mind which lies at the root of all gaiety.

Again, a man cannot be permanently happy unless he has a just sense of proportion.   He who is too big for his boots must needs limp; and he who has a swollen head is in perpetual discomfort.   The history of the lives of men, the history of the nations, gives one a fairer sense of proportion than does almost any other study.   In the great company of the men of old he cannot fail to assess his true value: if he has any conceit there is a greater than he to snub him;   if he has a poor opinion of his powers there is many a fool with whom to contrast himself favourably.   If he would risk his fortune on the spinning of a coin, being aware of the prevalence of his good-luck, archæology will tell him that the best luck will change ; or if, when in sore straits, he ask whether ever a man was so unlucky, archæology will answer him that many millions of men have been more unfavoured than he. Archæology provides a precedent for almost every event or occurrence where modern inventions are not involved ; and, in this manner, one may reckon their value and determine their trend. Thus many of the small worries which cause so leaden a weight to lie upon the heart and mind are by the archæologist ignored ; and many of the larger calamities by him are met with serenity.

But not only does the archæologist learn to estimate himself and his actions ; he learns also to see the relationship in which his life stands to the course of Time. Without archæology a man may be disturbed lest the world be about to come to an end : after a study of history he knows that it has only just begun ; and that gaiety which is said to have obtained " when the world was young " is to him, therefore, a present condition. By studying the ages the archæologist learns to reckon in units of a thousand years ; and it is only then that that little unit of threescore-and-ten falls into its proper proportion. " A thousand ages in Thy sight are like an evening gone ", says the hymn, but it is only the archæologist who knows the meaning of the words ; and it is only he who can explain that great discrepancy in the Christian faith between the statement " Behold, I come quickly " and the actual fact. A man who knows where he is in regard to his fellows, and realises where he stands in regard to Time, has learnt a lesson of archæology which is as necessary to his peace of mind as his peace of mind is necessary to his gaiety.

It is not needful, however, to continue to point out the many ways in which archæology may be shown to be necessary to happiness. The reader will have comprehended the trend of the argument, and, if he be in sympathy with it, he will not be unwilling to develop the theme for himself. Only one point, therefore, need here be taken up. It has been reserved to the end of this chapter, for, by its nature, it closes all arguments. I refer to Death.

Death, as we watch it around us, is the black menace of the heavens which darkens every man's day ; Death, coming to our neighbour, puts a period to our merry-making ; Death, seen close beside us, calls a halt in our march of pleasure. But let those who would wrest her victory from the grave turn to a study of the Past, where all is dead yet still lives, and they will find that the horror of life's cessation is materially lessened. To those who are familiar with the course of history, Death seems, to some extent, but the happy solution of the dilemma of life. So many men have welcomed its coming that one begins to feel that it cannot be so very terrible. Of the death of a certain Pharaoh an ancient Egyptian wrote : " He goes to heaven like the hawks, and his feathers are like those of the geese ; he rushes at heaven like a crane, he kisses heaven like the falcon, he leaps to heaven like the locust " ; and we who read his words can feel that to rush eagerly at heaven like the crane would be a very fine ending of the story. Archæology, and especially Egyptology, in this respect is a bulwark to those who find the faith of their fathers wavering ; for, after much study, the triumphant assertion which is so often found in Egyptian tombs—" Thou dost not come dead to thy sepulchre, thou comest living "—begins to take hold of the imagination. Death has been the parent of so much goodness, dying men have cut such a dash, that one looks at it with an awakening interest. Even if the sense of the misfortune of death is uppermost in an archæologist's mind, he may find not a little comfort in having before him the example of so many good men, who, in their hour, have faced that great calamity with squared shoulders.

" When Death comes ", says a certain sage of ancient Egypt, " it seizes the babe that is on the breast of its mother as well as him that has become an old man. When thy messenger comes to carry thee away, be thou found by him *ready* ". Why, here is our chance ; here is the opportunity for that flourish which modesty, throughout our life, has forbidden to us ! John Tiptoft, Earl of Worcester, when the time came for him to lay his head upon the block, bade the executioner smite it off with three strokes as a courtesy to the Holy Trinity. King Charles the Second, as he lay upon his death-bed, apologised to those who stood around him for " being such an unconscionable time adying ". The story is familiar of Napoleon's aide-de-camp, who, when he had been asked whether he were wounded, replied, " Not wounded, killed ", and thereupon expired. The Past is full of such incidents ; and so inspiring are they that Death comes to be regarded as a most stirring adventure. The archæologist, too, better than any other, knows the vastness of the dead men's majority ; and, if, like the ancients, he believe in the Elysian fields, where no death is and decay is unknown, he alone will realise the excellent nature of the company into which he will there be introduced.

There is, however, far more living going on in the world than dying ; and there is more happiness (thanks be !) than sorrow. Thus the archæologist has a great deal more of pleasure than of pain to give us for our enrichment. The reader will here enter an objection. He will say : " This may be true of archæology in general, but in the case of Egyptology, with which we are here mostly concerned, he surely has to deal with a sad and solemn people ". The answer is that no nation in the world's history has been so gay, so light-hearted as the ancient Egyptians ; and Egyptology furnishes, perhaps, the most convincing proof that archæology is, or should be a merry science, very necessary to the gaiety of the world. I defy a man suffering from his liver to understand the old Egyptians ; I defy a man who does not appreciate the pleasure of life to make anything of them. Egyptian archæology presents a pageant of such brilliancy that the archæologist is often carried along by it as in a dream, down the valley and over the hills, till, Past blending with Present, and Present with Future, he finds himself led to a kind of Island of the Blest, where death is forgotten and only the joy of life, and life's good deeds, still remain ; where pleasure-domes, and all the ancient " miracles of rare device ", rise into the air from above the flowers ; and where the damsel with the dulcimer beside the running stream sings to him of Mount Abora, and of the old heroes of the days gone by.   If the Egyptologist or the archæologist could revive within him one-hundredth part of the elusive romance, the delicate gaiety, the subtle humour, the intangible tenderness, the unspeakable goodness, of much that is to be found in his province, one would have to cry, like Coleridge :—

> " Beware, beware !
> Weave a circle round him thrice,
> And close your eyes with holy dread,
> For he on honey-dew hath fed,
> And drunk the milk of Paradise."

CHAPTER III

THE MISFORTUNES OF WENAMON

In the previous chapter it has been suggested that the archæologist is, to some extent, enamoured of the Past because it can add to the stock of things which are likely to tickle the fancy. So humorous a man is he, so fond of the fair things of life, so stirred by its adventures, so touched by its sorrows, that he must needs go to the Past to augment the supplies provided by the Present.

Here, then, is the place to give an example of the entertainment which he is likely to find in this province of his ; and if the reader can detect any smell of dust or hear any creak of dead bones in the story which follows, it will be a matter of surprise to me.

In the year 1891, at a small village in Upper Egypt named El Hibeh, some natives unearthed a much-damaged roll of papyrus which appeared to them to be very ancient. Since they had heard that antiquities have a market value they did not burn it along with whatever other scraps of inflammable material they had collected for their evening fire, but preserved it, and finally took it to a dealer who gave them in exchange for it a small sum of money. From the dealer's hands it passed into the possession of Monsieur Golenischeff, a Russian Egyptologist, who happened to be travelling in Egypt ; and by him it was carried to Petrograd, or St. Petersburg, as it was then called, where it now rests, if it has not been destroyed during the troubles there. This *savant* presently published a translation of the document, which at once caused a sensation in the Egyptological world ; and during the next few years four amended translations were made by different scholars. The interest shown in this

D

tattered roll was due to the fact that it had been found
to contain the actual report written by an official named
Wenamon to his chief, the High Priest of Amon-Ra,
relating his adventures in the Mediterranean while pro-
curing cedar-wood from the forests of Lebanon.   The
story which Wenamon tells is of the greatest value to
Egyptology, giving as it does a vivid account of the
political conditions obtaining in Syria and Egypt during
the reign of the Pharaoh Rameses XII ; but it also has
a very human interest, and the misfortunes of the writer
may excite one's sympathy and amusement, after this
lapse of three thousand years, as though they had occurred at the present day.

In the time at which Wenamon wrote his report Egypt
had fallen on evil days.   A long line of incapable descendants of the great Rameses II and Rameses III had ruled
the Nile valley ; and now a wretched ghost of a Pharaoh,
Rameses XII, sat upon the throne, bereft of all power, a
ruler in name only.   The government of the country lay
in the hands of two great nobles : in Upper Egypt,
Herhor, High Priest of Amon-Ra, was undisputed master ;
and in Lower Egypt, Nesubanebded, a prince of the
city of Tanis (the Zoan of the Bible), virtually ruled as
king of the Delta.   Both these persons ultimately
ascended the throne of the Pharaohs ; but at the time
of Wenamon's adventure the High Priest was the more
powerful of the two, and could command the obedience of
the northern ruler, at any rate in all sacerdotal matters.
The priesthood of Amon-Ra was the greatest political
factor in Egyptian life.   That god's name was respected
even in the courts of Syria, and though his power was now
on the wane, fifty years previously the great religious
body which bowed the knee to him was feared throughout
all the countries neighbouring to Egypt.   The main cause
of Wenamon's troubles was the lack of appreciation of
this fact that the god's influence in Syria was not as great
as it had been in the past ; and this report would certainly
not have been worth recording here if he had realised

that prestige is, of all factors in international relations, the least reliable.

In the year 1113 B.C. the High Priest undertook the construction of a ceremonial barge in which the image of the god might be floated upon the sacred waters of the Nile during the great religious festivals at Thebes ; and for this purpose he found himself in need of a large amount of cedar-wood of the best quality. He therefore sent for Wenamon, who held the sacerdotal title of " Eldest of the Hall of the Temple of Amon ", and instructed him to proceed to the Lebanon to procure the timber. It is evident that Wenamon was no traveller, and we may perhaps be permitted to picture him as a rather portly gentleman of middle age, not wanting either in energy or pluck, but given, like some of his countrymen, to a fluctuation of the emotions which would jump him from smiles to tears, from hope to despair, in a manner amazing to any but an Egyptian. To us he often appears as an overgrown baby, and his misfortunes have a farcical nature which makes its appeal as much through the medium of one's love of the ludicrous as through that of one's interest in the romance of adventure. Those who are acquainted with Egypt will see in him one of those types of naïve, delightful children of the Nile, whose decorous introduction into the parlour of the nations of to-day is requiring such careful rehearsal.

For his journey the High Priest gave Wenamon a sum of money, and as credentials he handed him a number of letters addressed to Egyptian and Syrian princes, and entrusted to his care a particularly sacred little image of Amon-Ra, known as Amon-of-the-Road, which had probably accompanied other envoys to the Kingdoms of the Sea in times past, and would be recognised as a token of the official nature of any embassy which carried it.

Thus armed Wenamon set out from El Hibeh—probably the ancient Hetbennu, the capital of the Eighteenth Province of Upper Egypt—on the sixteenth day of the eleventh month of the fifth year of the reign of Rameses

XII (1113 B.C.), and travelled down the Nile by boat to Tanis, a distance of some 200 miles. On his arrival at this fair city of the Delta, whose temples and palaces rose on the borders of the swamps at the edge of the sea, Wenamon made his way to the palace of Nesubanebded, and handed to him the letters which he had received from the High Priest. These were caused to be read aloud ; and Nesubanebded, hearing that Wenamon was desirous of reaching the Lebanon as soon as possible, made the necessary arrangements for his immediate despatch upon a vessel which happened then to be lying at the quay under the command of a Syrian skipper named Mengebet, who was about to set out for the Asiatic coast. On the first day of the twelfth month, that is to say fourteen days after his departure from his native town, Wenamon set sail from Tanis, crossing the swamps and heading out into " the Great Syrian Sea ".

The voyage over the blue rippling Mediterranean was calm and prosperous as the good ship sailed along the barren shores of the land of the Shashu, along the more mountainous coast of Edom, and thence northwards past the cities of Askalon and Ashdod. To Wenamon, however, the journey was fraught with anxiety. He was full of fears as to his reception in Syria, for the first of his misfortunes had befallen him. Although he had with him both money and the image of Amon-of-the-Road, in the excitement and hurry of his departure he had entirely forgotten to obtain again the bundle of letters of introduction which he had given Nesubanebded to read ; and thus there were reasons for supposing that his mission might prove a complete failure. Mengebet was evidently a stern old salt who cared not a snap of the fingers for Amon or his envoy, and whose one desire was to reach his destination as rapidly as wind and oars would permit ; and it is probable that he refused bluntly to return to Tanis when Wenamon informed him of the oversight. This and the inherent distrust of an Egyptian for a foreigner led Wenamon to regard the captain and his men with suspicion ; and one must imagine him seated in the rough deck-cabin gloomily guarding the divine image and his store of money. He had with him a secretary and probably two or three servants ; and one may picture these unfortunates anxiously watching the Syrian crew as they slouched about the deck. It is further to be remembered that, as a general rule, the Egyptians suffer excessively from sea-sickness.

After some days the ship arrived at the little city of Dor, which nestled at the foot of the Ridge of Carmel ; and here they put in to replenish their supplies. Wenamon states in his report that Dor was at that time a city of the Thekel or Sicilians, some wandering band of sea-rovers having left their native Sicily to settle here, at first under the protection of the Egyptians, but now independent of them. The King of Dor, by name Bedel, hearing that an envoy of the High Priest of Amon-Ra had arrived in his harbour, very politely sent down to him a joint of beef, some loaves of bread, and a jar of wine, upon which Wenamon must have set to with an appetite, after subsisting upon the scanty rations of the sea for so long a time.

It may be that the wine was more potent than that to which the Egyptian was accustomed ; or perhaps the white buildings of the city, glistening in the sunlight, and the busy quays, engrossed his attention too completely : anyhow, the second of his misfortunes now befell him. One of the Syrian sailors seized the opportunity to slip into his cabin and to steal the money which was hidden there. Before Wenamon had detected the robbery the sailor had disappeared for ever amidst the houses of Dor. That evening the distracted envoy, seated upon the floor of his cabin, was obliged to chronicle the list of stolen money, which list was afterwards incorporated in his report in the following manner :—

One vessel containing gold amounting to   ..   5 debens
Four vessels containing silver amounting to   20 debens
One wallet containing silver amounting to   ..   11 debens

Total of what was stolen : gold, 5 debens ; silver, 31 debens. A deben weighed about 100 grammes, and thus the robber was richer by 500 grammes of gold, which in those days would have the purchasing value of about £600 in our money, and 3,100 grammes of silver, equal to about £2,200.[1]

Wenamon must have slept little that night, and early on the following morning he hastened to the palace of King Bedel to lay his case before him. Fortunately Bedel did not ask him for his credentials but with the utmost politeness gave his consideration to the affair. Wenamon's words, however, were by no means polite, and one finds in them a blustering assurance which suggests that he considered himself a personage of extreme consequence, and regarded a King of Dor as nothing in comparison with an envoy of Amon-Ra.

" I have been robbed in your harbour,"[2] he cried, so he tells us in the report, " and, since you are the king of this land, you must be regarded as a party to the crime. You must search for my money. The money belongs to Nesubanebded, and it belongs to Herhor, my lord " (no mention, observe, of the wretched Rameses XII), "and to the other nobles of Egypt. It belongs also to Weret, and to Mekmel, and to Zakar-Baal the Prince of Byblos." These latter were the persons to whom it was to be paid.

The King of Dor listened to this outburst with Sicilian politeness, and replied in the following very correct terms : " With all due respect to your honour and excellency," he said, " I know nothing of this complaint which you have lodged with me. If the thief belonged to my land and went on board your ship in order to steal your money, I would advance you the sum from my treasury while they were finding the culprit. But the thief who robbed you belonged to your ship. Tarry, however, a few days here with me and I will seek him."

---

[1] See my *Catalogue of Weights and Balances in the Cairo Museum,* p. xvi.

[2] The translation is based on that of Prof. Breasted.

Wenamon, therefore, strode back to the vessel, and there remained, fuming and fretting, for nine long days. The skipper Mengebet, however, had no reason to remain at Dor, and seems to have told Wenamon that he could wait no longer. On the tenth day, therefore, Wenamon retraced his steps to the palace, and addressed himself once more to Bedel. "Look," he said to the king, when he was ushered into the royal presence, "you have not found my money, and therefore you had better let me go with my ship's captain and with those . . ." The rest of the interview is lost in a lacuna, and practically the only words which the damaged condition of the papyrus permits one now to read are, "He said, 'Be silent!'" which indicates that even the patience of a King of Dor could be exhausted.

When the narrative is able to be resumed one finds that Wenamon has set sail from the city, and has travelled along the coast to the proud city of Tyre, where he arrived one afternoon penniless and letterless, having now nothing left but the little Amon-of-the-Road and his own audacity. The charms of Tyre, then one of the great ports of the civilised world, were of no consequence to the destitute Egyptian, nor do they seem to have attracted the skipper of his ship, who, after his long delay at Dor, was in no mood to linger. At dawn the next morning, therefore, the journey was continued, and once more an unfortunate lacuna interrupts the passage of the report. From the tattered fragments of the writing, however, it seems that at the next port of call—perhaps the city of Sidon—a party of inoffensive Sicilian merchants was encountered, and immediately the desperate Wenamon hatched a daring plot. By this time he had come to place some trust in Mengebet, the skipper, who, for the sake of his own good standing in Egypt, had shown himself willing to help the envoy of Amon-Ra in his troubles, although he would not go so far as to delay his journey for him; and Wenamon therefore admitted him to his councils. On some pretext or another a party led by the Egyptian paid a visit to these merchants and entered into conversation with them. Then, suddenly overpowering them, a rush was made for their cash-box, which Wenamon at once burst open. To his disappointment he found it to contain only thirty-one debens of silver, which happened to be precisely the amount of silver, though not of gold, which he had lost. This sum he pocketed, saying to the struggling merchants as he did so, " I will take this money of yours, and will keep it until you find my money. Was it not a Sicilian who stole it, and no thief of ours ? I will take it."

With these words the party raced back to the ship, scrambled on board, and in a few moments had hoisted sail and were scudding northwards towards Byblos, where Wenamon proposed to throw himself on the mercy of Zakar-Baal, the prince of that city. Wenamon, it will be remembered, had always considered that he had been robbed by a Sicilian of Dor, notwithstanding the fact that only a sailor of his own ship could have known of the existence of the money, as King Bedel seems to have pointed out to him. The Egyptian, therefore, did not regard this forcible seizure of silver from these other Sicilians as a crime. It was a perfectly just appropriation of a portion of the funds which belonged to him by rights. Let us imagine ourselves robbed at our hotel by Hans the German waiter : it would surely give us the most profound satisfaction to take Herr Schnupfendorff, the piano-tuner, by the throat when next he visited us, and go through his pockets. He and Hans, being of the same nationality, must suffer for one another's sins, and if the magistrate thinks otherwise he must be regarded as prejudiced by too much study of the law.

Byblos stood at the foot of the hills of Lebanon, in the very shadow of the great cedars, and it was therefore Wenamon's destination. Now, however, as the ship dropped anchor in the harbour, the Egyptian realised that his mission would probably be fruitless, and that he himself would perhaps be flung into prison for illegally

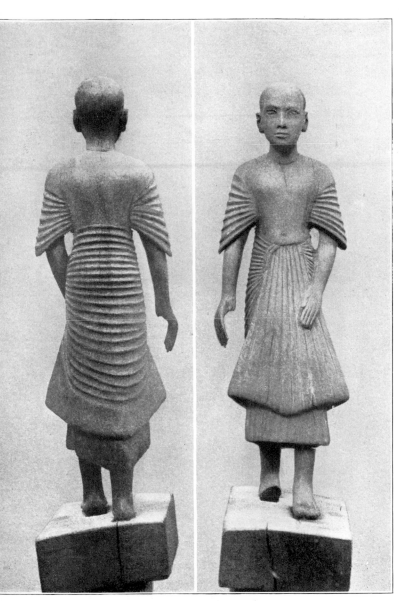

An Egyptian Priest or Religious Official
From a wooden statuette of about B.C. 1300, now in Cairo

having in his possession the famous image of the god to which he could show no written right. Moreover, the news of the robbery of the merchants might well have reached Byblos overland. His first action, therefore, was to conceal the idol and the money; and this having been accomplished he sat himself down in his cabin to await events.

The Prince of Byblos certainly had been advised of the robbery; and as soon as the news of the ship's arrival was reported to him he sent a curt message to the captain saying simply " Get out of my harbour." At this Wenamon gave up all hope, and, hearing that there was then in port a vessel which was about to sail for Egypt, he sent a pathetic message to the Prince asking whether he might be allowed to travel by it back to his own country.

No satisfactory answer was received, and for the best part of a month Wenamon's ship rode at anchor, while the distracted envoy paced the deck, vainly pondering upon a fitting course of action. Each morning the same brief order, " Get out of my harbour," was delivered to him by the harbour-master; but the indecision of the authorities as to how to treat this Egyptian official prevented the order being backed by force. Meanwhile Wenamon and Mengebet judiciously spread through the city the report of the power of Amon-of-the-Road, and hinted darkly at the wrath which would ultimately fall upon the heads of those who suffered the image and its keeper to be turned away from the quays of Byblos. No doubt, also, a portion of the stolen debens of silver was expended in bribes to the priests of the city, for, as we shall presently see, one of them took up Wenamon's cause with the most unnatural vigour.

All, however, seemed to be of no avail, and Wenamon decided to get away as best he could. His worldly goods were quietly transferred to the ship which was bound for the Nile; and, when night had fallen, with Amon-of-the-Road tucked under his arm, he hurried along the deserted quay. Suddenly out of the darkness there appeared a group of figures, and Wenamon found himself confronted by the stalwart harbour-master and his police. Now, indeed, he gave himself up for lost. The image would be taken from him, and no longer would he have the alternative of leaving the harbour. He must have groaned aloud as he stood there in the black night, with the cold sea wind threatening to tear the covers from the treasure under his arm. His surprise, therefore, was unbounded when the harbour-master addressed him in the following words : "Remain until morning here near the prince."

The Egyptian turned upon him fiercely. "Are you not the man who came to me every day saying 'Get out of my harbour' ?" he cried. "And now are you not saying 'Remain in Byblos' ?—your object being to let this ship which I have found depart for Egypt without me, so that you may come to me again and say 'Go away'."

The harbour-master in reality had been ordered to detain Wenamon for quite another reason. On the previous day, while the prince was sacrificing to his gods, one of the noble youths in his train, who had probably seen the colour of Wenamon's debens, suddenly broke into a religious frenzy, and so continued all that day, and far into the night, calling incessantly upon those around him to go and fetch the envoy of Amon-Ra and the sacred image. Prince Zakar-Baal had considered it prudent to obey this apparently divine command, and had sent the harbour-master to prevent Wenamon's departure. Finding, however, that the Egyptian was determined to board the ship, the official sent a messenger to the prince, who replied with an order to the skipper of the vessel to remain that night in harbour.

Upon the following morning a deputation, evidently friendly, waited on Wenamon, and urged him to come to the palace, which he finally did, incidentally attending on his way the morning service which was being celebrated upon the sea-shore. "I found the prince," writes

Wenamon in his report, " sitting in his upper chamber, leaning his back against a window, while the waves of the Great Syrian Sea beat against the wall below. I said to him ' The mercy of Amon be with you ! ' He said to me ' How long is it from now since you left the abode of Amon ? ' I replied ' Five months and one day from now '."

The prince then said " Look now, if what you say is true, where is the writing of Amon which should be in your hand ? Where is the letter of the High Priest of Amon which should be in your hand ? "

" I gave them to Nesubanebded," replied Wenamon.

" Then," says Wenamon, " he was very wroth, and he said to me ' Look here, the writings and the letters are not in your hand. And where is the fine ship which Nesubanebded would have given you, and where is its picked Syrian crew ? He would not put you and your affairs in charge of this skipper of yours, who might have had you killed and thrown into the sea. Whom would they have sought the god from then ?—and you, whom would they have sought you from then ? ' So he said to me, and I replied to him ' There are indeed Egyptian ships and Egyptian crews that sail under Nesubanebded, but he had at the time no ship and no Syrian crew to give me '."

The prince did not accept this as a satisfactory answer, but pointed out that there were ten thousand ships sailing between Egypt and Syria, of which number there must have been one at Nesubanebded's disposal.

" Then," writes Wenamon, " I was silent in this great hour. At length he said to me ' On what business have you come here ? ' I replied ' I have come to get wood for the great and august barge of Amon-Ra, king of the gods. Your father supplied it, your grandfather did so, and you too shall do it.' So spoke I to him."

The prince admitted that his fathers had sent wood to Egypt, but he pointed out that they had received proper remuneration for it. He then told his servants to go and find the old ledger in which the transactions were recorded, and this being done, it was found that a thousand debens of silver had been paid for the wood. The prince now argued that he was in no way the servant of Amon, for if he had been he would have been obliged to supply the wood without remuneration. "I am," he proudly declared, "neither your servant nor the servant of him who sent you here. If I cry out to the Lebanon the heavens open and the logs lie here on the shore of the sea." He went on to say that if, of his condescension, he now procured the timber, Wenamon would have to provide the ships and all the tackle. "If I make the sails of the ships for you," said the prince, "they may be top-heavy and may break, and you will perish in the sea when Amon thunders from heaven; for skilled workmanship comes only from Egypt to reach my place of abode." This seems to have upset the composure of Wenamon to some extent, and the prince took advantage of his uneasiness to say "Anyway, what is this miserable expedition that they have had you make (without money or equipment)?"

At this Wenamon appears to have lost his temper. "O guilty one!" he said to the prince, "this is no miserable expedition on which I am engaged. There is no ship upon the Nile which Amon does not own, and his is the sea, and his this Lebanon of which you say 'It is mine.' Its forests grow for the barge of Amon, the lord of every ship. Why Amon-Ra himself, the king of the gods, said to Herhor, my lord, 'Send me'; and Herhor made me go bearing the statue of this great god. Yet see, you have allowed this great god to wait twenty-nine days after he had arrived in your harbour, although you certainly knew he was there. He is indeed still what he once was: yes, now while you stand bargaining for the Lebanon with Amon its Lord. As for Amon-Ra, the king of the gods, he is the lord of life and health, and he was the lord of your fathers, who spent their lifetime offering to him. You also, you are the servant of Amon. If you will say to Amon 'I will do this', and you execute his command, you shall live and be prosperous and be healthy, and you shall be popular with your whole country and people. Wish not for yourself a thing belonging to Amon-Ra, king of the gods. Truly the lion loves his own ! Let my secretary be brought to me that I may send him to Nesubanebded, and he will send you all that I shall ask him to send, after which, when I return to the south, I will send you all, all your trifles again."

" So spake I to him," says Wenamon in his report, as with a flourish of his pen he brings this fine speech to an end. No doubt it would have been more truthful in him to say " So would I have spoken to him had I not been so flustered " ; but of all types of lie this is probably the most excusable. At all events, he said sufficient to induce the prince to send his secretary to Egypt ; and as a token of good faith Zakar-Baal sent with him seven logs of cedar-wood. In forty-eight days' time the messenger returned, bringing with him five golden and five silver vases, twenty garments of fine linen, 500 rolls of papyrus, 500 ox-hides, 500 coils of rope, twenty measures of lentils, and five measures of dried fish. At this present the prince expressed himself most satisfied, and immediately sent 300 men and 300 oxen with proper overseers to start the work of felling the trees. Some eight months after leaving Tanis, Wenamon's delighted eyes gazed upon the complete number of logs lying at the edge of the sea, ready for shipment to Egypt.

The task being finished, the prince walked down to the beach to inspect the timber, and he called to Wenamon to come with him. When the Egyptian had approached, the prince pointed to the logs, remarking that the work had been carried through although the remuneration had not been nearly so great as that which his fathers had received. Wenamon was about to reply when inadvertently the shadow of the prince's umbrella fell upon his head. What memories or anticipations this trivial incident aroused one cannot now tell with certainty. One of the gentlemen-in-waiting, however, found cause in it to whisper to Wenamon " The shadow of Pharaoh, your lord, falls upon you "—the remark, no doubt, being accompanied by a sly dig in the ribs. The prince angrily snapped " Let him alone " ; and with the picture of Wenamon gloomily staring out to sea, we are left to worry out the meaning of the occurrence. It may be that the prince intended to keep Wenamon at Byblos until the uttermost farthing had been extracted from Egypt in further payment for the wood, and that therefore he was to be regarded henceforth as Wenamon's king and master. This is perhaps indicated by the following remarks of the prince.

" Do not thus contemplate the terrors of the sea," he said to Wenamon. " For if you do that you should also contemplate my own. Come, I have not done to you what they did to certain former envoys. They spent seventeen years in this land, and they died where they were." Then, turning to an attendant, " Take him," he said, " and let him see the tomb in which they lie."

" Oh, don't let me see it," Wenamon tells us that he cried in anguish ; but, recovering his composure, he continued in a more valiant strain. " Mere human beings," he said, " were the envoys who were then sent. There was no god among them (as there now is)."

The prince had recently ordered an engraver to write a commemorative inscription upon a stone tablet recording the fact that the king of the gods had sent Amon-of-the-Road to Byblos as his divine messenger and Wenamon as his human messenger, that timber had been asked for and supplied, and that in return Amon had promised him ten thousand years of celestial life over and above that of ordinary persons. Wenamon now reminded him of this, asking him why he should talk so slightingly of the Egyptian envoys when the making of this tablet showed that in reality he considered their presence an honour. Moreover, he pointed out that when in future years an envoy from Egypt should read this tablet, he would of course pronounce at once the magical prayers which would procure for the prince, who would probably then be in hell after all, a draught of water. This remark seems to have tickled the prince's fancy, for he gravely acknowledged its value, and spoke no more in his former strain. Wenamon closed the interview by promising that the High Priest of Amon-Ra would fully reward him for his various kindnesses.

Shortly after this the Egyptian paid another visit to the sea-shore to feast his eyes upon the logs. He must have been almost unable to contain himself in the delight and excitement of the ending of his task and his approaching return in triumph to Egypt ; and we may see him jauntily walking over the sand, perhaps humming a tune to himself. Suddenly he observed a fleet of eleven ships sailing towards the town, and the song must have died upon his lips. As they drew nearer he saw to his horror that they belonged to the Sicilians of Dor, and we must picture him biting his nails in his anxiety as he stood amongst the logs. Presently they were within hailing distance, and some one called to them asking their business. The reply rang across the water, brief and terrible : " Arrest Wenamon ! Let not a ship of his pass to Egypt." Hearing these words the envoy of Amon-Ra, king of the gods, just now so proudly boasting, threw himself upon the sand and burst into tears.

The sobs of the wretched man penetrated to a chamber in which the prince's secretary sat writing at the open window, and he hurried over to the prostrate figure. " Whatever is the matter with you ? " he said, so we are told, tapping the man on the shoulder.

Wenamon raised his head. " Surely you see these birds which descend on Egypt," he groaned. " Look at them ! They have come into the harbour, and how long shall I be left forsaken here ? Truly you see those who have come to arrest me."

With these words one must suppose that Wenamon returned to his weeping, for he says in his report that the sympathetic secretary went off to find the prince in order that some plan of action might be formulated. When the news was reported to Zakar-Baal, he too began to lament ; for the whole affair was menacing and ugly. Looking out of the window he saw the Sicilian ships anchored as a barrier across the mouth of the harbour, he saw the logs of cedar-wood strewn over the beach, he saw the writhing figure of Wenamon pouring sand and dust upon his head and drumming feebly with his toes ; and his royal heart was moved with pity for the Egyptian.

Hastily speaking to his secretary, he told him to procure two large jars of wine and a ram, and to give them to Wenamon on the chance that they might stop the noise of his lamentations. The secretary and his servants procured these things from the kitchen, and, tottering down with them to the envoy, placed them by his side. Wenamon, however, merely glanced at them in a sickly manner, and then buried his head once more. The failure must have been observed from the window of the palace, for the prince sent another servant flying off for a popular Egyptian lady of no reputation, who happened to be living just then at Byblos in the capacity of a dancing-girl. Presently she minced into the room, very much elated, no doubt, at this indication of the royal favour. The prince at once ordered her to hasten down on to the beach to comfort her countryman. " Sing to him," he said, " Don't let his heart feel apprehension."

Wenamon seems to have waved the girl aside, and we may picture the prince making urgent signs to the lady from his window to renew her efforts. The moans of the miserable man, however, did not cease, and the prince had recourse to a third device. This time he sent a servant to Wenamon with a message of calm assurance. " Eat and drink," he said, " and let not your heart feel apprehension. You shall hear all that I have to say in the morning." At this Wenamon roused himself, and, wiping his eyes, consented to be led back to his rooms, ever turning, no doubt, to cast nervous glances in the direction of the silent ships of Dor.

On the following morning the prince sent for the leaders of the Sicilians and asked them for what reason they had come to Byblos. They replied that they had come in search of Wenamon, who had robbed some of their countrymen of thirty-one debens of silver. The prince was placed in a difficult position, for he was desirous to avoid giving offence either to Dor or to Egypt from whence he now expected further payment ; but he managed to pass out on to clearer ground by means of a simple stratagem.

" I cannot arrest the envoy of Amon in my territory," he said to the men of Dor. " But I will send him away, and you shall pursue him and arrest him."

The plan seems to have appealed to the sporting instincts of the Sicilians, for it appears that they drew off from the harbour to await their quarry. Wenamon was then informed of the scheme, and one may suppose that he showed no relish for it. To be chased across a bilious sea by sporting men of hardened stomach was surely a torture for the damned ; but it is to be presumed that Zakar-Baal left the Egyptian some chance of escape. Hastily he was conveyed on board a ship, and his misery must have been complete when he observed that outside the harbour it was blowing a gale. Hardly had he set out into the " Great Syrian Sea " before a terrific storm burst, and in the confusion which ensued we lose sight of the waiting fleet. No doubt the Sicilians put into Byblos once more for shelter, and deemed Wenamon at the bottom of the ocean as the wind whistled through their own bare rigging.

The Egyptian had planned to avoid his enemies by beating northwards when he left the harbour, instead of southwards towards Egypt ; but the tempest took the ship's course into its own hands and drove the frail craft north-westwards towards Cyprus, the wooded shores of which were, in course of time, sighted. Wenamon was now indeed 'twixt the devil and the deep sea, for behind him the waves raged furiously, and before him he perceived a threatening group of Cypriots awaiting him upon the wind-swept shore. Presently the vessel grounded upon the beach, and immediately the ill-starred Egyptian and the entire crew were prisoners in the hands of a hostile mob. Roughly they were dragged to the capital of the island, which happened to be but a few miles distant, and with ignominy they were hustled, wet and bedraggled, through the streets towards the palace of Hetebe, the Queen of Cyprus.

As they neared the building the queen herself passed by, surrounded by a brave company of nobles and soldiers. Wenamon burst away from his captors, and bowed himself before the royal lady, crying as he did so, " Surely there is somebody amongst this company who understands Egyptian." One of the nobles, to Wenamon's joy, replied " Yes, I understand it."

" Say to my mistress," cried the tattered envoy, " that I have heard even in far-off Thebes, the abode of Amon, that in every city injustice is done, but that justice obtains in the land of Cyprus. Yet see, injustice is done here also this day."

This was repeated to the queen, who replied " Indeed ! —what is this that you say ? "

Through the interpreter Wenamon then addressed himself to Hetebe. " If the sea raged," he said, " and the wind drove me to the land where I now am, will you let these people take advantage of it to murder me, I who am an envoy of Amon ? I am one for whom they will seek unceasingly ! And as for these sailors of the prince of Byblos, whom they also wish to kill, their lord will undoubtedly capture ten crews of yours, and will slay every man of them in revenge."

This seems to have impressed the queen, for she ordered the mob to stand on one side, and to Wenamon she said, " Pass the night . . . "

Here the torn writing comes to an abrupt end, and the remainder of Wenamon's adventures are for ever lost amidst the dust of El Hibeh. One may suppose that

Hetebe took the Egyptian under her protection, and that ultimately he arrived once more in Egypt, whither Zakar-Baal had perhaps already sent the timber. Returning to his native town, it seems that Wenamon wrote his report, which for some reason or other was never despatched to the High Priest. Perhaps the envoy was himself sent for, and thus his report was rendered useless ; or perhaps our text is one of several copies.

There can be no question that he was a writer of great power, and this tale of his adventures must be regarded as one of the jewels of the ancient Egyptian language. The brief description of the Prince of Byblos, seated with his back to the window, while the waves beat against the wall below, brings vividly before one that far-off scene, and reveals a lightness of touch most unusual in writers of that time. There is surely, too, an appreciation of a delicate form of humour observable in his account of some of his dealings with the prince. It is appalling to think that the peasants who found this roll of papyrus might have used it as fuel for their evening fire ; and that, had not a drifting rumour of the value of such articles reached their village, this little tale of old Egypt and the long-lost Kingdoms of the Sea would have gone up to empty heaven in a puff of smoke.

CHAPTER IV

THE PRESERVATION OF ANTIQUITIES

In the Dresden *Nachrichten*, a newspaper of considerable standing, an article appeared in the second year of the late war, in which a well-known German writer advocated a ruthless attack upon the antiquities and art treasures of Italy.

" If Italian statesmen," he said, " have imagined that the art treasures in their country are a species of insurance against a too energetic conduct of the War on Germany's part, they will experience some very bitter disappointments." He tells the Italian people that the well-being of the least significant German soldier—that is to say, any oaf from the lowest grade of German life—is of more value than the most magnificent gem of ancient or modern art ; and in conclusion he declares that " when the monuments and cathedrals, the statues and the pictures, the churches and the palaces, of Venice, Milan, Florence and Rome, feel the sharpness of the German sword, it will be—and God knows that it will be—a just judgment that overtakes them."

The views thus recorded are not to be regarded as the expression of an individual idiosyncrasy. The German treatment of the historical monuments of France and Belgium proved clearly enough that the Teutonic mind had discarded (let us hope temporarily) all reverence for ancient works of art as being a sentiment which was incompatible with the general policy of the nation ; and we had abundant proof that the existence of what we reckon the greatest and most permanent treasures of civilisation was believed by our late enemies to be of infinitely less account than the smallest and most transient operation of their aggressive warfare. Of course, there were certain artistic people in Germany who would have regretted the destruction of the great masterpieces and might have felt concerned on receiving the news of such a catastrophe ; but there is hardly a man of Teutonic race who would not have found excuses for the soulless creatures who then directed the activities of the nation, and would not repeat the criminal heresy that national necessity abrogates international obligations.

It is the irony of fate that the Germanic enemies of Italy, under the stress of war embraced a doctrine which was first preached by an Italian—a very young and unbalanced personage named Marinetti—who in his initial Manifesto of Futurism, dated 1909, declared that his sect " wished to destroy the museums and libraries which cover Italy with as many cemeteries."

" Would you," he wrote, " waste the best of your strength by a useless admiration of the past ? To admire an old picture is to pour our sensitiveness into a funeral urn instead of casting it forward in violent gushes of action. The admirable past may be balsam for invalids and for prisoners ; but we will have none of it, we, the young, the strong, the living Futurists. Come, then, seize the pickaxes and hammers ! Sap the foundations of the venerable cities. We stand upon the extreme promontory of the centuries : why should we look behind us ? "

This whole manifesto, indeed, might well have been written by a Prussian officer of the school which one trusts the war has dislodged ; and the ninth article of the Futurist doctrine, which says " We wish to glorify war, militarism, patriotism, the destructive arm of the anarchist, the beautiful inventions that kill, and the contempt for women," reveals a startling similarity to the creed of the German, as one saw it in those terrible years.

Our late enemies did not destroy valued historical monuments in the manner of savages who knew no better ; they destroyed them because the reasoned doctrines upon which their Culture was founded declared that one living German was of greater value than all the revered works of dead masters, one blow for Germany more precious than all the art treasures in the world. The only essential difference between the teachings of Futurism, at which we laughed, and of Pan-Germanism, against which we fought with such astounding intensity, is that the Futurist advocated the wholesale destruction of all relics of the past, whereas Pan-Germanism tolerated the retention of those monuments and works of art which, owing to their situation, did not interfere in the slightest degree with the paramount activities of the day. In other words, the Germans regarded the safeguarding of these works of art as a matter quite secondary to all practical considerations. They had no objection to the protection of their own monuments, which, they realised, had some sort of patriotic worth; but they did not consider that antiquities had an ethical value in themselves, and they did not regard the destruction of foreign works of art with any real regret at the time.

The point of view held, then and now, by the rest of the civilised world, is entirely different. While we recognise that national monuments or treasures of art are an asset to the country which produced them, we are accustomed to consider them more as assets of the whole human race, irrespective of nationality. We feel that a beautiful antiquity has an intrinsic value, and it is a matter of conscience with us to hand on to the future the treasures which we have received from the past. Cologne Cathedral or the castles of the Rhine would have been as little likely to be damaged intentionally by us as our own ancient buildings. The cathedral of Rheims, though it be stocked with memories of our early struggles with France, is as beloved by every intelligent Englishman as is Westminster Abbey; and the burning of Louvain evoked in England a feeling of distress no less sincere than that which would have been aroused by the destruction of Oxford or Cambridge. Ancient masterpieces are the possession of the whole world: they are the records of the development of the whole human race, and we treasure them without regard to creed, nationality, or faction. The German threat to destroy the monuments of Italy or France could only be received with horror by us, and the sense of outrage would not have been different had we ourselves been at war with the Italian or French peoples. Each nation, we believe, is but the steward of its antiquities on behalf of the whole world, and warfare does not disrupt that stewardship.

This attitude towards the relics of bygone days is not usually defined by us. It is a sense so rooted in our minds that we have felt no need to find for it a reasoned explanation. But, since our late enemies, in the excitement of warfare, widely and openly preached a doctrine of destruction which we had believed to be held only by a few madmen of the Futurist sect, it is necessary for us to inquire into the unconsidered arguments upon which our sentiments in this regard are based. What, then, is the value of an ancient work of art? Why do we feel that buildings or objects of this kind are entitled to respect no matter how fierce the international struggle which surges around them? Let us search for an answer to these questions in order that the attitude dictated to us by intuitive sentiment may be justified by some process of definite thought. Here in the following pages are briefly outlined the main arguments which have presented themselves to the mind of one whose business for several years it has been to safeguard the treasures of the past from thoughtless or intentional damage, and who, in the stress of that labour, has often searched for the foundations of the instinctive desire to preserve intact to future generations the ancient glories of an alien race.

"Long memories make great peoples," said Montalembert, and it is largely for this reason that the preservation of antiquities is desirable. Antiquities, whether they be works of art or objects of archæological interest, are the illustrations in the book of history, by means of which we are able to visualise the activities of past ages. The buildings and objects created by any period in a nation's existence have a value more or less equal to the written records of that age. On the one hand the documentary records sometimes tell us of matters upon which structural or artistic relics throw no light ; and on the other hand monuments and objects often give information to us which no written word could convey. Antiquities and histories are inseparable. The one kind of record supplements the other ; and it is as difficult to read history aright without the aid of these tangible illustrations as it would be to study Euclid without linear diagrams. Thus to destroy antiquities is to destroy history.

The Germans of course did not attempt to make a distinction between objects and documents in their threat to Italy, or in their destructive policy in France and Belgium. Public libraries were necessarily endangered by the menace to public museums, galleries, and buildings ; and the attack therefore was openly made upon the national archives themselves, both in their documentary and their material form. The cranks of the Futurist movement desired to annihilate historical records because they considered them to be of no value to human progress : the Germans were willing to obliterate these records because they considered them to be of less value than the temporary operations of their armies. There is very little difference between the two points of view.

Any person of intelligence will quickly recognise that the mind which looks with complacency upon the destruction of a part of the world's archives will regard with equanimity the destruction of the entire record of man's past activities. Ancient buildings, objects and documents are not so numerous that the loss of a few specimens can pass unnoticed ; but even if the number were unlimited the crime of the destruction of some of that number would not be diminished. A thief who steals a handy hundred pounds from a public fund is not less culpable because he leaves untouched the bulk of the capital sum, which happens to be out of his reach. This aspect of the

A human-faced lion, probably dating from the reign of Pharaoh Amenemes III,
B.C. 1825. One of the great masterpieces of ancient Egyptian art. Now in Cairo

matter thus resolves itself into a question whether a knowledge of history is of any practical value to the man of the present day, or whether it is merely a hindrance to the progress of his original thought. The Futurist definitely accepts the latter view.

" Would you poison yourselves," says his Manifesto, " by a knowledge of history ? Do you want to decay ? Would you waste your strength by a useless admiration of the past, from which you can but emerge exhausted, reduced, downtrodden ? "

The German seemed to take the same attitude towards history, with this one qualification—that he was prepared to tolerate, to a certain extent, the history of his own nation. In his blind agony he saw a certain use in the study of the development of Germanic thought, but recognised none in the lessons conveyed by the history of other nations. German antiquities had some sort of value to him because they were German, not because they were antiquities. Like the Futurist, he felt that he " stood upon the summit of the world " ; he believed that he had the right to make new laws, to upset accustomed habits ; he would not be bound by the old traditions of which the growth is recorded by history. Confident in the freedom and maniacal strength which he derived from his destruction of tradition, he bounded forward, to use the words of the Manifesto, " scratching the air with hooked fingers, and sniffing at the academy doors the odour of the rotting minds within ; warming his hands at the fire made by the burning of the old books ; while injustice, strong and healthy, burst forth radiantly in his eyes."

Like the Futurist, the militant German hated the restrictions placed upon him by calm, sedate history ; he detested the admonitions of accumulated experience ; and, regarding himself as superman, he wished to be rid of all records, documentary or material, which tended to pull his thoughts down from the untrodden paths of his high attainment to the unchanging plains of the world.

Just as in warfare he brushed aside every restraint which experience and custom had placed upon all military actions, and stopped his ears to the voice of history which counselled moderation, so in regard to the treatment of art treasures he adopted a policy of deliberate destructiveness based on the argument that the world's art, the world's history, the world's accumulations of experience, the world's very soul, was as nothing compared with Germany's needs of the moment.

" Come, good incendiaries with your charred fingers," he cried, in the words of the Futurist Manifesto, " set fire to the shelves of the libraries ! Flood the museums, that the glorious canvases may drift hopelessly away ! Destroy the venerable cities ! " So might Germany, untrammelled by obsolete codes, reign supreme over a new earth.

The uses of history are most readily shown in the irresistible opposition which it presents to this attitude ; and herein lies the practical value of all records of the past in whatever form they are placed before us. The simple consciousness that we who live in the present day are figures silhouetted against the luminous curtain of former ages produces in our minds a definite sense of proportion and decorum which is our surest defence against anarchy and uncontrol. Man's knowledge of good and evil, of right and wrong, whether divinely inspired or not, is the result of his accumulated experience. It is an inherited instinct, derived like the instinct of self-defence, from the teachings of the past ; and on that intuitive sense is based all law, all order, and all righteousness. To destroy antiquities, and consequently to obliterate a piece of history, is to help in the undermining of the very basis of orderly society and the weakening of the foundations upon which the peace of the world is to be built. The mind which can regard with equanimity the deliberate destruction of a glorious relic of bygone activities can have little love for the human race, and can hold in no esteem the traditional codes from which the goodness and the balance of mankind are mainly derived.

It is ridiculous to suppose that common sense and natural morality will direct our lives upon the true course. If we have no traditions, if the past experiences of our race be obliterated, we may stray from the road as the Germans strayed, and be utterly lost in the howling wilderness of materialism, where the qualities long-loved and endeared to us by time are forgotten, and the soul of mankind is shed.

Though we do not always realise the fact, it is the consciousness of history which gives us individually that natural discipline discarded by the Germans in place of an artificial obedience. It is the inherent sense of history that is the source of the strength and the sweetness of liberalism and democracy, for it gives to every individual a feeling of responsibility which causes him to act with a kind of reasonable sobriety on all occasions. I do not mean to say that a man is more decorous because he has learnt that William the Conqueror landed in England in 1066 ; I am not referring to a knowledge of the details of historical events, but rather to a consciousness of history in its widest aspect, a consciousness not necessarily derived at all from the study of books And it is the presence around us of ancient buildings and other relics of the past which prevents this consciousness from becoming dimmed in the hurly-burly of to-day's activities.

Let us ask ourselves this question : Are acquired knowledge and established custom, or is a vacuum the better base for human advancement ? If organising energy, creative faculty, and orderliness be so strong in us that we need no foundation for our efforts ; if, in the divine manner, we are prepared to create something out of nothing ; then, I suppose, we may reply that vacuum, with its freedom from impurities and useless habits, has its advantages. But if we have no pretension to divinity or to super-manhood, then it is clear that we cannot hope to improve the lot of humanity unless we set out upon our task of progress girt with the accumulated experience of former generations, that is to say, girt with history.

Moreover, history hands down to us that most precious of human assets—our conscience. It is history that arms us individually with the sword and buckler of instinctive orderliness ; and every antiquity or ancient work of art serves as a reminder to us of our responsibilities to God and man.   History is the silver thread which passes from a man back to his Creator ; and woe be to him who breaks that thread.

In the above remarks antiquities have been regarded simply as the relics of an earlier epoch ; but let us now ask ourselves what is the value of antiquities regarded as works of art.   In this aspect we must note that the value does not merely lie in the age of the object ; for no distinction can be made artistically between an ancient and a modern piece of work.   The splendours of art transcend time, their manifestations appearing sporadically in all periods ; and therefore, when we ask what is the value from this point of view of an ancient work of art we are in reality questioning what is the value of such a work, of any period, ancient or modern.   It is obvious that we cannot simply reply that these works are to be safeguarded because they are beautiful, or because they are finely inspired.   That would lead only to the question as to what *is* beauty or what *is* inspiration ; and the answer would vary according to the taste of the individual. A more practical, a more concrete reason must be given for the need of preserving these things.

Works of art, no matter what may be the material or the medium employed, are primarily expressions of a point of view which cannot be communicated by the written or the spoken word.   A painting, a piece of sculpture, an edifice, or any other work of art, is essentially a statement.   The creative impulse felt by the artist, the inspiration which impels him to set to work, is actually his desire to communicate some aspect of his thought to his fellow-men.   He has something to say, a message to deliver, an angle of vision to represent, a sensation or an emotion to express, which can be conveyed by no other means. Words are not the only method of intellectual communication between individuals ; and upon certain planes of thought they entirely fail to effect a sympathetic juncture. The artist must make use of other methods of intercourse. Rhythm, symmetry, the composition of lines, the grouping of colours and forms, go to make up his language ; and in this manner he unburdens his heart to his fellow-men. Thus the greatest value of a work of art lies in its action as a medium of high intercourse by means of vision and aspect in place of language.

When we look at the works of a master in this art of spiritual expression we are stirred and stimulated by the sensations which he himself has experienced, we read off the message which he has put before us, we see things from his point of view ; and a bond of emotional and intellectual sympathy is created between us which could have been established by no other means. In most cases the message thus conveyed is of an ideal nature, telling of emotions which are exalted altogether above the common incidents of the day, and placing us in touch with those beauties of life which are usually regarded as being in some manner God-given. The galleries of pictures and statuary which the Germans ransacked, the groups of splendid monuments and edifices which they blew to pieces, are the libraries of men's souls, where, through our eyes, we may receive the spiritual communications of the masters, and may be linked one to another by sympathy and understanding. In this manner works of art constitute the most powerful bond between the nations ; for they connect man to man without regard to nationality. Where a babel of languages leads to confusion and mis-understanding, Art speaks with a voice that men of all races can comprehend ; it speaks through the senses, and the language of the senses is common to all mankind.

The writer in the Dresden *Nachrichten* told his readers that the destruction of Italian works of art would be Italy's just punishment ; and evidently he had no belief that the loss would also be felt by his own nation. In his

warlike frenzy he had no wish to come into touch with
the point of view of other people ; and, moreover, his
war-dedicated mind regarded with mistrust all consideration of what may be called a spiritual subject. His stern
philosophy dulled his brains and blunted his wits ; and
he refused to admit either the possibility or the desir-
ability of receiving any stimulation from the work of
foreign hands. A picture for him was simply paint and
canvas, and Italian paint and canvas were enemy goods.
Similarly in regard to the French cathedrals which he
shot nearly to pieces he admitted the sanctity of neither
the art nor the religion of France. Or if there were a
glimmering in his mind that such works were the medium
for the expression of a point of view, and as such were the
cherished vehicles of international sympathy, he shunned
with so much the more decision the contamination of
non-Germanic ideals. The essence of his system was
anti-democratic : it was entirely opposed to internationalisation or to any tolerant and benevolent understanding between the peoples of the world ; and anything
that led to such a condition was scorned by him as being
incompatible with those tyrannical doctrines of the mailed
fist, to which in his frenzy he clung.

It is not necessary here to discuss the many arguments
of an idealistic kind which can be advanced in favour of
the preservation of antiquities. I have stated simply two
practical lines of thought—namely, that antiquities regarded as relics of a past age have the same value as
documentary records, and illustrate the story of the
development of the soul of mankind ; and that, regarded
as works of art, they serve as an international bond,
putting us in touch with the aspirations and the high
endeavour of all races and of all periods. In either case,
antiquities are seen to be of untold value to the world.
On the one hand, they put the people of to-day *au fait*
with the movement of the intellect of other ages ; they
keep us in touch with past experience, and give us the
benefit of earlier effort. On the other hand, they enlarge

the breadth of our outlook and put the thought of the different races of the world before us in its spiritual aspect more clearly than written records could put it. In either case they perform a function which is essential to that unity of mankind and that international tolerance upon which the future peace of the earth must be based. We fought for the maintenance of what may be termed the soul of the world ; and to destroy antiquities is to destroy the record and the manifestation of that soul. We fought, or so we believed, for the cessation of international misunderstanding, and to destroy works of art is to destroy a vital bond of sympathy between the nations. We fought for the happiness and well-being of our children's children ; and we must hand on to them intact the good things that we receive from the past and the present : not only the things that we, in our own phase of thought, consider good, but all those which the past has cherished and the future may find of value. To obliterate now anything which may be the inspiration of our descendants is against the principles for which we should strive. The Germans of the old *régime* deliberately destroyed the records of early ideals as worthless to their materialistic civilisation. We fought, and toiled, and poured out our blood and our treasure, that idealism, sympathy, tolerance, understanding, and good will might be established on this earth for ever. The dream has not been realized after all, but a right appreciation of the value of the records of the past will assuredly help towards its attainment.

CHAPTER V

THE MORALITY OF EXCAVATION

I AM asked with great frequency by travellers in Egypt and persons interested in Egyptology why it is that the excavation of ancient tombs is permitted. Surely, they say, the dead ought to be left to rest in peace. How would *we* like it were foreigners to come to England and ransack our graveyards? Is it not a sacrilege to expose to view once more the sepulchres and the mummies of the Pharaohs?

Questions of this kind, suggesting disapprobation of the primary actions of archæology, were at first inclined to take the breath away; but it soon became clear that in every case they were asked in all sincerity and were deserving of a studied reply. Moreover, there is no doubt that the whole subject of the morality of excavation, and the circumstances under which it is justifiable or unjustifiable, has been much neglected, and is liable to considerable misapprehension. I therefore venture here to play the part of an apologist and to explain the attitude assumed towards excavation by the small group of Egyptologists of what may be called the modern school, that it may serve as a response, halting but sincere, to this recurrent inquiry.

The main argument in favour of the excavation of tombs by archæologists is easily stated. The careful opening of an ancient Egyptian sepulchre saves for science information and antiquities which otherwise would inevitably be scattered to the four winds of heaven by native plunderers. In spite of the strenuous efforts of the Department of Antiquities, a considerable amount of robbery takes place in the ancient cemeteries. Tombs are rifled, coffins are broken open, mummies torn to pieces in the search for gold, heavy objects smashed into portable fragments, and valuable papyri ripped into several parts to be apportioned among the thieves. It will not be easy for the reader to picture in his mind the disorder of a plundered tomb. There lies the overturned sarcophagus, there sprawls the dead body with the head rent from the shoulders, there are the shattered remains of priceless vases believed by the robbers to have been of no great value. It is as though the place had been visited at full moon by demented monkeys.

Compare this with scientific excavation. The archæologist records by means of photographs, drawings, plans, and copious notes, everything that there is to be recorded in the tomb. Before he raises the lid of the shell in which the dead man lies he has obtained pictures of the intact coffin at every angle; before he unrolls the bandages from the mummy he has photographed it again and again. There is a rough decency in his dealings with the dead, and a care in handling the contents of the graves which would have been gratifying to their original owner. Every object is taken from the sepulchre in an orderly manner, and the body itself is either buried once more or is sent to the workroom of the archæologist or anthropologist. A tomb which might be thoroughly plundered in half an hour occupies the earnest attention of an archæologist for several days; and the mummy which would have been rapidly torn to pieces in the search for jewels is laboured over for many an hour by men of science.

Which, then, is the better course: to leave the tombs to be rifled by ignorant thieves, or to clear them of their contents in an orderly manner? I do not see how there can be any doubt as to the answer.

But let us assume for the sake of argument that there is no illegal robbery to be feared, and that the question is simply as to whether these ancient tombs should be excavated or left undisturbed. What can be said in favour of the molesting of the dead? What can be brought forward to justify this tampering with oblivion?

F

Firstly, it is to be remembered that without the excavation of the tombs a large part of the dynastic and industrial history of ancient Egypt could not be reconstructed ; and the question thus largely resolves itself into the query as to whether the history of Egypt is worth studying or not. The ancient Egyptians buried in their sepulchres a great quantity of " funeral furniture ", as it is called—beds, chairs, tables, boxes, chests, vases, utensils, weapons, clothing, jewellery, and so forth. Almost all the objects of this kind which are exhibited in our museums have been found in ancient sepulchres, almost all the pictures which give us scenes from the daily life of ancient Egypt have been discovered upon the walls of the mortuary chapels ; and if there had been no excavation of the tombs very little would have been known about the manners and customs of this antique race.

It was the discovery of the body of Akhnaton, and the consequent determination of his age at death, that made the writing of his biography possible : it was upon the walls of a tomb that his great hymn was inscribed. The invaluable biographies of the nobles of the various dynasties of Egyptian history were mostly recorded upon the walls of their mortuary chapels and tombs ; famous texts such as that upon the " Carnarvon tablet ", which relates a part of the history of the Hyksos wars, were found in the graves of the dead ; the beautiful " Song of the Harper " was engraved upon the wall of a tomb ; and so on. If a scruple had held the Egyptologist from interfering with the dead, these inscriptions would be unknown, and man would be the less understood.

The complex character of a human being is expounded only by the study of his forefathers. If we would appreciate the value of a race or nation we must of necessity sit down seriously to a detailed examination of its past. It is as futile to attempt to understand the modern Egyptians from a survey of this little moment of their present existence as it would be at a single interview to gauge the character of a butler or groom who brings no testimonials with him. The testimonials, credentials, references, and certificates of the Egyptian race are to be found in her ancient tombs ; and, say what you will, those who would leave them unexcavated and unstudied are like the trusting and much deceived young house-keepers who place their confidence in servants whose " characters " are not forthcoming. The study of Egyptology is a political necessity, and for this reason alone the tombs must be opened and their contents recorded. Lord Cromer, in a letter to the present writer, speaks of the " value of archæology, which is really only another name for history, *to the practical politician of the present day* ". " Incidents in ancient history," he writes, " frequently brought to my mind the facts with which I had to deal during my tenure of office in Egypt " ; while both in his Reports and in his *Ancient and Modern Imperialism* he enlarges upon this same theme.

Thucydides said that history was philosophy learnt from examples. " To philosophise on mankind," wrote Taine, " exact observation is not sufficient, but requires to be completed, and knowledge of the present must be supplemented from the history of the past." " History," says Seeley, " lies before science as a mass of materials out of which a political doctrine may be deduced . . . The ultimate object of all my teaching (of history) is to establish this fundamental connection, to show that politics and history are only different aspects of the same study . . . What can be more plainly political than the questions—What ought to be done with India ? What ought to be done with our Colonies ? But they are questions which need the aid of history. We cannot delude our-selves . . . so as to fancy that commonsense or common morality will suffice to lead us to a true opinion."

These words are especially applicable to Egypt, where there is a complete sequence of many thousands of years of history, and where the historian may watch the Egyptian in his every mood, and may observe his actions under innumerable combinations of circumstances. The race has not changed its character since the days of the Pharaohs, and in order to know of what the nation is capable in the future we must ascertain what it has done in the past. It is our particular business in Egypt to work for the future, to build up a nation out of the wreck which confronted us in 1882 ; but, as Edmund Burke said, " people will not look forward to posterity who never look backward to their ancestors." It is an incontestable fact that the contents of the ancient sepulchres do give us the material to form the basis of the only reasonable study of the Egyptian question—the study of the Present in the light of the Past with an eye to the Future. The records which are discovered in the tombs tell us what Egyptian individuals can accomplish ethically, while the antiquities themselves show us of what they are capable artistically, industrially, technically, and scientifically.

It is to obtain this knowledge, and also, of course, to add to our general material for the study of art, religion, literature, and so forth, that the ancient tombs must be excavated and recorded, and the dead disturbed. Moreover, the mummies and bones of the dead men are of considerable value to science. The work of Professor G. Elliot Smith, F.R.S., and his assistants has led to most important discoveries in connection with the history of disease ; and his minute examination of thousands of mummies has been most extraordinarily fruitful. Studies in the origin and growth of such diseases as tuberculosis or plague cannot fail to be of importance ; but without the excavation of ancient tombs no such work can be undertaken. I venture to think, too, that the fight against disease is invigorated by the knowledge that certain maladies are of modern growth, and that the known world was at one time free of them.

There is, however, a very widespread feeling against any meddling with the dead. A sentiment which has a large part of its origin in the belief that the spirits of the departed have still some use for their bodies forbids one to disturb the bones which have been committed to

the earth. There is the fear lest the disturbing of the
dead should offend the susceptibilities of the living members of the family to which the deceased belonged. A
body from which the life has gone assumes, also, a sanctity derived from the mystery of death. It has passed
beyond the sphere of our understanding. The limbs
which in life were apparently independent of Heaven
have suddenly fallen back upon God, and are become the
property of the Infinite. A corpse represents the total
collapse of our expediencies, the absolute paralysis of our
systems and devices ; and thus, as the incitement to the
mental search for the permanency which must somewhere
exist, the lifeless bones become consecrate.

The question, however, is a somewhat different one in
the case of the embalmed bodies of the ancient Egyptians.
No modern family traces its descent back to the days of
the Pharaohs ; and the mummies which are found in the
old tombs, although often those of historical characters,
and therefore in a special sense the property of the
Egyptian nation, compel the family consideration of no
particular group of persons. Like other antique objects,
they fall under the care of the Department of Antiquities,
which acts on behalf of the people of Egypt and the
scientists of the world. They have been such aeons dead
that they no longer suggest the fact of death ; like
statues, they seem never to have been alive. It is with
an effort that in the imagination one puts motion into
the stiff limbs, and thoughts into the hard, brown skulls.
They have lost to a great extent that awful sanctity
which more recent bones possess, for the soul has been so
long departed from them that even the recollection of its
presence is forgotten. People who would be terrified to
pass the night in a churchyard will sleep peacefully in an
ancient Egyptian necropolis camped amidst the tombs.

After all, what virtue do our discarded bodies possess
that we should dislike to turn them over ? What right
have we to declare that the mummies must be left undisturbed, when their examination will give us vitally

important information regarding the history and early development of diseases—information which is of real, practical value to mankind ? Is it just for us to object to the opening of tombs which contain matter and material so illuminating and of such value to Egypt and the world ? Those who hold orthodox religious opinions sometimes point out that the dead should not be interfered with, firstly, because the bodies are temples of the spirit, and, secondly, because they will rise again at the call of the last trump. " All that are in the graves shall hear His voice, and shall come forth ? " says the Gospel of St. John (v. 28) ; and the belief in the Second Advent seems, at first sight, to necessitate the preservation of the dead in the tombs. In answer to these contentions, however, one may point out that the mummies of the ancient Egyptians are the notable exception to the general law of total destruction which overtakes the ancient dead in all countries, and which leaves to the present day hardly a trace of the millions of bodies of our remote ancestors. The dissection and scattering of all the mummies in Egypt would add infinitesimally to the number of corpses already reduced to dust and blown about the world. Moreover one may call attention to the words of our Lord : " Let the dead bury their dead," which seem to indicate that no extreme consideration for them is required.

It is often argued, and with far more justice, that the mummies should not be disturbed or removed from their tombs because it is obvious that the ancients took extreme care to prevent any tampering of this kind, and most passionately desired their bones to be left where they were laid. There are many Churchmen who, tracing an historic growth in religion, maintain that the consecration ceremony made by the priests of long ago in all sincerity, and accepted by the people in like manner, is of the same eternal value as any Christian committal of the dead body ; and that therefore one is actually sacrilegious in touching a body laid to rest in the name of the elder gods.

In stating the answer of the archæologist we must

return to the subject of illegal excavation, and must point
out that scientific excavation prevents the desecration of
the tombs by the inevitable plunderer, and the violent
smashing up of the mummies in the crazy search for gold.
I have come upon whole cemeteries ransacked by native
thieves, the bodies broken and tossed about in all directions.   I have seen mummies sticking up out of the sand
like the " Aunt Sallies " of a country fair to act as a
target for the stone-throwing of Egyptian boys.   In the
Middle Ages mummies were dragged from their tombs and
exported to Europe to be used in the preparation of
medicines.   " The Egyptian mummies," says Sir Thomas
Browne in *Urn Burial*, " which Cambyses or time hath
spared, avarice now consumeth.   Mummy is become
merchandise, Mizraim cures wounds, and Pharaoh is sold
for balsams."   There is some reason, also, to suppose that
Pharaoh was sold for common manure.

The scientific excavator anticipates the robber whenever it is possible to do so ; and if, in the cause of science,
the mummies, like the bodies of paupers in the dissecting-
room, are sometimes exposed to what may appear to be
indignities, these are surely not so great as the insults
which they might suffer at the hands of the modern
Egyptians, who, in this regard, care not a snap of the
fingers for sentiment.

Nevertheless, I am of opinion that the ancient dead
should be treated with very great respect, and that they
should be left in their tombs whenever it is consistent with
scientific work to do so.   Though the religious point of
view may not be accepted, it is usually undesirable to act
without regard to inherited sentiment ; and as regards
the dead, there is a very distinct feeling at the back of all
our minds against any form of desecration.   It is, no
doubt, a survival which cannot be defended, but it should
not be lightly dismissed on that account.   Certain mummies of necessity must be examined and dissected, and
for this purpose it is often necessary to remove them to
scientific institutions ; others, in certain cases, require to

be available for public examination in museums. But there is no reason why the bones of one of the Pharaohs, for example, should now lie jumbled in a dusty old box under the table of a certain museum workroom ; nor does there seem to be any particular object served in exposing other bodies, which do not happen to have the protective dignity of the mummies of Rameses the Second and Sethos the First, to the jibes and jests of the vulgar.

It seems reasonable to hold that the mummies of Pharaohs and other historical characters should be available for study at any moment, and should not be buried again beneath the tons of sand and rock from which they have been removed. But most assuredly they should be placed with decency and solemnity in a room set aside for the purpose in the Cairo Museum, and should only be seen by special permission. Certain exceptions might be made to this rule. The mummies of Rameses the Second, Sethos the First, Thutmosis the Fourth, Prince Yuaa, Princess Tuau, and one or two others have such inherent dignity that, in rather more serious and impressive surroundings, they might well remain on regular exhibition in Cairo. It is a pity that they cannot be placed once more in their tombs at Thebes, where they might be visited, as is the tomb and mummy of Amenophis the Second among the hills of the western desert. But there is too grave a danger from the native plunderer, who, in spite of bolts, bars, and police, on one occasion burst into the tomb of this Amenophis and bashed in the breast of the mummy in the vain search for gold. At present there are seven watchmen in the Valley of the Tombs of the Kings, and it would be quite absurd to replace more of the royal mummies there with such inadequate protection. The tomb of Rameses the Second, moreover, is now destroyed, and the alabaster sarcophagus of Sethos the First is in London ; thus neither of these two mummies could be properly enshrined.

The public exhibition of the mummies of the ancient Egyptians in the galleries of the museums of the world,

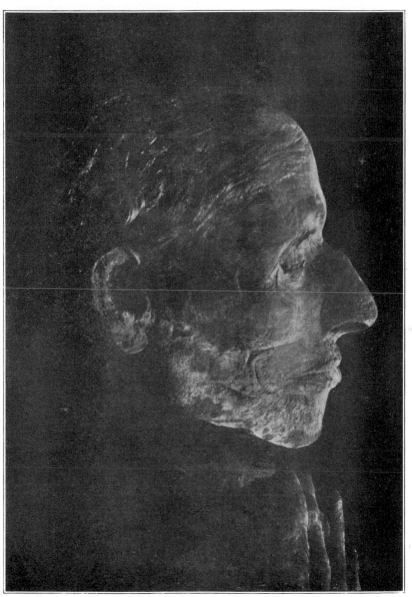

The mummy of Prince Yuaa. The photograph was taken by the Author
on the day of its discovery. The mummy is now in the Cairo Museum

where they are generally stuffed into glass cases amidst
dusty collections of pots and pans and sticks and stones,
is always objectionable. One does not care to think of
the body of a Pharaoh who ruled a mighty empire exposed to the giggling comments of the members of a school
treat, or to the hard jests of the American tourist. The
only three justifications for the removal of the body from
the tomb are that it could not safely be left in its sepulchre, that it is of use to scientists, and that it is of value
in the education of the public. Now, the first two of these
points do not give reason for its exhibition at all, and the
third obviously requires the " setting " to be impressive
and conducive to serious and undistracted thought. We
are not called upon to amuse the public by means of
the earthly remains of a great king : we may leave the
business of entertainment to the circus proprietor.

The fact that excavation so often involves the disturbance of the dead makes it a very serious matter, not
to be entered into in any but a purely scientific spirit.
But there are also other reasons for regarding excavation
as in no way a sport.

The archæologist who lays bare an intact burial takes
upon himself a grave responsibility. If we admit that the
study of the ancient Egyptians is of any value to mankind, then we must also allow that the excavator has a
duty to the world to perform when he enters an ancient
sepulchre and is confronted by the antiquities which are
stored there. The objects which he sees in front of him
are not his own : they belong to all men ; and it is his
business on behalf of the public to get from them as much
information as possible. In the present stage of the
development of archæology the value of a " find " of
antiquities often rests far more in the original arrangement of the objects than in the objects themselves. The
sole interest of a scarab, for example, may be in the fact
that it rested on the first and not the second finger of the
mummy ; and the main value of the mummy may be
found in the manner of its orientation as it lies in the

tomb. Such evidence as this, however trifling it may seem, must of necessity be the basis of all real knowledge of the history of a race ; and the excavator who omits to record by means of photographs, drawings, and notes every scrap of evidence with which he meets, commits a far greater crime than he could at once comprehend, and has failed in his duty to the public. An item is for ever lost : and the history of Egypt is built up by means of items.

Some years ago I excavated a few tombs in Lower Nubia which were in danger of robbery. I photographed the contents *in situ*, recorded the positions of the skeletons and all the objects placed around them, measured and photographed the skulls, and went away believing that my duty to science had been fulfilled. Some months later I showed the photographs of the skulls to a certain *savant*, who examined them closely.

" I notice in these pictures," said he, " that some of the front teeth are missing from the jaws. Had they dropped out in the grave, or had they been knocked out during life ? You could, of course, tell from the condition of the jawbone." And it was with considerable shame that I was obliged to admit that I had not made the required observations. The point was an important one. Certain African tribes break out the front teeth for ornamental reasons, and the origin and geographical distribution of this strange custom, which can now be traced back to Pharaonic times, is a matter of far-reaching value to ethnology.

The excavator must be prepared to record everything he sees, and his general knowledge must be such that he will not, by ignorance of what to search for, overlook matters of this kind ; for it is a patent fact that, in general, we do not see what we do not look for. The number of tombs in Egypt is limited, and the person who excavates any one of them has an opportunity for observation which can never be exactly repeated. When he has removed the antiquities to the museum he has necessarily obliterated for ever the source of his information, and, unless the contents of the tomb are all duly photographed and recorded *in situ*, that obliteration is as calamitous as the actual destruction of the antiquities themselves. He may carry off to his museum, let us say, four bronze statuettes of no particular artistic merit or individuality. Their real value to the scholar may have rested almost solely in the fact that they stood at the four corners of the tomb to ward off the evil spirits of the north, south, east, and west ; and it is that piece of information rather than the somewhat mediocre objects themselves which must at all costs be preserved.

Thus the responsibility of the excavator is very great, and he must honestly feel capable of meeting the demands which such work makes upon him, and must enter upon his labours *in full consciousness of his obligations to the public*. It may fall to his lot to dig through the stratified remains of a Roman fortress in order to reach the ruins of an Egyptian temple buried far below. To a large extent the Roman walls and buildings must be destroyed, and scholars will afterwards possess only so much information regarding the fortress as the excavator has had the ability to record. If his notes are incomplete, then he may justly be accused of destroying valuables which can never be replaced ; and I can see very little difference between him and the crazy villain who cuts a slice out of a famous painting or smashes the nose off a statue. The rarity of antiquities and ancient remains constitutes their special value. Information once destroyed can never be recovered. A stroke of the spade or pick, made before the necessary records are taken, may nullify the labours of many an ancient Egyptian's lifetime. An old priest's philosophy may have been summed up in the burial of a magical figure of Osiris in the earth floor under his bed as a protection against evil, and a too hasty stroke of the pick may lay bare the statuette but at the same time obliterate the traces of the position of the bed, thus rendering the magical little god as meaningless as the thousands of others just like it which line our museum shelves. The point of an arrow lying below the dust of a royal skeleton may be shown by close observation to have been the cause of death, and a fact will thus be added to history which might have been lost had a rough hand scattered the ashes.

Dead men are not useless ; and the excavator must not cheat the world of any part of its great perquisite. The dead are the property of the living, and the archæologist is the world's agent for the estate of the grave. The fact that the world does not yet realise the value of its possessions in this respect is no justification for bad stewardship. A *dilettante* can no more amuse himself by excavating carelessly because the world is not looking than the agent can play the fool with property which is neglected by its owner. Excavation is only moral when it is conducted on the strictest scientific lines for the benefit of mankind. Bad excavating, that is to say, digging for antiquities and not for information, is not the less dishonest because it happens to break no law. It cheats the living men of their rightful possessions which, believe me, are of real practical value to them. It cheats the dead of their utility, and gives in very truth a sting to death and the victory to the grave.

In past years professed archæologists have been surprisingly remiss in regard to the moral principles of excavation. The work of such famous men as Mariette can only be described as legalised plundering, and there are not a few diggers at the present day who have no possible right to touch ancient ground. Mariette made practically no useful records during the course of his work. For example, we do not know with certainty from what tomb came the famous statue of *Shêkh-el-beled*, perhaps the greatest art treasure in Egypt ; we do not know how it was found ; we do not know whether it was the *ka*-statue of the deceased standing behind the altar, or whether it had some other function in the sepulchre ; we do not even know its exact date. It was Mariette's custom to send a native overseer to conduct the work for him, and it was his boast that numerous excavations under his direction

were being carried on throughout Egypt at one and the
same time. The antiquities were dug out at a terrific
rate, and were hurled pell-mell into the museum in cart-
loads. In more recent years European gentlemen, and
even native antiquity-dealers, have been given excavating concessions, and have ransacked the ancient tombs
and temples in a mad search for loot, no records being
made and no scientific information being gleaned.

All antiquities found in Egypt, except those discovered
on private property, belong by law to the Egyptian
Government ; and it has been the custom for many years
to allow natives to excavate, should they so desire, on the
understanding that they pay all expenses and receive in
return one half of the objects found, the work being conducted under the supervision of a native *ghaffir*, or watchman, employed by the Department. The antiquities
handed over to the native promotor of the work (not to
mention those which he has retained illicitly), are sold by
him to dealers and merchants, and the enterprise is often
a very profitable one. No records whatsoever are made,
and there is a total loss of every scrap of interesting information. Of course, since this is a long-established
custom, it is perhaps a difficult one to stop ; and, doubtless, there are arguments to be recorded in its favour.
I was permitted, however, to put an end to it in my own
district of Upper Egypt ; and, whilst I was there, no
person, native or European, who was not a competent
archæologist, or who did not employ a competent archæologist to do the work for him, was allowed to excavate
for antiquities or new material. Nor was any person
permitted to excavate who desired to do so simply for
pecuniary gain and who intended to sell on the open
market the objects which fell to his share.

For many years European or American millionaires,
bored with life's mild adventure, have obtained excavating
concessions in Egypt, and have dallied with the relics of
bygone ages in the hope of receiving some thrill to stimulate their sluggard imagination. They call it " treasure

hunting ", and their hope is to find a king lying in state with his jewelled crown upon his head. With this romantic desire for excitement one feels a kind of sympathy ; but, nevertheless, it is a tendency which requires to be checked. The records of the past are not ours to play with : in the manner of big game in Uganda, they have to be carefully preserved ; and the tombs, like elephants, should only be disturbed by those provided with a strictly worded licence. That licence should prohibit merchandise in the relics of the dead, all foolery with the things of the past, and all pseudo-archæological endeavours. None but the honest and disinterested expert can get full value out of a " find ", and excavation is not moral unless full value is obtained. What would have happened to the fragile objects found recently by Lord Carnarvon and Mr. Carter in the tomb of Tutankhamen if those two gentlemen had not been trained archæologists working for science and not for loot ?

Another aspect of the subject must now be examined. Archæologists whose intentions are perfectly honest often dig out monuments, sepulchres, and temples which require to be protected as soon as exposed ; but they do not first consider whether such protection is available. They are overwhelmed by the desire to make discoveries, and they go on digging and digging without any regard for the immovable but frangible objects which are left exposed to destruction in their wake. " Oh, the Government will look after them," say they, not realising that the Government is already straining every nerve and expending every available penny upon such works of preservation, and can do no more. People sometimes believe that the British are vandals ; and I must therefore observe in passing that under British direction more money has been spent upon antiquities in Egypt in proportion to the budget of the country than in any other part of the world. During the four or five years previous to the war nearly £300,000 was spent by the Egyptian Government on archæological works ; and surely no more can be asked.

In archæological work there is nothing more harmful than the craze for discovery. The archæologist often thinks that it is his business to find antiquities with which to fill the museum which he represents ; or, again, he thinks it is necessary to make some startling discovery which will redound to his credit and to that of his institution. This attitude is generally forced upon him by the fact that the persons or societies who have financed his work desire to see a tangible return for their money, and are not satisfied with the heavy records of a dull piece of work such as the planning and clearing up of an empty fortress of Roman date. They insist on their representative going for the plums ; and they do not seem to realise that in so doing they are encouraging him to excavate in an unprincipled manner. An archæologist cannot accomplish his duty to the world unless he digs out the unfruitful site as conscientiously and diligently as he would the plenteous one, and records everything minutely, whether it happens to thrill him or leave him cold. This is the first principle of honest work, based upon the quite obvious truth that at the present time we cannot always tell exactly which of our records of the past are going to be considered of value to the future.

In digging thus for the plums, it is the excavator's object to obtain as large a concession from the Government as possible, and to tap as many sites as he may. The result is that far more ruins are left exposed to the scant mercies of the weather, the native robber, and the unscrupulous tourist than would be the case were he to confine himself to working thoroughly over one set of remains. The excavator has no right to expose any immovable monument unless and until he can secure its protection—at his own expense if need be. Being responsible, as I was, for the preservation of hundreds of ancient remains, I felt with peculiar bitterness the callous behaviour of certain archæologists who in past years have opened up ruins which could in no way be protected, and which have now been smashed up and defaced. The peasants will hack out pieces of bas-reliefs from stone walls to sell to the dealers, or sometimes for superstitious reasons, or again from sheer maliciousness, will break up the most precious treasures of art. No ancient monument in Egypt is safe unless it is walled in, or placed under lock and key in the charge of a custodian ; and I do not hesitate to say that it is the bounden duty of the excavator to make full arrangements for such protective measures or ever he puts pick in the ground.

Excavation is being carried on in Egypt on a scale wholly disproportionate to the number of trained field-workers available. Yet it would not be easy for the Government to refuse the desired concessions, since they are generally presented in the name of institutions of high standing ; but at the same time the would-be excavator should remember that the Government ought not to give a licence to anybody through a sort of generosity or desire to show magnanimity. It sometimes happens that ancient cemeteries or ruins are situated so far from the nearest police outpost that they are in real danger of illegal plundering by native robbers ; and in such cases it is desirable that they should be excavated as quickly as possible even though the persons who conduct the work are not absolutely first-class men. But it should be clearly understood that such danger from unauthorised diggers is the only possible justification for excavations which are not conducted on the strictest scientific lines and under the close supervision of first-rate men. By a first-rate man I mean an archæologist who has been trained in his work ; who is imbued with the highest principles, and is aware of his responsibility to the world ; who subordinates personal interests and the interests of the institution which he serves to those of science in general ; who works for the benefit of his fellow-men, desiring only to give them in complete measure the full value of the property they possess in the regions of the dead ; whose general knowledge is such that he will not overlook any item of evidence in the " finds " which he makes ; who is prepared to sit or stand over his work all day long no matter how trying the conditions ; who is deft with his fingers as well as with his brain, being able to photograph, draw, plan, mend, and write fluently ; and who can organise and control his men. There is no harm in allowing a wealthy amateur to excavate provided that he employs a trained archæologist to do the work for him and does not interfere in it himself, and also provided that he intends to make available to the public the antiquities which fall to his share and all the information which has been gleaned. But there is very real harm done in giving concessions without the most strictly-worded licences, in which are clauses precluding all un-scientific work and frustrating all enterprises undertaken entirely for personal gain. The exploiting of the ancient tombs simply for mercenary purposes gives the excavator far too much the appearance and character of a ghoul.

The archæologist, so eager to add to his knowledge by new discoveries, should remember that there is already quite enough material on hand to keep him busy for the rest of his life, material which urgently requires his attention and his protection. The standing monuments of Egypt are still unstudied in any degree of completeness ; and if only the various antiquarian societies would send out their scholars to make careful records of the remains which are already accessible, instead of urging them to unearth something new, Egyptology would be established on a much more solid basis. What scholars are thoroughly acquainted with the vast stores of Egyptological material in the museums of the world, or with the wonderful paintings and reliefs upon the walls of the temples, tombs, and mortuary chapels now in view throughout Egypt ? Why excavate more remains until these are studied, unless the desired sites are in danger, or unless some special information is required ? Why fill up our museums with antiquities before public opinion has been sufficiently educated to authorise the employment of larger numbers of curators ? Why add to the burden of Egypt by

G

increasing the number of monuments which have to be protected ? It is to be remembered that in some cases the longer an excavation is postponed the better chance there will be of recording the discoveries adequately. Our methods improve steadily, our knowledge grows, the number of expert excavators increases ; and each year finds us more fit than we were formerly for the delicate and onerous task of searching the dead.

It will be seen, then, that excavation is not a thing which may be lightly entered upon. It is a very serious business, and involves a grave duty to the public. Even if the arguments in favour of scientific research which I have suggested at the beginning of this paper are considered to be those of a casuist, as no doubt they will be by a certain class of readers, no one will deny that the study of the past has a broadening influence upon our minds, and therefore is not to be trifled with.

In Egypt, where scientific excavations are conducted entirely by Europeans and Americans, one has to consider, finally, one's duty to the Egyptians, who care not one jot for their history, but who, nevertheless, as the living descendents of the Pharaohs should be the nominal stewards of their ancient possessions. What right have we as foreigners to dig out the graves of the ancient Egyptians ?

Our right is a limited one. The Egyptians of the present day have no interest in antiquities except when considered as merchandise. They have no idea of what is called scientific work, and excavations conducted by them have not the slightest similarity to those under the supervision of modern archæologists. Yet neither the activities of the native plunderer nor the pressing need for the study of the history of the Nile Valley permits the Government to refrain altogether from allowing excavation ; and therefore the work has to be done by trained archæologists without regard to their nationality. This internationalisation of the work can be justified also on the ground that antiquities of so ancient a kind are in many respects the property of the whole world ; and, following out this argument, it will at once be apparent that archæologists must work solely for the benefit of mankind in general, since they are dealing with the property of all men. By admitting the right of non-Egyptian scientists to excavate in Egypt because all the world has the right to hold shares in these mines of information, one admits the existence of the excavator's duty to the world. That duty must never be overlooked. It consists in getting the greatest possible amount of information out of a discovery with the least possible damage to the things found. Any excavations authorised in Egypt which are not of an absolutely scientific character are injustices to the Egyptians and to all men. It is the business of the Egyptologist to work for the welfare of Egypt as well as for the benefit of the world ; and if he fail to make the relics of the Pharaohs yield their *full* burden and act to their *utmost* capacity for the purpose of teaching the Egyptians of the future the qualities of their race, and assisting the occupying Power and the world at large to estimate those qualities and their bearing on modern thought, then his excavations are not moral and should not be authorised.

To the few Egyptologists of what one may call the modern scientific school these principles are so obvious that it may seem somewhat absurd to put them into words as I have done here. I am, however, answering repeated inquiries ; and, moreover, it is an unfortunate fact that high principles on the subject of excavation are conspicuously absent among all but this small group of Egyptologists. The *savant* is often possessed only by the joy of discovery and the mad desire to find something new. He rushes into excavation like a fighter into the fray, and the consequence is disastrous. He should realise far more keenly than he sometimes does the seriousness of his undertakings and the great responsibilities which are involved. It is only by this realisation that he can justify his labours in the field. It is only by the most scrupulously conscientious work that he can convince the interested public at all of the morality of excavation.

CHAPTER VI

THE TEMPERAMENT OF THE ANCIENT EGYPTIANS

A CERTAIN school geography book, now out of date, condenses its remarks upon the character of our Gallic cousins into the following pregnant sentence : " The French are a gay and frivolous nation, fond of dancing and red wine." The description would so nearly apply to the ancient inhabitants of Egypt, that its adoption here as a text to this chapter cannot be said to be extravagant. The unbiased enquirer into the affairs of ancient Egypt must discover ultimately, and perhaps to his regret that the dwellers on the Nile were a " gay and frivolous people," festive, light-hearted, and mirthful, " fond of dancing and red wine," and pledged to all that is brilliant in life. There are very many people, naturally, who hold to those views which their forefathers held before them, and picture the Egyptians as a sombre, gloomy people ; replete with thoughts of Death and of the more melancholy aspect of religion ; burdened with the menacing presence of a multitude of horrible gods and demons, whose priests demanded the erection of vast temples for their appease-ment ; having little joy of this life, and much uneasy conjecture about the next ; making entertainment in solemn gatherings and ponderous feasts ; and holding merriment in holy contempt. Of the five startling classes into which the dictionary divides the human temperament, namely, the bilious or choleric, the phleg-matic, the sanguine, the melancholic, and the nervous, it is probable that the first, second, and the fourth would be those assigned to the Ancient Egyptians by these people. This view is so entirely false that one will be forgiven if, in the attempt to dissolve it, the gaiety of the race is thrust before the reader with too little qualification. The sanguine, and perhaps the nervous, are the classes of temperament under which the Egyptians must be docketed. It cannot be denied that they were an industrious and even a strenuous people, that they indulged in the most serious thoughts, and attempted to study the most complex problems of life, and that the ceremonial side of their religion occupied a large part of their time. But there is abundant evidence to show that, like their descendants of the present day, they were one of the least gloomy peoples of the world, and that they took their duties in the most buoyant manner, allowing as much sunshine to radiate through their minds as shone from the cloudless Egyptian skies upon their dazzling country.

It is curiously interesting to note how general is the present belief in the solemnity of this ancient race's attitude towards existence, and how little their real character is appreciated. Already the reader will be protesting, perhaps, that the application of the geographer's summary of French characteristics to the ancient Egyptians lessens in no wise its ridiculousness, but rather increases it. Let the protest, however, be held back for a while. Even if the Egyptians were not always frivolous, they were always uncommonly gay, and any slight exaggeration will be pardoned in view of the fact that old prejudices have to be violently overturned, and the stigma of melancholy and ponderous sobriety torn from the national name. It would be a matter of little surprise to some good persons if the products of excavations in the Nile Valley consisted largely of antique black gloves.

Like many other nations the ancient Egyptians rendered mortuary service to their ancestors, and solid tomb-chapels had to be constructed in honour of the more important dead. Both for the purpose of preserving the mummy intact, and also in order to keep the ceremonies going for as long a period of time as possible, these chapels were constructed in a most substantial manner, and many of them have withstood successfully the siege of the years.   The dwelling-houses, on the other hand, were seldom delivered from father to son ; but, as in modern Egypt, each grandee built a palace for himself, designed to last for a lifetime only, and hardly one of these mansions still exists even as a ruin.

Moreover the tombs were constructed in the dry desert or in the solid hillside, whereas the dwelling-houses were situated on the damp earth, where they had little chance of remaining undemolished.   And so it is that the main part of our knowledge of the Egyptians is derived from a study of their tombs and mortuary temples.   How false would be our estimate of the character of a modern nation were we to glean our information solely from its church-yard inscriptions !   We should know absolutely nothing of the frivolous side of the life of those whose bare bones lie beneath the gloomy declaration of their Christian virtues.   It will be realised how sincere was the light-heartedness of the Egyptians when it is remembered that almost everything in the following record of their gaieties is derived from a study of the tombs, and of objects found therein.

Light-heartedness is the key-note of the ancient philosophy of the country, and in this assertion the reader will, in most cases, find cause for surprise.   The Greek travellers in Egypt, who returned to their native land impressed with the wonderful mysticism of the Egyptians, committed their amazement to paper, and so led off that feeling of awed reverence which is felt for the philosophy of Pharaoh's subjects.   But in their case there was the presence of the priests and wise men eloquently to baffle them into a state of respect, and there were a thousand unwritten arguments, comments, articles of faith, and controverted points of doctrine heard from the mouths of the believers in them, to surprise them into a reverential attitude.   But we of the present day have left to us only the more outward and visible remains of the Egyptians.

There are only the fundamental doctrines to work on, the more penetrating notes of the harmony to listen to. Thus the outline of the philosophy is able to be studied without any complication, and we have no whirligig of priestly talk to confuse it. Examined in this way, working only from the cold stones and dry papyri, we are confronted with the old " Eat, drink, and be merry," which is at once the happiest and most dangerous philosophy conceived by man. It is to be noticed that this way of looking at life is to be found in Egypt from the earliest times down to the period of the Greek occupation of the country, and, in fact, until the present day. That is to say, it was a philosophy inborn in the Egyptian—a part of his nature.

Imhotep, the famous philosopher of Dynasty III, about B.C.3000, said to his disciples : " Behold the dwellings of the dead. Their walls fall down, their place is no more ; they are as they had never existed " ; and he drew from this the lesson that man is soon done with and forgotten, and that therefore his life should be as happy as possible. To Imhotep must be attributed the earliest known exhortation to man to resign himself to his candle-end of a life, and to the inevitable snuffing-out to come, and to be merry while yet he may. There is a poem dating from about B.C.2000, from which the following is taken :—

" Walk after thy heart's desire so long as thou livest. Put myrrh on thy head, clothe thyself in fine linen, anoint thyself with the true marvels of god. . . Let not thy heart concern itself, until there cometh to thee that great day of lamentation. Yet he who is at rest can hear not thy complaint, and he who lies in the tomb can understand not thy weeping. Therefore, with smiling face, let thy days be happy, and rest not therein. For no man carrieth his goods away with him ; O, no man returneth again who is gone thither."

Again we have the same sentiments expressed in a tomb of about B.C.1350, belonging to a certain Neferhotep, a priest of Amon. It is quoted elsewhere in these pages, and here we need only note the ending :

" Come, songs and music are before thee. Set behind thee all cares ; think only upon gladness, until that day cometh wherein thou shalt go down to the land which loveth silence."

A Ptolemaic description quoted more fully towards the end of this chapter reads : " Follow thy desire by night and by day. Put not care within thy heart."

The ancient Egyptian peasants, like their modern descendants, were fatalists, and a happy carelessness seems to have softened the strenuousness of their daily tasks. The peasants of the present day in Egypt so lack the initiative to develop the scope of their industries that their life cannot be said to be strenuous. In whatever work they undertake, however, they show a wonderful degree of cheerfulness, and a fine disregard for misfortune. Their forefathers, similarly, went through their labours with a song upon their lips. In the tombs at Sakkâra, dating from the Old Empire, there are scenes representing flocks of goats treading in the seed on the newly-sown ground, and the inscriptions give the song which the goat-herds sing :—

> " The goat-herd is in the water with the fishes,—
> He speaks with the *nar*-fish, he talks with the pike ;
> From the west is your goat-herd ; your goat-herd is from the west."

The meaning of the words is not known, of course, but the song seems to have been a popular one. A more comprehensible ditty is that sung to the oxen by their driver, which dates from the New Empire :—

> " Thresh out for yourselves, ye oxen, thresh out for yourselves.
> Thresh out the straw for your food, and the grain for your masters.
> Do not rest yourselves, for it is cool to-day."

Some of the love-songs have been preserved from destruction, and these throw much light upon the subject of the Egyptian temperament. A number of songs, supposed to have been sung by a girl to her lover, form themselves into a collection entitled " The beautiful and gladsome songs of thy sister, whom thy heart loves, as she walks in the fields." The girl is supposed to belong to the peasant class, and most of the verses are sung while she is at her daily occupation of snaring wild duck in the marshes. One must imagine the songs warbled without

any particular refrain, just as in the case of the modern
Egyptians, who pour out their ancient tales of love and
adventure in a series of bird-like cadences, full-throated,
and often wonderfully melodious. A peculiar sweetness
and tenderness will be noted in the following examples, and,
though they suffer in translation, their airy lightness and
refinement is to be distinguished. One characteristic
song, addressed by the girl to her lover, runs :—

> " Caught by the worm, the wild-duck cries,
> But in the love-light of thine eyes
> I, trembling, loose the trap. So flies
>   The bird into the air.
> What will my angry mother say ?
> With basket full I come each day,
> But now thy love hath led me stray,
>   And I have set no snare."

Again, in a somewhat similar strain, she sings :—

> " The wild duck scatter far, and now
> Again they light upon the bough
>   And cry unto their kind ;
> Anon they gather on the mere—
> But yet unharmed I leave them there,
>   For love hath filled my mind."

Another song must be given here in prose form. The girl
who sings it is supposed to be making a wreath of flowers,
and as she works she cries :—

" I am thy first sister, and to me thou art as a garden which I
have planted with flowers and all sweet-smelling herbs. And I
have directed a canal into it, that thou mightest dip thy hand into
it when the north wind blows cool. The place is beautiful where
we walk, because we walk together, thy hand resting in mine,
our mind thoughtful and our heart joyful. It is intoxicating
to me to hear thy voice, yet my life depends upon hearing it.
Whenever I see thee it is better for me than food and drink."

One more song must be quoted, for it is so artless and so
full of human tenderness that I may risk the accusation of
straying from the main argument in repeating it. It
runs :—

> " The breath of thy nostrils alone
> Is that which maketh my heart to live.
> I found thee :
> God grant thee to me
> For ever and ever."

It is really painful to think of these words as having fallen from the lips of what is now a resin-smelling lump of bones and hardened flesh, perhaps still unearthed, perhaps lying in some museum show-case, or perhaps kicked about in fragments over the hot sand of some tourist-crowded necropolis. Mummies are the most lifeless objects one could well imagine. It is impossible even for those whose imaginations are the most powerful to infuse life into a thing so utterly dead as an embalmed body ; and this fact is partly responsible for that atmosphere of stark melancholy sobriety and aloofness which surrounds the affairs of ancient Egypt. In reading these verses, it is imperative for their right understanding that the mummies and their resting places should be banished from the thoughts. It is not always a simple matter for the student to rid himself of the atmosphere of the museum, where the beads which should be jangling on a brown neck are lying numbered and labelled on red velvet ; where the bird trap, once the centre of such feathered commotion, is propped up in a glass case as " D, 18, 432 " ; and where even the document in which the verses are written is the lawful booty of the grammarian and philologist in the library. But it is the first duty of an archæologist to do away with that atmosphere.

Let those who are untrammelled, then, pass out into the sunshine of the Egyptian fields and marshes, where the wild duck cry to each other as they scuttle through the tall reeds. Here in the early morning comes our songstress, and one may see her as clearly as one can that Shulamite of King Solomon's day, who has had the good fortune to belong to a land where stones and bones, being few in number, do not endanger the atmosphere of the literature. One may see her, her hair moving in the breeze " as a flock of goats that appear from Mount Gilead " ; her teeth white " as a shorn sheep which came up from the washing " ; and her lips " like a thread of scarlet." Through such imaginings alone can one appreciate the songs, or realise the lightness of the manner in which they were sung.

With such a happy view of life among the upper classes
as is indicated by their philosophy, and with that merry
disposition amongst the peasants which shows itself in
their love of song, it is not surprising to find that asceticism
is practically unknown in ancient Egypt before the time
of Christ. At first sight, in reflecting on the mysteries and
religious ceremonies of the nation, we are apt to endow
the priests and other participators with a degree of
austerity wholly unjustified by the facts. We picture the
priest chanting his formulæ in the dim light of the temple,
the atmosphere about him heavy with incense ; and we
imagine him as an anchorite who has put away the things
of this world. But in reality there seems to have been not
even such a thing as a celibate amongst the priests.
Each man had his wife and his family, his house, and his
comforts of food and fine linen. He indulged in the usual
pastimes and was present at the merriest of feasts. The
famous wise men and magicians, such as Uba-ana of the
Westcar Papyrus, had their wives, their parks, their
pleasure-pavilions, and their hosts of servants. Great
dignitaries of the Amon Church, such as Amenhotepsase,
the Second Prophet of Amon in the time of Thutmosis IV,
are represented as feasting with their friends, or driving
through Thebes in richly-decorated chariots drawn by
prancing horses, and attended by an array of servants. A
monastic life, or the life of an anchorite, was held by the
Egyptians in scorn ; and indeed the state of mind which
produces the monk and the hermit was almost entirely
unknown to the nation in dynastic times. It was only in
the Ptolemaic and Roman periods that asceticism came to
be practised ; and some have thought that its introduction into Egypt is to be attributed to the preachings of the
Hindoo missionaries sent from India to the court of the
Ptolemies. It is not really an Egyptian characteristic ;
and its practice did not last for more than a few centuries.

The religious teachings of the Egyptians before the
Ptolemaic era do not suggest that the mortification of the
flesh was a possible means of purifying the spirit. An

appeal to the senses and to the emotions, however, was
considered as a legitimate method of reaching the soul.
The Egyptians were passionately fond of ceremonial
display. Their huge temples, painted as they were with
the most brilliant colours, formed the setting of processions and ceremonies in which music, rhythmic
motion, and colour were brought to a point of excellence.
In honour of some of the gods dances were conducted;
while celebrations, such as the fantastic Feast of Lamps,
were held on the anniversaries of religious events. In these
gorgeously spectacular ceremonies there was no place for
anything sombre or austere, nor could they have been
conceived by any but the most life-loving temperaments.

As in his religious functions, so in his home, the
Egyptian regarded brilliancy and festivity as an edifica-
tion. When in trouble or distress, he was wont to
relieve his mind as readily by an appeal to the vanities of
this world as by an invocation of the powers of Heaven.
Thus, when King Sneferu, of Dynasty IV, was oppressed
with the cares of state, his councillor Zazamankh constructed for him a pleasure boat which was rowed around
a lake by the most beautiful damsels obtainable. And
again, when Wenamon, the envoy of Herhor of Dynasty
XXI, had fallen into trouble with the pirates of the
Mediterranean, his depression was banished by the gift of
a dancing-girl, two vessels of wine, a young goat of tender
flesh, and a message which read—" Eat and drink, and
let not thy heart feel apprehension."

An intense craving for brightness and cheerfulness is to
be observed on all sides, and the attempt to cover every
action of life with a kind of lustre is perhaps the most
apparent characteristic of the race. At all times the
Egyptians decked themselves with flowers, and rich and
poor alike breathed what they called " the sweet north
wind " through a screen of blossoms. At their feasts and
festivals each guest was presented with necklaces and
crowns of lotus-flowers, and a specially selected bouquet
was carried in the hands. Constantly, as the hours

passed, fresh flowers were brought in to them, and the guests are shown in the tomb paintings in the act of burying their noses in the delicate petals with an air of luxury which even the conventionalities of the draughts- man cannot hide. In the woman's hair a flower was pinned which hung down before the forehead ; and a cake of ointment, concocted of some sweet-smelling unguent, was so arranged upon the head that, as it slowly melted, it re-perfumed the flower. Complete wreaths of flowers were sometimes worn, and this was the custom as much in the dress of the home as in that of the feast. The common people also arrayed themselves with wreaths of lotuses at all galas and carnivals. The room in which a feast was held was decorated lavishly with flowers. Blossoms crept up the delicate pillars to the roof ; garlands twined themselves around the tables and about the jars of wine ; and single buds lay in every dish of food. Even the dead were decked in the tombs with a mass of flowers, as though the mourners would hide with the living delights of the earth the misery of the grave.

The Egyptian loved his garden, and filled it with all manner of beautiful flowers. Great parks were laid out by the Pharaohs, and it is recorded of Thutmosis III, that he brought back from his Asiatic campaigns vast quantities of rare plants with which to beautify Thebes. Festivals were held at the season when the flowers were in full bloom, and the light-hearted Egyptian did not fail to make the flowers talk to him, in the imagination, of the delights of life. In one case a fig-tree is made to call to a passing maiden to come into its shade.

" Come," it says, " and spend this festal day, and to-morrow, and the day after to-morrow, sitting in my shadow. Let thy lover sit at thy side, and let him drink . . . Thy servants will come with the dinner things—they will bring drink of every kind, with all manner of cakes, flowers of yesterday and of to-day, and all kinds of refreshing fruit."

Than this one could hardly find a more convincing indication of the gaiety of the Egyptian temperament. In the eighteenth and nineteenth centuries A.D., the people were so oppressed that any display of luxury was discouraged, and a happy smile brought the tax-collector to the door to ascertain whether it was due to financial prosperity. But the carrying of flowers, and other indications of a kind of unworried contentment, are now again becoming apparent on all sides.

The affection displayed by the Egyptians for bright colours would alone indicate that their temperament was not melancholic. The houses of the rich were painted with colours which would be regarded as crude had they appeared in the Occident, but which are admissible in Egypt, where the natural brilliancy of the sunshine and the scenery demands a more extreme colour-scheme in decoration. The pavilions in which the nobles " made a happy day," as they phrased it, were painted with the most brilliant wall-decorations, and the delicately shaped lotus columns supporting the roof were striped with half a dozen colours, and were hung with streamers of linen. The ceilings and pavements seem to have afforded the artists a happy field for a display of their originality and skill, and it is on these stretches of smooth-plastered surface that gems of Egyptian art are often found. A pavement from the palace of Akhnaton at Tell el Amarna shows a scene in which a cow is depicted frisking through the reeds, and birds are represented flying over the marshes. In the palace of Amenophis III at Gurneh there was a ceiling decoration representing a flight of doves, which, in its delicacy of execution and colouring, is not to be classed with the crude forms of Egyptian decoration, but indicates an equally light-hearted temperament in its creator. It is not probable that either bright colours or daintiness of design would emanate from the brains of a sombre-minded people.

Some of the feminine garments worn in ancient Egypt were exceedingly gaudy, and they made up in colour all that they lacked in variety of design. In the Middle and New Empires the robes of the men were as many-hued as their wall decorations, and as rich in composition. One may take as a typical example the costume of a certain priest who lived at the end of Dynasty XVIII. An elaborate wig covers his head ; a richly ornamented necklace surrounds his neck ; the upper part of his body is clothed in a tunic of gauze-like linen ; as a skirt there is swathed around him the most delicately coloured fine linen, one end of which is brought up and thrown gracefully over his arm ; decorated sandals cover his feet and curl up over his toes ; and in his hand he carries a jewelled wand surmounted by feathers. It would be an absurdity to state that these folds of fine linen hid a heart set on things higher than this world and its vanities. Nor do the objects of daily use found in the tombs suggest any austerity in the Egyptian character. There is no reflection of the Underworld to be looked for in the ornamental bronze mirrors, nor smell of death in the frail perfume pots. Religious abstraction is not to be sought in lotus-formed drinking-cups, and mortification of the body is certainly not practised on golden chairs and soft cushions. These were the objects buried in the tombs of the priests and religious teachers.

The puritanical tendency of a race can generally be discovered by a study of the personal names of the people. The names by which the Egyptians called their children are as gay as they are pretty, and lack entirely the Puritan character. " Eyes-of-love," " My-lady-is-as gold," " Cool-breeze," " Gold-and-lapis-lazuli," " Beautiful-morning," are Egyptian names very far removed from " Through-trials-and-tribulations-we-enter-into-the Kingdom-of-Heaven-Jones," which is the actual name of a modern scion of a Puritan family. And the well-known " Praise-God Barebones " has little to do with the Egyptian " Beautiful-Kitten," " Little-Wild-Lion," " I-have-wanted-you," " Sweetheart," and so on.

The nature of the folk-tales is equally indicative of the temperament of a nation. The stories which have come down to us from ancient Egypt are often as frivolous as they are quaint. Nothing delighted the Egyptians more than listening to a tale told by an expert story-teller; and it is to be supposed that such persons were in as much demand in the old days as they are now. One may still read of the adventures of the Prince who was fated to die by a dog, a snake, or a crocodile; of the magician who made the waters of the lake heap themselves up that he might descend to the bottom dry-shod to recover a lady's jewel; of the fat old wizard who would cut a man's head off and join it again to his body; of the fairy godmothers who made presents to a new-born babe; of the ship-wrecked sailor who was thrown up on an island inhabited by a serpent with a human nature; of the princess in the tower whose lovers spent their days in attempting to climb to her window—and so on. The stories have no moral, they are not pompous: they are purely amusing, interesting and romantic. As an example one may quote the story which is told of Prince Setna, the son of Rameses II. This Prince was one day sitting in the court of the temple of Ptah, when he saw a woman pass, "beautiful exceedingly, there being no woman of her beauty." There were wonderful golden ornaments upon her, and she was attended by fifty-two persons, themselves of some rank and much beauty. "The hour that Setna saw her, he knew not the place on earth where he was"; and he called to his servants and told them to "go quickly to the place where she is, and learn what comes under her command." The beautiful lady proved finally to be named Tabubna, the daughter of a priest of Bast, the Cat. Setna's acquaintance with her was later of a most disgrace-ful character; and, from motives which are not clear, she made him murder his own children to please her. At the critical moment, however, when the climax is reached, the old, old joke is played upon the listener, who is told that Setna then woke up, and discovered that the whole affair had been an afternoon dream in the shade of the temple court.

The Egyptians often amused themselves by drawing comic pictures and caricatures, and there is an interesting series still preserved in which animals take the place of human beings, and are shown performing all manner of antics. One sees a cat walking on its hind legs driving a flock of geese, while a wolf carrying a staff and knapsack leads a herd of goats. There is a battle of the mice and cats, and the king of the mice in his chariot drawn by two dogs, is seen attacking the fortress of the cats. A picture which is worthy of Edward Lear shows a ridiculous hippopotamus seated amidst the foliage of a tree, eating from a table, whilst a crow mounts a ladder to wait upon him. There are caricatures showing women of fashion rouging their faces, unshaven and really amusing old tramps, and so forth. Even upon the walls of t\e tombs there are often comic pictures, in which one may see little girls fighting and tearing each other's hair, men tumbling one over another as they play, and the like ; and one must suppose that these were the scenes which the owner of the tomb wished to perpetuate throughout the eternity of Death.

The Egyptians took keen delight in music. In the sound of the trumpet and on the well-tuned cymbals they praised God in Egypt as merrily as the Psalmist could wish. The strings and the pipe, the lute and the harp, made music at every festival—religious, national, or private. Plato tells us that " nothing but beautiful forms and fine music was permitted to enter into the assemblies of young people " in Egypt ; and he states that music was considered as being of the greatest consequence for its beneficial effects upon youthful minds. Strabo records the fact that music was largely taught in Egypt, and the numbers of musical instruments buried in the tombs or represented in the decorations confirm his state-ment. The music was scientifically taught and a know-ledge of harmony is apparent in the complicated forms of the instruments. The harps sometimes had as many as twenty-two strings ; the long-handled guitars, fitted with three strings, were capable of wide gradations ; and the flutes were sufficiently complicated to be described by early writers as " many-toned." The Egyptian did not

H

merely bang a drum with his fist because it made a noise, nor blow blasts upon a trumpet as a means of expressing the inexpressible. He was an educated musician, and he employed the medium of music to encourage his lightness of heart and to render his gaiety more gay.

One sees representations of the women in a rich man's harîm amusing themselves by dancing and singing. In the tomb of Ay there is a scene showing the interior of the women's quarters, and here the ladies are shown dancing, playing guitars, feasting or adorning themselves with their jewellery ; while the store-rooms are seen to be filled with all manner of musical instruments, as well as mirrors, boxes of clothes, and articles of feminine use. At feasts and banquets a string band played during the meal, and songs were sung to the accompaniment of the harp. At religious festivals choruses of male and female voices were introduced. Soldiers marched through the streets to the sound of trumpets and drums, and marriage processions and the like were led by a band. At the feasts it was customary for all the dancing girls, who were employed for the amusement of the guests, to perform their dances and to play a guitar or a flute at the same time. One sees representations of girls, their heads thrown back and their long hair flying, merrily twanging a guitar as they skip round the room. In the civil and religious processions many of the participators danced along as though from sheer lightness of heart ; and on some occasions even the band footed it down the high-road, circling, jumping, and skipping as they played.

The words for " rejoice " and " dance " were synonymous in the literature of the Egyptians. In early days dancing naturally implied rejoicing, and rejoicing was most easily expressed by dancing. But the Egyptians of the refined periods more often danced to amuse themselves, regarding it, just as we do at the present day, as an exhilaration. Persons of the upper classes, however, did not indulge very freely in it, but preferred to watch the performances of professional dancers. At all banquets dancing was as indispensable as wine, women and song, and it rather depended on the nature of the wine and women as to whether the guests joined personally in the sport or sat still while the dancers swayed around the room. The professionals were generally women, but sometimes men were employed, and one sees representations of a man performing some difficult solo while a chorus of women sings and marks time by clapping the hands. Men and women danced together on occasions, but as a general rule the Egyptian preferred to watch the movements of the more graceful sex by themselves. The women sometimes danced naked, to show off the grace of their poses and the suppleness of their muscles ; sometimes they were decked with ribbons only ; and sometimes they wore transparent dresses made of linen of the finest texture. It was not unusual for them to carry tambourines and castanets with which to beat time to their dances. On the other hand, there were delicate and sober performances, unaccompanied by music. The paintings show some of the poses to have been exceedingly graceful, and there were character dances enacted in which the figures must have been highly dramatic and artistic. For example, the tableau which occurs in one dance, and is called " The Wind," shows two of the dancing-girls bent back like reeds when the wind blows upon them, while a third figure stands over them in protection, as though symbolising the immovable rocks.

But more usually the merry mood of the Egyptian asserted itself, as it so often does at the present day, in a demand for something approaching nearer to buffoonery. The dancers whirled one another about in the wildest manner, often tumbling head over heels on the floor. A trick, attended apparently with success, consisted in the attempt by the dancers to balance the body upon the head without the support of the arms. This buffoonery was highly appreciated by the audience which witnessed it ; and the banqueting-room must have been full of the noise of riotous mirth.   One cannot, indeed, regard a feast as pompous or solemn at which the banging of the tambourines and the click of castanets vied with the clatter of the dishes and the laughter of the guests in creating a general hullabaloo.   Let those state who will that the Egyptian was a gloomy individual, but first let them not fail to observe that same Egyptian trying to stand upon his head amidst the roars of laughter of his friends.

Dancing as a religious ceremony is to be found in many primitive countries, and in Egypt it exists at the present day in more than one form.   In the days of the Pharaohs it was customary to institute dances in honour of some of the gods, more especially those deities whose concerns were earthly—that is to say, those connected with love, joy, birth, death, fertility, reproduction, and so on.   It will be remembered how David danced before the ark of the Lord, and how his ancestors danced in honour of the golden calf.   In Egypt the king was wont to dance before the great god Min of the crops, and at harvest-time the peasants performed their thanksgiving before the figures of Min in this manner.   Hathor and Bast, the two great goddesses of pleasure, were worshipped in the dance. Hathor was mistress of sports and dancing, and patron of amusements and mirth, joy and pleasure, beauty and love ;   and in regard to the happy temperament of the Egyptians, it is significant that this goddess was held in the highest esteem throughout the history of the nation.

Bast was honoured by a festival which for merriment and frivolity could not well be equalled.   The festival took place at Bubastis, and is described by Herodotus in the following words :—

" This is the nature of the ceremony on the way to Bubastis. They go by water, and numerous boats are crowded with persons of both sexes.   During the voyage several women strike the cymbals, some men play the flute, the rest singing and clapping their hands.   As they pass near a town they bring the boat close to the bank.   Some of the women continue to sing and play the cymbals ;   others cry out as long as they can, and utter mocking jests against the people of the town, who begin to dance, while the former pull up their clothes before them in a scoffing manner.

The same is repeated at every town they pass on the river. Arrived at Bubastis, they celebrate the festival of Bast, sacrificing a great number of victims, and on that occasion a greater consumption of wine takes place than during the whole of the year."

At this festival of Bast half the persons taking part in the celebrations must have become intoxicated. The Egyptians were always given to wine-drinking, and Athenaeus goes so far as to say that they were a nation addicted to systematic intemperance. The same writer on the authority of Hellanicus, states that the vine was cultivated in the Nile Valley at a date earlier than that at which it was first grown by any other people ; and it is to this circumstance that Dion attributes the Egyptian's love of wine. Strabo and other writers speak of the wines of Egypt as being particularly good, and various kinds emanating from different localities are mentioned. The wines made from grapes were of the red and white varieties ; but there were also fruit wines, made from pomegranates and other fruits. In the list of offerings inscribed on the walls of temples and tombs one sees a large number or varieties recorded—wines from the north, wines from the south, wines provincial, and wines foreign. Beer, made of barley, was also drunk very largely, and this beverage is heartily commended by the early writers. Indeed, the wine and beer-bibber was so common an offender against the dignity of the nation, that every moralist who arose had a word to say against him. Thus, for example, in the maxims of Ani one finds the moralist writing :—

" Do not put thyself in a beer-house. An evil thing are words reported as coming from thy mouth when thou dost not know that they have been said by thee. When thou fallest thy limbs are broken, and nobody givest thee a hand. Thy comrades in drink stand up, saying ' Away with this drunken man '."

The less thoughtful members of society, however, considered drunkennsss as a very good joke, and even went so far as to portray it in their tomb decorations. One seees men carried home from the feast across the shoulders of three of their companions, or ignominiously hauled out of the house by their ankles and the scruff of their neck. In the tomb of Paheri at El Kab women are represented at a feast, and scraps of their conversation are recorded, such, for instance, as " Give me eighteen cups of wine, for I should love to drink to drunkenness : my inside is as dry as straw." There are actually representations of women overcome with nausea through immoderate drinking, and being attended by servants who have hastened with basins to their assistance. In another tomb-painting, a drunken man is seen to have fallen against one of the delicate pillars of the pavilion with such force that it has toppled over, to the dismay of the guests around.

In the light of such scenes as these one may picture the life of an Egyptian in the elder days as being not a little depraved. One sees the men in their gaudy raiment, and the women luxuriously clothed, staining their garments with the wine spilt from the drinking bowls as their hands shake with their drunken laughter ; and the vision of Egyptian solemnity is still further banished at the sight. It is only too obvious that a land of laughter and jest, feasting and carouse, must be situated too near a Pompeian volcano to be capable of endurance and the inhabitants too purposeless in their movements to avoid at some time or other running into the paths of burning lava. The people of Egypt went merrily through the radiant valley in which they lived, employing all that the gods had given them—not only the green palms, the thousand birds, the blue sky, the hearty wind, the river and its reflections, but also the luxuries of their civilisation —to make for themselves a frail feast of happiness. And when the last flowers, the latest empty drinking-cup, fell to the ground, nothing remained to them but that sodden, drunken night of disgrace which so shocks one at the end of dynastic history, and which inevitably led to the fall of the nation. Christian asceticism came as the natural reaction and Mohammedan strictness followed in due course ; and it required the force of both these movements to put strength and health into the people once more.

One need not dwell, however, on this aspect of the Egyptian temperament. It is more pleasing, and as pertinent to the argument, to follow the old lords of the Nile into the sunshine once more, and to glance for a moment at their sports. Hunting was a pleasure to them, in which they indulged at every opportunity. One sees representations of this with great frequency upon the walls of the tombs. A man will be shown standing in a reed boat which has been pushed in amongst the waving papyrus. A boomerang is in his hand, and his wife by his side helps him to locate the wild duck, so that he may penetrate within throwing-distance of the birds before they rise. Presently up they go with a whir, and the boomerang claims its victims ; while all manner of smaller birds dart amidst the reeds, and gaudy butterflies pass startled overhead. Again one sees the hunter galloping in his chariot over the hard sand of the desert, shooting his arrows at the gazelle as he goes. Or yet again with his dogs he is shown in pursuit of the long-eared Egyptian hare, or of some other creature of the desert. When not thus engaged he may be seen excitedly watching a bull-fight, or eagerly judging the merits of rival wrestlers, boxers, and fencers. One may follow him later into the seclusion of his garden, where, surrounded by a wealth of trees and flowers, he plays draughts with his friends, romps with his children, or fishes in his artificial pond.

There is much evidence of this nature to show that the Egyptian was as much given to these healthy amusements as he was to the mirth of the feast. Josephus states that the Egyptians were a people addicted to pleasure, and the evidence brought together in the foregoing pages shows that his statement is to be confirmed. In sincere joy of living they surpassed any other nation of the ancient world. Life was a thing of such delight to the Egyptian, that he shrank equally from losing it himself and from taking it from another. His prayer was that he might live to be a centenarian. In spite of the many wars of the Egyptians, there was less unnecessary bloodshed in the

Nile Valley than in any other country which called itself civilised.   Death was as terrible to them as it was inevitable, and the constant advice of the thinker was that the living should make the most of their life.   When a king died, it was said that " he went forth to heaven having spent life in happiness," or that " he rested after life, having completed his years in happiness."   It is true that the Egyptians wished to picture the after-life as one of continuous joy.   One sees representations of a man's soul seated in the shade of the fruit-trees of the Underworld, while birds sing in the branches above him, and a lake of cool water lies before him ; but they seemed to know that this was too pleasant a picture to be a real one. A woman, the wife of the high priest, left upon her tombstone the following inscription, addressed to her husband :

" O, brother, husband, friend," she says, " thy desire to drink and to eat has not ceased.   Therefore be drunken, enjoy the love of women—make holiday.   Follow thy desire by night and by day.   Put not care within thy heart.   Lo ! are not these the years of thy life upon earth ?   For as for the Underworld, it is a land of slumber and heavy darkness, a resting-place for those who have passed within.   Each sleepeth there in his own room, they never awake to see their fellows, they behold not their fathers nor their mothers, their heart is careless of their wives and children."

She knows that she will be too deeply steeped in the stupor of the Underworld to remember her husband, and unselfishly she urges him to continue to be happy after the manner of his nation.   Then, in a passage which rings down the years in its terrible beauty, she tells of her utter despair, lying in the gloomy Underworld, suffocated with the mummy bandages, and craving for the light, the laughter, and the coolness of the day.

" The water of life," she cries " with which every mouth is moistened, is corruption to me, the water that is by me corrupteth me.   I know not what to do since I came into this valley.   Give me running water ; say to me, ' Water shall not cease to be brought to thee '.   Turn my face to the north wind upon the edge of the water.   Verily thus shall my heart be cooled and refreshed from its pain."

It is, however, the glory of life, rather than the horror of death which is the dominant note in the inscription and reliefs. The scenes in the tomb decorations seem to cry out for very joy. The artist has imprisoned in his representations as much sheer happiness as was ever infused into cold stone. One sees there the gazelle leaping over the hills as the sun rises, the birds flapping their wings and singing, the wild duck rising from the marshes, and the butterflies flashing overhead. The fundamental joy of living—the gaiety of life which the human being may feel in common with the animals—is shown in these scenes as clearly as is the merriment in the representations of feasts and dancing. In these paintings and reliefs one finds an exact illustration to the joyful exhortation of the Psalmist as he cries, " Let the heavens rejoice, and let the earth be glad ; . . . let the fields be joyful, and all that is therein." In a land where, to quote one of their own poems, " the tanks are full of water and the earth overflows with love," where " the cool north wind " blows merrily over the fields, and the sun never ceases to shine, it would be a remarkable phenomenon if the ancient Egyptians had not developed the sanguine temperament. The foregoing pages have shown them at their feasts, in their daily occupations, and in their sports, and the reader will find that it is not difficult to describe them, in the borrowed words of the old geographer, as a people always gay and never-ceasingly " fond of dancing and red wine."

CHAPTER VII

EXCAVATIONS IN EGYPT

THERE came to the camp of a certain professor, who was engaged in excavating the ruins of an ancient Egyptian city, a young and faultlessly-attired Englishman, whose thirst for dramatic adventure had led him to offer his services as an unpaid assistant digger. This immaculate personage had read in novels and tales many an account of the wonders which the spade of the excavator could reveal, and he firmly believed that it was only necessary to set a " nigger " to dig a little hole in the ground to open the way to the treasuries of the Pharaohs. Gold, silver, and precious stones gleamed before him, in his imagination, as he hurried along subterranean passages to the vaults of long-dead kings. He expected to slide upon the seat of his very well-made breeches down the staircase of the ruined palace which he had entered by way of the skylight, and to find himself, at the bottom, in the presence of the bejewelled dead. In the intervals between such experiences he was of opinion that a little quiet gazelle shooting would agreeably fill in the swiftly passing hours ; and at the end of the season's work he pictured himself returning to the bosom of his family with such a tale to tell that every ear would be opened to him.

On his arrival at the camp he was conducted to the site of his future labours ; and his horrified gaze was directed over a large area of mud-pie, knee-deep in which a few bedraggled natives slushed their way downwards. After three weeks' work on this distressing site, the professor announced that he had managed to trace through the mud the outline of the palace walls, once the feature of the city, and that the work here might now be regarded as finished.   He was then conducted to a desolate spot in the desert, and until the day on which he fled back to England he was kept to the monotonous task of super-intending a gang of natives whose sole business it was to dig a very large hole in the sand, day after day and week after week.

It is, however, sometimes the fortune of the excavator to make a discovery which almost rivals in dramatic interest the tales of his youth.   Such an experience fell to the lot of Emil Brugsch Pasha when he was lowered into an ancient tomb and found himself face to face with a score of the Pharaohs of Egypt, each lying in his coffin ; or when Howard Carter and Lord Carnarvon climbed into the tomb of Tutankhamen, and saw before them the glorious funeral paraphernalia of the Pharaoh ; or again, when Monsieur de Morgan discovered the great mass of royal jewels in one of the pyramids at Dachour.   But such finds can be counted on the fingers, and more often an ex-cavation is a fruitless drudgery.   Moreover, the life of a digger is not always a pleasant one.

It will perhaps be of interest to the reader of romances to illustrate the above remarks by the narration of some of my own experiences ; but there are only a few interest-ing and unusual episodes in which I have had the pecu-liarly good fortune to be an actor.   There will probably be some drama to be felt in the account of the more important discoveries (for there certainly is to the antiquarian himself) ; but it should be pointed out that the interest of these rare finds pales before the description which many of us have heard, of how the archæologists of a past century discovered the body of Charlemagne clad in his royal robes and seated upon his throne—which, by the way, is quite untrue.   In spite of all that is said to the contrary, truth is seldom stranger than fiction ; and the reader who desires to be told of the discovery of buried cities whose streets are paved with gold should take warning in time and return at once to his novels.

If the dawning interest of the reader has now been thoroughly cooled by these words, it may be presumed that it will be utterly annihilated by the following narration of my first fruitless excavation ; and thus one will be able to continue the story with the relieved consciousness that nobody is attending.

In the capacity of assistant to Professor Flinders Petrie, I was set, many years ago, to the task of excavating a supposed royal cemetery in the desert behind the ancient city of Abydos, in Upper Egypt. Two mounds were first attacked ; and after many weeks of work in digging through the sand, the superstructure of two great tombs was bared. In the case of the first of these several fine passages of good masonry were cleared, and at last the burial chamber was reached. In the huge sarcophagus which was there found great hopes were entertained that the body and funeral-offerings of the dead prince would be discovered ; but when at last the interior was laid bare the solitary article found was a copy of a French newspaper left behind by the last, and equally disgusted, excavator. The second tomb defied the most ardent exploration, and failed to show any traces of a burial. The mystery was at last solved by Professor Petrie, who, with his usual keen perception, soon came to the conclusion that the whole tomb was a dummy, built solely to hide an enormous mass of rock chippings, the presence of which had been a puzzle for some time. These mason's chippings were evidently the output from some large cutting in the rock, and it became apparent that there must be a great rock tomb in the neighbourhood. Trial trenches in the vicinity presently revealed the existence of a long wall, which, being followed in either direction, proved to be the boundary of a vast court or enclosure built upon the desert at the foot of a conspicuous cliff. A ramp led up to the entrance ; but as it was slightly askew and pointed to the southern end of the enclosure, it was supposed that the rock tomb, which presumably ran into the cliff from somewhere inside this area, was situated at that end. The next few weeks were occupied in the tedious task of probing the sand hereabouts, and at length in clearing it away altogether down to the surface of the underlying rock. Nothing was found, however ; and sadly we turned to the exact middle of the court, and began to work slowly to the foot of the cliff. Here, in the very middle of the back wall, a pillared chamber was found, and it seemed certain that the entrance to the tomb would now be discovered.

The best men were placed to dig out this chamber, and the excavator—it was many years ago—went about his work with the weight of fame upon his shoulders and an expression of intense mystery upon his sorely sun-scorched face. How clearly memory recalls the letter home that week, " We are on the eve of a great discovery " ; and how vividly rises the picture of the baking desert sand into which the sweating workmen were slowly digging their way ! But our hopes were short-lived, for it very soon became apparent that there was no tomb entrance in this part of the enclosure. There remained the north end of the area, and on to this all the available men were turned. Deeper and deeper they dug their way, until the mounds of sand thrown out formed, as it were, the lip of a great crater. At last, some forty or fifty feet down, the underlying rock was struck, and presently the mouth of a great shaft was exposed leading down into the bowels of the earth. The royal tomb had at last been discovered, and it only remained to effect an entrance. The days were now filled with excitement, and, the thoughts being concentrated on the question of the identity of the royal occupant of the tomb, it was soon fixed in our minds that we were about to enter the burial-place of no less a personage than the great Pharaoh Senusert III (Sesostris), the same king whose jewels were found at Dachour.

One evening, just after I had left the work, the men came down to the distant camp to say that the last barrier was now reached and that an entrance could be

effected at once.   In the pale light of the moon, therefore,
I hastened back to the desert with a few trusted men.
As we walked along, one of these natives very cheerfully
remarked that we should all probably get our throats
cut, as the brigands of the neighbourhood had got wind
of the discovery, and were sure to attempt to enter the
tomb that night.   With this pleasing prospect before us
we walked with some caution over the silent desert.
Reaching the mound of sand which surrounded our
excavation, we crept to the top and peeped over into the
crater.   At once we observed a dim light below us, and
almost immediately an agitated but polite voice from the
opposite mound called out in Arabic, " Go away, mister.
We have all got guns."   This remark was followed by
a shot which whistled past me ; and therewith I slid down
the hill once more, and heartily wished myself safe in my
bed.   Our party then spread round the crater, and at
a given word we proposed to rush the place.   But the
enemy was too quick for us, and after the briefest scrim-
mage, and the exchanging of a harmless shot or two, we
found ourselves in possession of the tomb, and were able
to pretend that we were not a bit frightened.

Then into the dark depths of the shaft we descended,
and ascertained that the robbers had not effected an
entrance.   A long night watch followed, and the next day
we had the satisfaction of arresting some of the criminals.
The tomb was found to penetrate several hundred feet
into the cliff, and at the end of the long and beautifully
worked passage the great royal sarcophagus was found—
empty ! So ended a very strenuous season's work.

If the experiences of a digger in Professor Petrie's camp
are to be regarded as typical, they will probably serve to
damp the ardour of eager young gentlemen in search of
ancient Egyptian treasure.   One lives in a bare little hut
constructed of mud, and roofed with cornstalks or corru-
gated iron ; and if by chance there happens to be a
rain storm, as there was when I was a member of the
community, one may watch the frail building gently

subside in a liquid stream upon one's bed and books. For seven days in the week one's work continues, and it is only to the real enthusiast that that work is not monotonous and tiresome.

A few years later it fell to my lot to excavate for the Government the funeral temple of Thutmosis III at Thebes, and a fairly large sum was spent upon the undertaking. Although the site was most promising in appearance, a couple of months' work brought to light hardly a single object of importance, whereas exactly similar sites in the same neighbourhood had produced inscriptions of the greatest value. Many years ago Lord Carnarvon began his work upon a site of my own selection, the net result of which, after six weeks' labour, was one mummified cat! To sit over the work day after day, as did that patient excavator, then new to this sort of adventure, with the flies buzzing around his face and the sun blazing down upon him from a relentless sky, was hardly a pleasurable task; and to watch the clouds of dust go up from the tip-heap, where tons of unprofitable rubbish rolled down the hillside all day long, was an occupation for the damned. Yet that is excavating as it is usually found to be.

Now let us consider the other side of the story. In the Valley of the Tombs of the Kings at Thebes excavations were conducted for some years at the expense of Mr. Theodore M. Davis, of Newport, Rhode Island, by special arrangement with the Department of Antiquities of the Egyptian Government; and as the representative of that Department I had to supervise the work. The finding of the tomb of Yuaa and Tuau during these excavations was an event only eclipsed by Lord Carnarvon's recent discovery, and one which came somewhere near to the standard of romance set by the novelists. Yuaa and Tuau were the parents of Queen Tiy, the discovery of whose tomb is recorded in the next chapter. When the entrance of their tomb was cleared, a flight of steps was exposed, leading down to a passage blocked by a wall of loose

stones.   In the top right hand corner a small hole, large
enough to admit a man, had been made in ancient times,
and through this we could look down into a dark passage.
As it was too late in the day to enter at once, we postponed
that exciting experience until the morrow, and some
police were sent for to guard the entrance during the
night.   I had slept the previous night over the mouth,
and there was now no possibility of leaving the place for
several more nights, so a rough camp was formed on the
spot.

Here I settled myself down for the long watch, and
speculated on the events of the next morning, when Mr.
Davis and one or two well-known Egyptologists were to
come to the valley to be present at the opening of the
sepulchre.   Presently, in the silent darkness, a slight
noise was heard on the hillside, and immediately the
challenge of the sentry rang out.   This was answered by
a distant call, and after some moments of alertness on our
part we observed two figures approaching us.   These, to
my surprise, proved to be a well-known American artist
and his wife,[1] who had obviously come on the expectation
that trouble was ahead ; but though in this they were
destined to suffer disappointment, still, out of respect for
the absolute unconcern of both visitors, it may be mentioned that the mouth of a lonely tomb already said by
native rumour to contain incalculable wealth is not
perhaps the safest place in the world.   Here, then, on
a level patch of rock we three lay down and slept fitfully
until the dawn.   Soon after breakfast the wall at the
mouth of the tomb was pulled down, and the party passed
into the low passage which sloped down to the burial
chamber.   At the bottom of this passage there was a
second wall blocking the way ; but when a few layers had
been taken off the top we were able to climb, one by one,
into the chamber.

Imagine entering a town house which had been closed
for the summer ; imagine the stuffy room, the stiff, silent

[1] Mr. and Mrs. Joseph Lindon Smith.

Excavating the Osireion at Abydos.   A chain of
boys handing up baskets of sand to the surface

[*Photograph by the Author*]

appearance of the furniture, the feeling that some ghostly occupants of the vacant chairs have just been disturbed, the desire to throw open the windows to let life into the room once more. That was perhaps the first sensation as we stood, really dumbfounded, and stared around at the relics of the life of over three thousand years ago, all of which were as new almost as when they graced the palace of Prince Yuaa. Three arm-chairs were perhaps the first objects to attract the attention : beautiful carved wooden chairs, decorated with gold. Belonging to one of these was a pillow made of down and covered with linen. It was so perfectly preserved that one might have sat upon it or tossed it from this chair to that without doing it injury. Here were fine alabaster vases, and in one of these we were startled to find a liquid, like honey or syrup, still unsolidified by time. Boxes of exquisite workmanship stood in various parts of the room, some resting on delicately wrought legs. Now the eye was directed to a wicker trunk fitted with trays and partitions, and ventilated with little apertures, since the scents were doubtless strong. Two most comfortable beds were to be observed, fitted with springy string mattresses and decorated with charming designs in gold. There in the far corner, placed upon the top of a number of large white jars, stood the light chariot which Yuaa had owned in his lifetime. In all directions stood objects gleaming with gold undulled by a speck of dust, and one looked from one article to another with the feeling that the entire human conception of Time was wrong. These were the things of yesterday, of a year or so ago. Why, here were meats prepared for the feasts in the Underworld ; here were Yuaa's favourite joints, each neatly placed in a wooden box as though for a journey. Here was his staff, and here were his sandals—a new pair and an old. In another corner there stood the magical figures by the power of which the prince was to make his way through Hades. The words of the mystical " Chapter of the Flame " and of the " Chapter of the Magical Figure

I

of the North Wall " were inscribed upon them ; and upon a great roll of papyrus twenty-two yards in length other efficacious prayers were written.

But though the eyes passed from object to object, they ever returned to the two lidless gilded coffins in which the owners of this room of the dead lay as though peacefully sleeping. First above Yuaa and then above his wife the electric lamps were held, and as one looked down into their quiet faces (from which the bandages had been removed by some ancient robber), there was almost the feeling that they would presently open their eyes and blink at the light. The stern features of the old man commanded one's attention, and again and again our gaze was turned from this mass of wealth to this sleeping figure in whose honour it had been placed here.

At last we returned to the surface to allow the thoughts opportunity to collect themselves and the pulses time to quiet down, for, even to the most unemotional, a discovery of this kind, bringing one into the very presence of the past, has really an unsteadying effect. Then once more we descended, and made the preliminary arrangements for the cataloguing of the antiquities. It was now that the real work began, and, once the excitement was passed, there was a monotony of labour to be faced which put a very considerable strain on the powers of all concerned. The hot days when one sweated over the heavy packing-cases, and the bitterly cold nights when one lay at the mouth of the tomb under the stars, dragged on for many a week ; and when at last the long train of boxes was carried down to the Nile *en route* for the Cairo Museum, it was with a sigh of relief that I returned to my regular work.

This, of course, was a very exceptional discovery. We afterwards made other great finds, but to me they did not equal in dramatic interest the discovery just recorded. Even in this royal valley, however, there is much drudgery to be faced, and for a large part of the season's work it is the excavator's business to turn over endless masses of rock chippings, and to dig huge holes which have no interest for the patient digger. Sometimes the mouth of a tomb is bared, and is entered with the profoundest hopes, which are at once dashed by the sudden abrupt ending of the cutting a few yards from the surface. At other times a tomb-chamber is reached and is found to be absolutely empty.

At another part of Thebes, the well-known Italian Egyptologist, Professor Schiaparelli, had excavated for a number of years without finding anything of much importance, when suddenly one fine day he struck the mouth of a large tomb which was evidently intact. I was at once informed of the discovery, and proceeded to the spot as quickly as possible. The mouth of the tomb was approached down a flight of steep, rough steps, still half-choked with *débris*. At the bottom of this the entrance of a passage running into the hillside was blocked by a wall of rough stones. After photographing and removing this, we found ourselves in a long, low tunnel, blocked by a second wall a few yards ahead. Both these walls were intact, and we realised that we were about to see what probably no living man had ever seen before : the absolutely intact remains of a rich Theban of the Imperial Age—*i.e.*, about 1200 or 1300 B.C. When this second wall was taken down we passed into a carefully cut passage high enough to permit of our standing upright.

At the end of this passage a plain wooden door barred our progress. The wood retained the light colour of fresh deal, and looked for all the world as though it had been set up but yesterday. A heavy wooden lock, such as is used at the present day, held the door fast. A neat bronze handle on the side of the door was connected by a string to a wooden knob set in the masonry door-post ; and this string was carefully sealed with a small dab of stamped clay. The whole contrivance seemed so modern that Professor Schiaparelli called to his servant for the key, who quite seriously replied, " I don't know where it is, sir." He then thumped the door with his hand to see whether it would be likely to give ; and, as the echoes reverberated through the tomb, one felt that the mummy, in the darkness beyond, might well think that his resurrection call had come.   One almost expected him to rise, like the dead knights of Kildare in the Irish legend, and to ask, " Is it time ? " for the three thousand years which his religion had told him was the duration of his life in the tomb was already long past.

Meanwhile we turned our attention to the objects which stood in the passage, having been placed there at the time of the funeral, owing to the lack of room in the burial-chamber.   Here a vase, rising upon a delicately shaped stand, attracted the eye by its beauty of form ; and here a bedstead caused us to exclaim at its modern appearance. A palm-leaf fan, used by the ancient Egyptians to keep the flies off their wines and unguents, stood near a now empty jar ; and near by a basket of dried-up fruit was to be seen.   This dried fruit gave the impression that the tomb was perhaps a few months old, but there was nothing else to be seen which suggested that the objects were even as much as a year old.   It was almost impossible to believe, and quite impossible to realise, that we were standing where no man had stood for well over three thousand years ; and that we were actually breathing the air which had remained sealed in the passage since the ancient priests had closed the entrance thirteen hundred years before Christ.

Before we could proceed farther, many flashlight photographs had to be taken, and drawings made of the doorway ; and after this a panel of the woodwork had to be removed with a fretsaw in order that the lock and seal might not be damaged.   At last, however, this was accomplished, and the way into the tomb-chamber was open.   Stepping through the frame of the door, we found ourselves in an unencumbered portion of the floor, while around us in all directions stood the funeral furniture, and on our left the coffins of the deceased noble and his wife loomed large.   Everything looked new and undecayed, and even the order in which the objects were arranged suggested a tidying-up done that very morning. The gravel on the floor was neatly smoothed, and not a speck of dust was anywhere to be observed. Over the large outer coffin a pall of fine linen was laid, not rotting and falling to pieces like the cloth of mediæval times we see in our museums, but soft and strong like the sheets of our beds. In the clear space before the coffin stood a wooden pedestal in the form of a miniature lotus column. On the top of this, resting on three wooden prongs, was a small copper dish, in which were the ashes of incense, and the little stick used for stirring them. One asked oneself in bewilderment whether the ashes here, seemingly not cold, had truly ceased to glow at a time when Rome and Greece were undreamt of, when Assyria did not exist, and when the Exodus of the Children of Israel was yet unaccomplished.

On low tables round cakes of bread were laid out, not cracked and shrivelled, but smooth and brown, with a kind of white-of-egg glaze upon them. Onions and fruit were also spread out ; and the fruit of the *dôm* palm was to be seen in plenty. In various parts of the chamber there were numerous bronze vessels of different shapes, intended for the holding of milk or wine.

Well supplied with food and drink, the senses of the dead man were soothed by a profusion of flowers, which lay withered but not decayed beside the coffin, and which at the time of the funeral must have filled the chamber with their sweetness. Near the doorway stood an upright wooden chest closed with a lid. Opening this, we found it to contain the great ceremonial wig of the deceased man, which was suspended from a rail passing across the top of the chest, and hung free of the sides and bottom. The black hair was plaited into hundreds of little tails, but in size the wig was not unlike those of the early eighteenth century in Europe. Chairs, beds, and other pieces of furniture were arranged around the room, and at one side there were a number of small chests and boxes piled up against the wall. We opened one or two of these, and found them to contain delicate little vases of glass, stone and metal, wrapped round with rags to prevent them breaking. These, like everything else in the tomb, were new and fresh, and showed no trace of the passing of the years.

The coffins, of course, were hidden by the great casing in which each rested, and which itself was partly hidden by the linen pall. Nothing could be touched for many days until photographs had been taken and records made ; and we therefore returned through the long passage to the light of the day.

There must have been a large number of intact tombs to be found when the first modern interest in Egyptian antiquities developed ; but the market thus created had to be supplied, and gangs of illicit diggers made short work of the most accessible tombs. This illegal excavation, of course, continues to some extent at the present day, in spite of all precautions, but the results are becoming less and less proportionate to the labour expended and risk taken. A native likes best to do a little quiet digging in his own back yard and to admit nobody else into the business. To illustrate this, I may mention a tragedy which was brought to my notice a few years ago. A certain native discovered the entrance of a tomb in the floor of his stable, and at once proceeded to worm his way down the tunnel. That was the end of the native. His wife, finding that he had not returned two hours or so later, went down the newly found tunnel after him. That was the end of her also. In turn, three other members of the family went down into the darkness, and that was the end of them. A native official was then called, and, lighting his way with a candle, penetrated down the winding passage. The air was so foul that he was soon obliged to retreat, but he stated that he was just able to see in the distance ahead the bodies of the unfortunate peasants, all of whom had been overcome by what he quaintly described as " the evil lighting and bad climate."

Various attempts at the rescue of the dead bodies during the day and the night having failed, I gave orders that this tomb should be regarded as their sepulchre, and that its mouth should be sealed up. According to the natives, there was evidently a vast hoard of wealth stored at the bottom of this tomb, and the would-be robbers had met their death at the hands of the demon in charge of it, who had seized each man by the throat as he came down the tunnel and had strangled him.

The Egyptian peasants have a very strong belief in the power of such creatures of the spirit world. A native who was attempting recently to discover hidden treasure in a certain part of the desert, sacrificed a lamb each night above the spot where he believed the treasure to lie, in order to propitiate the *djin* who guarded it. On the other hand, however, they have no superstition as regards the sanctity of the ancient dead, and they do not hesitate on that ground to rifle the tombs. Thousands of graves have been desecrated by these seekers after treasure, and it is very largely the result of this that scientific excavation is often so fruitless nowadays. When an excavator states that he has discovered a tomb, one takes it for granted that he means a *plundered* tomb, unless he definitely says that it was intact, in which case one calls him a lucky fellow and regards him with green envy.

And thus we come back to my remarks at the beginning of this chapter, that there is a painful disillusionment awaiting the man who comes to dig in Egypt in the hope of finding the golden cities of the Pharaohs or the bejewelled bodies of their dead.

CHAPTER VIII

THE TOMB OF TIY AND AKHNATON[1]

In January 1907 the excavations in the Valley of the Tombs of the Kings at Thebes, which were being conducted each year under my supervision at the expense of Mr. Davis, brought to light the entrance of a tomb which, by its style, appeared to be that of a royal personage of the XVIIIth Dynasty. The Valley lies behind the cliffs which form the western boundary of Thebes, and is approached by a long winding road running between the rocks and rugged hills of the Lybian desert. Here the Pharaohs of the XVIIIth to the XXth Dynasties were buried in large sepulchres cut into the sides of the hills; and the excavations had for their object the removal of the *débris* which had collected at the foot of these hills, in order that the tombs hidden beneath might be revealed. About sixty tombs are now open, some of which were already known to Greek and Roman travellers; and there are palpably not more than two or three still to be discovered.

When this new tomb-entrance was uncovered I was at once notified, and proceeded with all despatch to the Valley. It was not long before we were able to enter the tomb. A rough stairway led down into the hillside, bringing us to the mouth of a passage which was entirely blocked by a wall of built stones. On removing this wall we found ourselves in a small passage, descending at a sharp incline to a chamber which could be seen a few yards further on. Instead of this passage being free from *débris*, however, as we had expected on finding the entrance-wall intact, it was partly filled with fallen stones which seemed to be the ruins of an earlier entrance-wall.

---

[1] A few paragraphs in this chapter also appear in my *Life and Times of Akhnaton, Pharaoh of Egypt.*

The entrance of the Tomb of Queen Tiy, with a native policeman guarding it. The large Tomb of Rameses X is to the left

On top of this heap of stones lay one of the sides of a large funeral shrine, almost entirely blocking the passage. This shrine, as we later saw, was in the form of a great box-like sarcophagus, made of cedar-wood covered with gold, and it had been intended as an outer covering for the coffin of the deceased person. It was, however, not put together : three sides of it were leaning against the walls of the burial-chamber, and the fourth was here in the passage. Either it was never built up, or else it was in process of being taken out of the tomb again when the work was abandoned.

To pass this portion of the shrine which lay in the passage without doing it damage was no easy matter. We could not venture to move it, as the wood was rotten ; and indeed, for over a year it remained in its original position. We therefore made a bridge of planks within a few inches of the low roof, and on this we wriggled ourselves across into the unencumbered passage beyond. In the funeral-chamber, besides the other portions of the shrine, we found at one corner a splendid coffin, in the usual form of a recumbent figure, inlaid in a dazzling manner with rare stones and coloured glass. The coffin had originally lain upon a wooden bier, in the form of a lion-legged couch ; but this had collapsed and the mummy had fallen to the ground, the lid of the coffin being partly thrown off by the fall, thus exposing the head and feet of the body, from which the bandages had decayed and fallen off. In the powerful glare of the electric light which we carried, the bare skull, with a golden vulture upon it, could be seen protruding from the remains of the linen bandages and from the sheets of flexible gold-foil in which, as we afterwards found, the whole body was wrapped. The inscription on the coffin, the letters of which were made of rare stones, gave the titles of Akhnaton, "the beautiful child of the Sun " ; but turning to the shrine we found other inscriptions stating that King Akhnaton had made it for his mother, Queen Tiy, and thus no immediate reply could be given to those at the mouth of the tomb who called to us to know which of the Pharaohs of Egypt had been found.

In a recess in the wall above the body there stood four alabaster "canopic" jars, each with a lid exquisitely sculptured in the form of a human head.   In another corner there was a box containing many little toilet vases and utensils of porcelain.   A few alabaster vases and other objects were lying in various parts of the chamber, arranged in some sort of rough order.

Nothing, of course, could yet be touched, and for several days, during the lengthy process of photographing and recording the contents of the tomb *in situ*, no further information could be obtained as to the identity of the owner of the tomb.   The shrine was certainly made for Queen Tiy, and so too were the toilet utensils, judging by an inscription upon one of them which gave the names of Tiy and her husband, King Amenophis III, the parents of Akhnaton. It was, therefore, not a surprise when a passing doctor declared the much broken bones to be those of a woman—that is to say, those of Queen Tiy. For reasons which will presently become apparent, it had been difficult to believe that Akhnaton could have been buried in this Valley, and one was very ready to suppose that the coffin bearing his name had but been given by him to his mother.

The important discovery was now announced, and caused considerable interest and excitement.   At the end of the winter the various archæologists departed to their several countries, and it fell to me to despatch the antiquities to the Cairo Museums, and to send the bones, soaked in wax to prevent their breakage, to Dr. Elliot Smith, to be examined by that eminent authority. It may be imagined that my surprise was considerable when I received a letter from him reading—" Are you sure that the bones you sent me are those which were found in the tomb? Instead of the bones of an old woman, you have sent me those of a young man.   Surely there is some mistake."

There was, however, no mistake. Dr. Elliot Smith later informed me that the bones were those of a young man of about thirty years of age, and at first this description did not seem to tally with that of Akhnaton, who was always thought to have been a man of middle age. But there is now no possibility of doubt that the coffin and mummy were those of this extraordinary Pharaoh, although the tomb and funeral furniture belonged to Queen Tiy. Dr. Elliot Smith's decision was, of course, somewhat disconcerting to those who had written of the mortal remains of the great Queen; but it is difficult to speak of Tiy without also referring to her famous son Akhnaton, and in these articles he had received full mention.

About the year B.C. 1500 the throne of Egypt fell to the young brother of Queen Hatshepsut, Thutmosis III, and under his vigorous rule the country rose to a height of power never again equalled. Amenophis II succeeeded to an empire which extended from the Sudân to the Euphrates and to the Greek Islands; and when he died he left these great possessions almost intact to his son, Thutmosis IV, the grandfather of Akhnaton. It is important to notice the chronology of this period. The mummy of Thutmosis IV has been shown by Dr. Elliot Smith to be that of a man of not more than twenty-six years of age; but we know that his son Amenophis III was old enough to hunt lions at about the time of his father's death, and that he was already married to Queen Tiy a year later. Thus one must suppose that Thutmosis IV was a father at the age of thirteen or fourteen, and that Amenophis III was married to Tiy at about the same age. The wife of Thutmosis IV was probably a Syrian princess, and it must have been during her regency that Amenophis III married Tiy, who was not of royal blood. Amenophis and Tiy introduced into Egypt the luxuries of Asia; and during their brilliant reign the Nile Valley was more open to Syrian influence than it had ever been before. The language of Babylon was perhaps the Court tongue, and the correspondence was written in cuneiform instead of in the hieratic script of Egypt. Amenophis III, as has been said, was probably partly

Asiatic ;   and there is, perhaps, some reason to suppose
that Yuaa, the father of Queen Tiy, was also a Syrian.
One has, therefore, to picture the Egyptian Court at this
time as being saturated with foreign ideas, which clashed
with those of the orthodox Egyptians.

Queen Tiy bore several children to the King ; but it was
not until they had reigned over twenty years that a son
and heir was born, whom they named Amenophis, that
being changed later to Akhnaton.   It is probable that he
first saw the light in the royal palace at Thebes, which
was situated on the edge of the desert at the foot of the
western hills.   It was an extensive and roomy structure
lightly built and gaily decorated.   The ceiling and pavements of its halls were fantastically painted with scenes
of animal life :   wild cattle ran through reedy swamps
beneath one's feet, and many-coloured fish swam in the
water ;   while overhead flights of pigeons, white against
a blue sky, passed across the hall, and the wild duck
hastened towards the open casements.   Through curtained
doorways one might obtain glimpses of a garden planted
with flowers foreign to Egypt ;   and on the east of the
palace the King had made a great pleasure-lake for the
Queen, surrounded by the trees of Asia.   Here, floating
in her golden barge, which was named *Aton-gleams*, the
Queen might look westwards over the tree-tops to the
splendid Theban hills towering above the palace, and
eastwards to the green valley of the Nile and the three
great limestone hills beyond.   Amenophis III has been
rightly called the " Magnificent," and one may well
believe that his son Akhnaton was born to the sound of
music and to the clink of golden wine-cups.   Fragments
of countless thousands of wine-jars and blue faience
drinking vessels have been found in the ruins of the
palace ;   and contemporary objects and paintings show
us some of the exquisitely wrought bowls of gold and
silver which must have graced the royal tables, and the
charming toilet utensils which were to be found in the
sleeping apartments.

While the luxurious Court rejoiced at the birth of this Egypto-Asiatic prince, one feels that the ancient priesthood of Amon-Ra must have stood aloof, and must have looked askance at the baby who was destined one day to be their master.   This priesthood was perhaps the proudest and most conservative community which conservative Egypt ever produced.   It demanded implicit obedience to its stiff and ancient conventions, and it refused to recognise the growing tendency towards religious speculation. One of the great gods of Syria was Aton, the god of the sun ; and his recognition at the Theban Court was a source of constant irritation to the ministers of Amon-Ra.

Probably they would have taken stronger measures to resist this foreign god had it not been for the fact that Atum of Heliopolis, an ancient god of Egypt, was on the one hand closely akin to Ra, the associated deity with Amon, and on the other hand to Aton of Syria.   Thus Aton might be regarded merely as another name for Ra or Amon-Ra ; but the danger to the old *régime* lay in the fact that with the worship of Aton there went a certain amount of free-thought.   The sun and its warm rays were the heritage of all mankind ; and the speculative mind of the Asiatic, always in advance of the less imaginative Egyptian, had not failed to attach to the Aton-worship a number of semi-philosophical teachings far broader than the strict doctrines of Amon-Ra could tolerate.

There is much reason to suppose that Queen Tiy was the prime factor in the new movement. It may, perhaps, be worth noting that her father was a priest of the Egyptian god Min, who corresponded to the North Syrian Aton in his capacity as a god of vegetation ; and she may have imbibed something of the broader doctrines from him.   It is the barge upon *her* pleasure-lake which is called *Aton-gleams*, and it is *her* private artist who is responsible for one of the first examples of the new style of art which begins to appear at this period.   Egyptian art was bound down by conventions jealously guarded by the priesthood, and the slight tendency to break away from these, which now becomes apparent, is another sign of the broadening of thought under the reign of Amenophis III and Tiy.

King Amenophis III does not seem to have been a man of strong character, and in the changes which took place at this time he does not appear to have taken so very large a part. He always showed the most profound respect for, and devotion to his Queen ; and one is inclined to regard him as a tool in her hands. According to some accounts he reigned only thirty years, but there are contemporary monuments dated in his thirty-sixth year, and it seems probable that for the last few years he was reigning only in name, and that in reality his ministers, under the regency of Queen Tiy, governed the land. Amenophis III was perhaps during his last years insane or stricken with some paralytic disease, for we read of an Asiatic monarch sending a miracle-working image to Egypt, apparently for the purpose of attempting to cure him. It must have been during these six years of absolute power, while Akhnaton was a boy, that the Queen pushed forward her reforms and encouraged the breaking down of the old traditions, especially those relating to the worship of Amon-Ra.

Amenophis III died in about the forty-ninth year of his age, after a total reign of thirty-six years ; and Akhnaton, who still bore the name of Amenophis, ascended the throne. One must picture him now as an enthusiastic boy, filled with the new thought of the age, and burning to assert the broad doctrines which he had learned from his mother and her friends, in defiance of the priests of Amon-Ra. He was already married to a lady named Nefertiti, and certainly before he was sixteen years of age he was the father of two daughters.

The new Pharaoh's first move, under the guidance of Tiy, was to proclaim Aton the only true god, and to name himself high priest of that deity. He then began to build a temple dedicated to Aton at Karnak; but it must have been distasteful to observe how overshadowed and dwarfed was this new temple by the mighty buildings in honour of the older gods which stood there. Moreover, there must have been very serious opposition to the new religion in Thebes, where Amon had ruled for so many centuries unchallenged. In whatever direction he looked he was confronted with some evidence of the worship of Amon-Ra : he might proclaim Aton to be the only god, but Amon and a hundred other deities stared down at him from every temple wall. He and his advisers, therefore, decided to abandon Thebes altogether and to found a new capital elsewhere.

Akhnaton selected a site for the new city on the west bank of the river, at a point now named El Amarna, about 160 miles above Cairo. Here the hills recede from the river, forming a bay about three miles deep and five miles long ; and in this bay the young Pharaoh decided to build his capital, which was named " Horizon of Aton." With feverish speed the new buildings were erected. A palace even more beautiful than that of his parents at Thebes was prepared for him ; a splendid temple dedicated to Aton was set up amidst a garden of rare trees and brilliant flowers ; villas for his nobles were erected, and streets were laid out. Queen Tiy, who seems to have continued to live at Thebes, often came down to El Amarna to visit her son ; but it seems to have been at his own wish rather than at her advice that he now took the important step which set the seal of his religion upon his life.

Around the bay of El Amarna, on the cliffs which shut if off so securely, the King caused landmarks to be made at intervals, and on these he inscribed an oath which some have interpreted to mean that he would never again leave his new city. He would remain, like the Pope in the Vatican, for the rest of his days within the limits of this bay ; and, rather than be distracted by the cares of state and the worries of empire, he would shut himself up with his god and would devote his life to his religion. He was but a youth still, and, to his inexperienced mind, this oath seemed nothing ; nor in his brief life does it seem that he broke it, though at times he must have longed to visit his domains.

The religion which this boy, who now called himself Akhnaton, " The Glory of Aton ", taught was by no means the simple worship of the sun. It was, without question, the most enlightened religion which the world at that time had ever known. The young priest-king called upon mankind to worship the unknown power, which is behind the sun, that power of which the brilliant sun was the visible symbol, and which might be discerned in the fertilising warmth of the sun's rays. Aton was originally the actual sun's disk ; but Akhnaton called his god " Heat which is in Aton ", and thus drew the eyes of his followers towards a Force far more intangible and distant than the dazzling orb to which they bowed down. Akhnaton's god was the energy which created the sun, the something which penetrated to this earth in the sun's heat and caused the vegetation to grow.

Amon-Ra and the gods of Egypt were for the most part but deified mortals, endued with monstrous, though limited, power, and still having around them tradition of exaggerated human deeds. Others had their origin in the natural phenomena—the wind, the Nile, the sky, and so on. All were terrific, revengeful, and able to be moved by human emotions. But Akhnaton's god was the intangible and yet ever-present Father of mankind, made manifest in sunshine. The youthful High Priest called upon his followers to search for their god not in the confusion of battle or behind the smoke of human sacrifices, but amidst the flowers and trees, amidst the wild duck and the fishes. He preached an enlightened nature-study ; he was perhaps the first apostle of the Simple Life. He strove to break down conventional religion, and ceaselessly urged his people to worship in Truth, simply, without excess of ceremonial. While the elder gods had been manifest in natural convulsions and in the more awful incidents of life, Akhnaton's kindly god could be seen in the chick which broke out of its egg, in the wind which filled the sails of the ships, in the fish which leapt from the water. Aton was the joy which caused the young sheep " to

Bust of Akhnaton found at Tell el Amarna and now in Berlin

dance upon their feet," and the birds to " flutter in their marshes." He was the god of the simple pleasures of life, and Truth was the watchword of his followers.

It may be understood how the boy longed for truth in all things when one remembers the thousand exaggerated conventions of Egyptian life at this time. Court etiquette had developed to a degree which rendered life to the Pharaoh an endless round of unnatural poses of mind and body. In the preaching of his doctrine of truth and simplicity, Akhnaton did not fail to call upon his subjects to regard their Pharaoh not as a god but as a man. It was usual for the Pharaoh to keep aloof from his people : Akhnaton was to be found in their midst. The Court demanded that their lord should drive in solitary state through the city : Akhnaton sat in his chariot with his wife and children, and allowed the artist to represent him joking with his little daughter, who has mischievously poked the horses with a stick. In representing the Pharaoh, the artist was expected to draw him in some conventional attitude of dignity : Akhnaton insisted upon being shown in all manner of natural attitudes—now leaning languidly upon a staff, now nursing his children, and now caressing his wife.

As has been said, one of the first artists to break away from the ancient conventions was in the service of Queen Tiy, and was probably under her influence. But in the radical change in the art which took place, Akhnaton is definitely stated to have been the leader, and the new school acknowledge that they were taught by the King. The new art is extraordinary, and it must be owned that its merit lies sometimes in its originality rather than in its beauty. An attempt is made to do away with the prescribed attitudes and the strict proportions, and to portray any one individual with his natural defects. Some of the sculptured heads, however, which have come down to us, and notably the four " canopic " heads found in this tomb, are of wonderful beauty, and have no trace of traditional mannerisms, though they are highly idealised.

The King's desire for light-heartedness led him to encourage the use of bright colours and gay decorations in the palace. Some of the ceiling and pavement paintings are of great beauty, while the walls and pillars inlaid with coloured stones must have given a brilliancy to the halls unequalled in Egypt at any previous time.

The group of nobles who formed the King's Court had all sacrificed much in coming to the new capital. Their estates around Thebes had been left, their houses abandoned, and the tombs which were in process of being made for them in the Theban hills had been rendered useless. The King, therefore, showered favours upon them, and at his expense built their houses and constructed sepulchres for them. It is on the walls of these tombs that one obtains the main portion of one's information regarding the teachings of this wonderful youth, who was now growing into manhood. Here are inscribed those beautiful hymns to Aton which rank so high in ancient literature. It is unfortunate that space does not allow of more than a few extracts from the hymns to be quoted here ; but something of their beauty may be realised from these.

" Thy dawning is beautiful in the horizon of heaven,
O living Aton, Beginning of life !
When thou risest in the eastern horizon of heaven
Thou fillest every land with thy beauty."

" Though thou art afar, thy rays are on earth ;
Though thou art on high, thy footprints are the day."

" When thou settest in the western horizon of heaven
The world is in darkness like the dead.
Men sleep in their chambers, their heads are wrapt up.
Every lion cometh forth from his den.
The serpents, they sting.
Darkness reigns, the world is in silence :
He that made them has gone to rest in his horizon."

" Bright is the earth when thou risest in the horizon . . .
When thou sendest forth thy rays
The two lands of Egypt are in daily festivity,
Awake and standing upon their feet,
For thou hast raised them up.
Their limbs bathed, they take their clothing,
Their arms uplifted in adoration to thy dawning.
Then in all the world they do their work."

" All cattle rest upon their herbage, all trees and plants flourish.
The birds flutter in their marshes, their wings uplifted in adoration
      to thee.
All the sheep dance upon their feet,
All winged things fly ; they live when thou hast shone upon them."

" The barques sail up-stream and down-stream alike,   . . .
The fish in the river leap up before thee,
And thy rays are in the midst of the great sea."

" Thou art he who createst the man-child in woman   . . .
Who giveth life to the son in the body of his mother ;
Who soothest him that he may not weep,
A nurse even in the womb."

" When the chick crieth in the egg-shell,
Thou givest him breath therein to preserve him alive   . . .
He cometh forth from the egg, to chirp with all his might.
He runneth about upon his two feet."

" How manifold are thy works !
They are hidden from before us." [1]

There are several verses of this hymn, which are almost
identical with Psalm civ, and those who study it closely
will be forced to one of two conclusions : either that Psalm
civ is derived from this hymn of the young Pharaoh, or
that both are derived from some early Syrian hymn to
the sun. Akhnaton may have only adapted this early
psalm to local conditions ; though, on the other hand, a
man capable of bringing to pass so great a religious revolution in Egypt may well be credited with the authorship of
this splendid song. There is no evidence to show that it
was written before the King had reached manhood.

Queen Tiy probably did not now take any further part
in a movement which had got so far out of her hands.
She was now nearly sixty years old, and this, to one who
had been a mother so early in life, was a considerable age.
It seems that she sometimes paid visits to her son at El
Amarna, but her interest lay in Thebes, where she had once
held so brilliant a Court. When at last she died, therefore,
it is not surprising to find that she was buried in the Valley
of the Tombs of the Kings. The tomb which has been
described above is most probably her original sepulchre,
and here her body was placed in the golden shrine made

---

[1] Professor Breasted's translation.

for her by Akhnaton, surrounded by the usual funeral furniture. She thus lay no more than a stone's throw from her parents, whose tomb was described in the last chapter, and was of very similar size and shape.

After her death, although preaching this gentle creed of love and simple truth, Akhnaton waged a bitter and stern war against the priesthoods of the old gods. It may be that the priesthood of Amon had again attempted to overthrow the new doctrines, or had in some manner called down the particular wrath of the Pharaoh. He issued an order that the name of Amon was to be erased and obliterated wherever it was found, and his agents proceeded to hack it out on all the temple walls. The names also of other gods were erased ; and it is noticeable in this tomb that the word *mut*, meaning " mother ", was carefully spelt in hieroglyphs which would have no similarity to those used in the word *Mut*, the goddess-consort of Amon. The name of Amenophis III, his own father, did not escape the King's wrath, and the first syllables were everywhere erased.

As the years went by Akhnaton seems to have given himself more and more completely to his new religion. He had now so trained one of his nobles, named Merira, in the teachings of Aton that he was able to hand over to him the high priesthood of that god, and to turn his attention to the many other duties which he had imposed upon himself. In rewarding Merira, the King is related to have said, " Hang gold at his neck before and behind, and gold on his legs, because of his hearing the teaching of Pharaoh concerning every saying in these beautiful places." Another official whom Akhnaton greatly advanced says : " My lord advanced me because I have carried out his teaching, and I hear his word without ceasing." The King's doctrines were thus beginning to take hold; but one feels, nevertheless, that the nobles followed the King rather for the sake of their material gains than for the spiritual comforts of the Aton-worship. There is reason to suppose that at least one of these nobles was degraded and banished from the city.

But while Akhnaton was preaching peace and goodwill amidst the flowers of the temple of Aton, his generals in Asia Minor were vainly struggling to hold together the great empire created by Thutmosis III. Akhnaton had caused a temple of Aton to be erected at one point in Syria at least, but in other respects he took little or no interest in the welfare of his foreign dominions. War was not tolerated in his doctrine : it was a sin to take away life which the good Father had given. One pictures the hardened soldiers of the empire striving desperately to hold the nations of Asia faithful to the Pharaoh whom they never saw. The small garrisons were scattered far and wide over Syria, and constantly they sent messengers to the Pharaoh asking at least for some sign that he held them in mind.

There is no more pathetic page of ancient history than that which tells of the fall of the Egyptian Empire. The Amorites, advancing along the sea-coast, took city after city from the Egyptians almost without a struggle. The chiefs of Tunip wrote an appeal for help to the King : " To the King of Egypt, my lord,—The inhabitants of Tunip, thy servant." The plight of the city is described and reinforcements are asked for. " And now," it continues, " Tunip thy city weeps, and her tears are flowing, and there is no help for us. For twenty years we have been sending to our lord the King, the King of Egypt, but there has not come a word to us, no, not one." The messengers of the beleaguered city must have found the King absorbed in his religion, and must have seen only priests of the sun where they had hoped to find the soldiers of former days. The Egyptian governor of Jerusalem, attacked by Aramaeans, writes to the Pharaoh, saying : " Let the King take care of his land, and . . . let him send troops . . . For if no troops come in this year, the whole territory of my lord the King will perish." To this letter is added a note to the King's secretary, which reads " Bring these words plainly before my lord the King : the whole land of my lord the King is going to ruin."

So city after city fell, and the empire, won at such cost, was gradually lost to the Egyptians. It is probable that Akhnaton had not realised how serious was the situation in Asia Minor. A few of the chieftains who were not actually in arms against him had written to him every now and then assuring him that all was well in his dominions ; and, strange to relate, the tribute of many of the cities had been regularly paid. The Asiatic princes, in fact, had completely fooled the Pharaoh, and had led him to believe that the nations were loyal while they themselves prepared for rebellion. Akhnaton, hating violence, had been only too ready to believe that the despatches from Tunip and elsewhere were unjustifiably pessimistic. He had hoped to bind together the many countries under his rule, by giving them a single religion. He had hoped that when Aton should be worshipped in all parts of his empire, and when his simple doctrines of love, truth, and peace should be preached from every temple throughout the length and breadth of his dominions, then war would cease and a unity of faith would hold the lands in harmony one with the other.

When, therefore, the tribute suddenly ceased, and the few refugees came staggering home to tell of the perfidy of the Asiatic princes and the fall of the empire, Akhnaton seems to have received his death blow. He was now not more than thirty years of age or so ; and though his portraits show that his face was already lined with care, and that his body was thinner than it should have been, he seems to have had plenty of reserve strength. He was the father of several daughters, but his queen had borne him no son to succeed him ; and thus he must have felt that his religion could not outlive him. With his empire lost, with Thebes his enemy, and with his treasury well-nigh empty, one feels that Akhnaton must have sunk to the very depths of despondency. His religious revolution had ruined Egypt, and had failed : did he, one wonders, find consolation in the sunshine and amidst the flowers ?

His death followed speedily ; and, resting in the splendid coffin in which we found him, he was laid in the tomb prepared for him in the hills behind his new capital. The throne fell to the husband of one of his daughters, Smenkhkara, who, after an ephemeral reign, gave place to another of the sons-in-law of Akhnaton, named Tutankhaton. This king was speedily persuaded to change his name to Tutankhamon, to abandon the worship of Aton, and to return to Thebes. Akhnaton's city fell into ruins, and soon the temples and palaces had become the haunt of jackals and the home of owls. The nobles returned with their new king to Thebes, and not one remained faithful to those " teachings " to which they had once pretended to be such earnest listeners.

The fact that the body in the new tomb was that of Akhnaton, and not of Queen Tiy, gives a new reading to the history of the burial. When Tutankhamon returned to Thebes, Akhnaton's memory was still, it appears, regarded with reverence, and it seems that there was no question of leaving his body in the neighbourhood of his deserted palace, where, until the discovery of this tomb, Egyptologists had expected to find it. It was carried to Thebes, together with some of the funeral furniture, and was placed in the tomb of Queen Tiy, which had been reopened for the purpose. But after some years had passed and the priesthood of Amon-Ra had again asserted itself, Akhnaton began to be regarded as a heretic and as the cause of the loss of Egypt's Asiatic dominions. These sentiments were vigorously encouraged by the priesthood, and soon Akhnaton came to be spoken of as " that criminal ", and his name was obliterated from his monuments. It was now felt that his body could no longer lie in state together with that of Queen Tiy in the Valley of the Tombs of the Kings. The sepulchre was therefore opened once more, and the name of Akhnaton was everywhere erased from the inscriptions. The tomb, polluted by the presence of the heretic, was no longer fit for Tiy, and the body of the Queen was therefore carried elsewhere, perhaps to the tomb of her husband Amenophis III. The shrine in which her mummy had lain was pulled to pieces and an attempt was made to carry it out of the tomb ; but this arduous task was presently abandoned, and one portion of the shrine was left in the passage, where we found it. The body of Akhnaton, his name erased, was now the sole occupant of the tomb. The entrance was blocked with stones, and sealed with the seal of Tutankhamon, a fragment of which was found ; and it was in this condition that it was discovered in 1907.

The bones of this extraordinary Pharaoh are in the Cairo Museum, but are not exhibited. The visitor to that Museum, however, may now see the " canopic " jars, the alabaster vases, the gold vulture, the gold necklace, the sheets of gold in which the body was wrapped, the toilet utensils, and parts of the shrine, all of which we found in the burial-chamber. The magnificent coffin has now been restored, and is also on view. Below the feet is inscribed a short prayer, which must have been composed by Akhnaton, and in which he addresses the god for whom he suffered so much. It reads : " I shall breathe the sweet breath which comes forth from Thy mouth. I shall behold Thy beauty every day. It is my desire that I may hear Thy sweet voice, even the North wind, that my limbs may rejuvenate with life through love of Thee. Give me Thy hands, holding Thy spirit, that I may receive it, and may live by it. Call Thou upon my name throughout eternity, and it shall never fail."

They are the most pathetic lines in all Egyptian history.

CHAPTER IX

THE TOMB OF HOREMHEB

IN the last chapter a discovery was recorded which, as experience has shown, is of considerable interest to the general reader. The romance and the tragedy of the life of Akhnaton form a really valuable addition to the store of good things which is our possession, and which the archæologist so diligently labours to increase. Another discovery, that of the tomb of Horemheb, was made in 1908; and, as it forms the natural sequel to the previous chapter, I may be permitted to record it here.

Akhnaton was succeeded by Smenkhkara, his son-in-law, who, after a brief reign, gave place to Tutankhamon, during whose reign of six or eight years the court returned to Thebes. A certain noble named Ay came next to the throne, but held it for only five years. The country was now in a chaotic condition, and was utterly upset and disorganised by the revolution of Akhnaton, and by the vacillating policy of the three weak kings who succeeded him, each reigning for so short a time. One cannot say to what depths of degradation Egypt might have sunk had it not been for the timely appearance of Horemheb, a wise and good ruler, who, though but a soldier of not particularly exalted birth, managed to raise himself to the vacant throne, and succeeded in so organising the country once more that his successors, Rameses I, Sety I, and Rameses II, were able to regain most of the lost dominions, and to place Egypt at the head of the nations of the world.

Horemheb, " The Hawk in Festival ", was born at Alabastronopolis, a city of the Eighteenth Province of Upper Egypt, during the reign of Amenophis III, who has rightly been named " The Magnificent ", and in whose reign Egypt was at once the most powerful, the most wealthy, and the most luxurious country in the world. There is reason to suppose that Horemheb's family were of noble birth, and it is thought by some that an inscription which calls King Thutmosis III " the father of his fathers " is to be taken literally to mean that the old warrior was his great—or great-great-grandfather. The young noble was probably educated at the splendid court of Amenophis III where the wit and intellect of the world was congregated, and where, under the presidency of the beautiful Queen Tiy, life slipped by in a round of revels.

As an impressionable young man, Horemheb must have watched the gradual development of free thought in the palace, and the ever-increasing irritation and chafing against the bonds of religious convention which bound all Thebans to the worship of the god Amon. Judging by his future actions, Horemheb did not himself feel any real repulsion to Amon, though the religious rut into which the country had fallen was sufficiently objectionable to a man of his intellect to cause him to cast in his lot with the movement towards emancipation. In later life he would certainly have been against the movement, for his mature judgment led him always to be on the side of ordered habit and custom as being less dangerous to the national welfare than a social upheaval or change.

Horemheb seems now to have held the appointment of captain or commander in the army, and at the same time, as a " Royal Scribe ", he cultivated the art of letters, and perhaps made himself acquainted with those legal matters which he was in later years destined to reform.

When Amenophis III died, the new king, Akhnaton, carried out the revolution which had been pending for many years, and absolutely banned the worship of Amon, with all that it involved. He built himself a new capital at El Amarna, and there he instituted the worship of the sun, or rather the heat or power of the sun, under the name of Aton. In so far as the revolution constituted a breaking away from tiresome convention, the young Horemheb seems to have been with the King. No one of intelligence could deny that the new religion and new philosophy which was preached at El Amarna was more worthy of consideration on general grounds than was the narrow doctrine of the Amon priesthood ; and all thinkers must have rejoiced at the freedom from bonds which had become intolerable. But the world was not ready, and indeed is still not ready, for the doctrines which Akhnaton propounded ; and the unpractical model-kingdom which was uncertainly developing under the hills of El Amarna must have already been seen to contain the elements of grave danger to the State.

Nevertheless the revolution offered many attractions. The frivolous members of the court, always ready for change and excitement, welcomed with enthusiasm the doctrine of moral and simple life which the King and his advisers preached, just as in the decadent days before the French Revolution the court, bored with licentiousness, gaily welcomed the morality-painting of the young Greuze. And to the more serious-minded, such as Horemheb seems to have been, the movement must have appealed in its imperial aspect. The new god Aton was largely worshipped in Syria, and it seems evident that Akhnaton had hoped to bind together the heterogeneous nations of the empire by a bond of common worship. The Asiatics were not disposed to worship Amon, but Aton appealed to them as much as any god, and Horemheb must have seen great possibilities in a common religion.

It is thought that Horemheb may be identified amongst the nobles who followed Akhnaton to El Amarna, and though this is not certain, there is little doubt that he was in high favour with the King at the time. To one whose tendency is neither towards frivolity nor towards fanaticism, there can be nothing more broadening than the influence of religious changes. More than one point of view is appreciated : a man learns that there are other ruts than that in which he runs, and so he seeks the smooth midway. Thus Horemheb, while acting loyally towards his King, and while appreciating the value of the new movement, did not exclude from his thoughts those teachings which he deemed good in the old order of things. He seems to have seen life broadly ; and when the new religion of Akhnaton became narrowed and fanatical, as it did towards the close of the tragic chapter of that king's short life, Horemheb was one of the few men who kept an open mind.

Like many other nobles of the period, he had constructed for himself a tomb at Sakkâra, in the shadow of the pyramids of the old kings of Egypt ; and fragments of this tomb, which of course was abandoned when he became Pharaoh, are now to be seen in various museums. In one of the scenes there sculptured Horemheb is shown in the presence of a king who is almost certainly Akhnaton; and yet in a speech to him inscribed above the reliefs, Horemheb makes reference to the god Amon whose very name was anathema to the King. The royal figure is drawn according to the canons of art prescribed by Akhnaton, and upon which, as a protest against the conventional art of the old order, he laid the greatest stress in his revolution ; and thus, at all events, Horemheb was in sympathy with this aspect of the movement. But the inscriptions which refer to Amon, and yet are impregnated with the Aton style of expression, show that Horemheb was not to be held down to any one mode of thought. Akhnaton was, perhaps, already dead when these inscriptions were added, and thus Horemheb may have had no further reason to hide his views ; or it may be that they constituted a protest against the narrowness which marred the last years of the idealist.

Those who read the history of the period in the last chapter will remember how Akhnaton came to persecute the worshippers of Amon, and how he erased that god's name wherever it was written throughout the length and breadth of Egypt. Evidently with this action Horemheb did not agree ; nor was this his only cause for complaint. As an officer, and now a highly placed general, of the army, he must have seen with feelings of the utmost bitterness the neglected condition of the Syrian provinces. Revolt after revolt occurred in these states ; but Akhnaton, dreaming and praying in the sunshine of El Amarna, would send no expedition to punish the rebels. Goodfellowship with all men was the King's watchword, and a policy more or less democratic did not permit him to make war on his fellow-creatures. Horemheb could smell battle in the distance, but could not taste of it. The battalions which he had trained were kept useless in Egypt ; and even when, during the last years of Akhnaton's reign, or under his immediate successor, he was made commander-in-chief of all the forces, there was no means of using his power to check the loss of the cities of Asia. Horemheb must have watched these cities fall one by one into the hands of those who preached the doctrine of the sword, and there can be little wonder that he turned in disgust from the doings at El Amarna.

During the times which followed, when Smenkhkara held the throne for a year or so, and afterwards, when Tutankhamon became Pharaoh, Horemheb seems to have been the leader of the reactionary movement. He did not concern himself so much with the religious aspect of the questions : there was as much to be said on behalf of Aton as there was on behalf of Amon. But it was he who knocked at the doors of the heart of Egypt, and urged the nation to awake to the danger in the East. An expedition against the rebels was organised, and one reads that Horemheb was the " companion of his Lord upon the battlefield on the day of the slaying of the Asiatics." Akhnaton had been opposed to warfare, and had dreamed that dream of universal peace which still is a far-off light to mankind. Horemheb was a practical man in whom such a dream would have seemed but weakness ; and, though one knows nothing more of these early campaigns, the fact that he attempted to chastise the enemies of the empire at this juncture stands to his account for all time.

Under Tutankhamon the court returned to Thebes, though not yet exclusively to the worship of Amon ; and the political phase of the revolution came to an end. The country once more settled into the old order of life, and Horemheb, having experienced the full dangers of philosophic speculation, was glad enough to abandon thought for action. He was now the most powerful man in the kingdom, and inscriptions call him " the greatest of the great, the mightiest of the mighty, presider over the Two Lands of Egypt, general of generals," and so on. The King " appointed him to be Chief of the Land, to administer the laws of the land as Hereditary Prince of all this land " ; and " all that was done was done by his command." From chaos Horemheb was producing order, and all men turned to him in gratitude as he reorganised the various government departments.

The offices which he held, such as Privy Councillor, King's Secretary, Great Lord of the People, and so on, are very numerous ; and in all of these he dealt justly though sternly, so that " when he came the fear of him was great in the sight of the people, prosperity and health were craved for him, and he was greeted as ' Father of the Two Lands of Egypt '." He was indeed the saviour and father of his country, for he had found her corrupt and disordered, and he was leading her back to greatness and dignity.

At this time he was probably a man of about forty years of age. In appearance he seems to have been noble and good to look upon. " When he was born," says the inscription, " he was clothed with strength : the hue of a god was upon him " ; and in later life, " the form of a god was in his colour," whatever that may mean. He was a man of considerable eloquence and great learning. "He astonished the people by that which came out of his mouth," we are told ; and " when he was summoned before the King the palace began to fear." One may picture the weak Pharaoh and his corrupt court, as they watched with apprehension the movements of this stern soldier, of whom it was said that his every thought was " in the footsteps of the Ibis,"—the ibis being the god of wisdom.

On the death of Tutankhamon, the question of inviting Horemheb to fill the vacant throne must have been seriously considered. A Hittite document recently discovered shows the late King's widow, Akhnaton's daughter, seeking an alliance with a Hittite prince, and promising to make him King of Eygpt; but there was another candidate, a certain Ay, who had been one of the most important nobles in the group of Akhnaton's favourites at El Amarna, and who was the father of the beautiful Nefertiti, Akhnaton's queen. Religious feeling was at the time running high, for the partizans of Amon and those of Aton seem to have been waging war on one another ; and Ay appears to have been regarded as the man most likely to bridge the gulf between the two parties. A favourite of Akhnaton, and once a devout worshipper of Aton, he was not averse to the cults of other gods ; and by conciliating both factions he managed to obtain the throne for himself. His power, however, did not last for long ; and as the priests of Amon regained the confidence of the nation at the expense of those of Aton, so the power of Ay declined. His past connections with Akhnaton told against him, and in five years or so he disappeared, leaving the throne vacant once more. We hear no more of Tutankhamon's widow or of her Hittite alliance.

There was now no question as to who should succeed. A princess named Mutnezem, the sister of Akhnaton's queen, and daughter of King Ay, was the heiress to the throne. All men turned to Horemheb in the hope that he would marry this lady, and thus reign as Pharaoh over them. He was now some forty-five years of age, full of energy and vigour, and passionately anxious to have a free hand in the carrying out of his schemes for the reorganisation of the government. It was therefore with joy that, in about the year 1345 B.C., he sailed up to Thebes in order to claim the crown.

He arrived at Luxor at a time when the annual festival of Amon was being celebrated, and all the city was *en fête*. The statue of the god had been taken from its shrine at

Karnak, and had been towed up the river to Luxor in a gorgeous barge, attended by a fleet of gaily-decorated vessels. With songs and dancing it had been conveyed into the Luxor temple, where the priests had received it standing amidst piled-up masses of flowers, fruit, and other offerings. It seems to have been at this moment that Horemheb appeared, while the clouds of incense streamed up to heaven, and the morning air was full of the sound of the harps and the lutes. Surrounded by a crowd of his admirers, he was conveyed into the presence of the divine figure, and was there and then hailed as Pharaoh.

From the temple he was carried amidst cheering throngs to the palace which stood near by ; and there he was greeted by the Princess Mutnezem, who fell on her knees before him and embraced him. That very day, it would seem, he was married to her, and in the evening the royal heralds published the style and titles by which he would be known in the future : " Mighty Bull, Ready in Plans ; Favourite of the Two Goddesses, Great in Marvels ; Golden Hawk, Satisfied with Truth ; Creator of the Two Lands," and so forth. Then, crowned with the royal helmet, he was led once more before the statue of Amon, while the priests pronounced the blessings of the gods upon him. Passing down to the quay before the temple, the figure of the god was placed once more upon the state barge and was floated down to Karnak ; while Horemheb was led through the rejoicing crowds back to the palace to begin his reign as Pharaoh.

In religious matters Horemheb at once adopted a strong attitude of friendship towards the Amon party which represented the old order of things. There is evidence to show that Aton was not at once persecuted ; yet one by one his shrines were abandoned, and the neglected temples of Amon and the elder gods once more rang with the hymns of praise. Inscriptions tell us that the King " restored the temples from the marshes of the Delta to Nubia. He fashioned a hundred images with all their bodies correct, and with all splendid costly stones. He

A statue of Tutankhamen, the Pharaoh whose tomb was
discovered by Lord Carnarvon in 1922.   Now in Cairo

established for them daily offerings every day. All the vessels of their temples were wrought of silver and gold. He equipped them with priests and with ritual-priests, and with the choicest of the army. He transferred to them lands and cattle, supplied with all equipment." By these gifts to the neglected gods, Horemheb was striving to bring Egypt back to its normal condition, and in no way was he prejudiced by any particular devotion to Amon.

A certain Patonemheb, who had been one of Akhnaton's favourites in the days of the revolution, was appointed High Priest of Ra—the older Egyptian form of Aton who was at this time identified with that god—at the temple of Heliopolis ; and this can only be regarded as an act of friendship to the Aton-worshippers. The echoing and deserted temples of Aton in Thebes and El Amarna, however, were now pulled down, and the blocks were used for the enlarging of the temple of Amon—a fact which indicates that their original dedication to Aton had not caused them to be accursed.

The process of restoration was so gradual that it could not have much disturbed the country. Horemheb's hand was firm but soothing in these matters, and the revolution seems to have been killed as much by kindness as by force. It was probably not till some years later that he showed any tendency to revile the memory of Akhnaton ; and the high feeling which at length brought the revolutionary king the name of " that criminal of El Amarna " did not rise for some considerable time. The difficulties experienced by Horemheb in steering his course between Amon and Aton, in quietly restoring the old equilibrium without in any way persecuting those who by religious convictions were Aton-worshippers, must have been immense ; and one cannot but feel that the King must have been a diplomatist of the highest standing. His unaffected simplicity won all hearts to him ; his toleration and broadness of mind brought all thoughtful men to his train ; and his strong will led them and guided them from chaos to order, from fantastic Utopia to the solid old

L

Egypt of the past. Horemheb was the preacher of Sanity, the apostle of the Normal, and Order was his watchword.

The inscriptions tell us that it was his custom to give public audiences to his subjects, and there was not a man amongst those persons whom he interviewed whose name he did not know, nor one who did not leave his presence rejoicing. Up and down the Nile he sailed a hundred times, until he was able truly to say, " I have improved this entire land ; I have learned its whole interior ; I have travelled it entirely in its midst." We are told that " his Majesty took counsel with his heart how he might expel evil and suppress lying. The plans of his Majesty were an excellent refuge, repelling violence and delivering the Egyptians from the oppressions which were around them. Behold, his Majesty spent the whole time seeking the welfare of Egypt, and searching out instances of oppression in the land."

It is interesting, by the way, to note that in the eighth year the King restored the tomb of Thutmosis IV, which had been robbed during the revolution ; and the inscription which the inspectors left behind them was found on the wall when Mr. Howard Carter discovered the tomb a few years ago. The plundering of the royal tombs is a typical instance of the lawlessness of the times. The corruption, too, which followed on the disorder was appalling ; and wherever the King went he was confronted with deceit, embezzlement, bribery, extortion, and official tyranny. Every Government officer was attempting to obtain money from his subordinates by illegal means ; and *bakshish*—that bogie of the Nile Valley— cast its shadow upon all men.

Horemheb stood this as long as he could ; but at last, regarding justice as more necessary than tact, we are told that " his Majesty seized a writing-palette and scroll, and put into writing all that his Majesty the King had said to himself." It is not possible to record here more than a few of the good laws which he then made, but the following examples will serve to show how near to his heart were the interests of his people.

It was the custom for the tax-collectors to place that portion of a farmer's harvest, which they had taken, upon the farmer's own boat, in order to convey it to the public granary. These boats often failed to be returned to their owners when finished with, and were ultimately sold by the officials for their own profit. Horemheb, therefore, made the following law :—

" If the poor man has made for himself a boat with its sail, and, in order to serve the State, has loaded it with the Government dues, and has been robbed of the boat, the poor man stands bereft of his property and stripped of his many labours. This is wrong, and the Pharaoh will suppress it by his excellent measures. If there be a poor man who pays the taxes to the two deputies, and he be robbed of his property and his boat, my majesty commands : that every officer who collects the taxes and takes the boat of any citizen, this law shall be executed against him, and his nose shall be cut off, and he shall be sent in exile to Tharu. Furthermore, concerning the tax of timber, my majesty commands that if any officer find a poor man without a boat, then he shall bring him a craft belonging to another man in which to carry the timber ; and in return for this let the former man do the loading of the timber for the latter."

The tax-collectors were wont to commandeer the services of all the slaves in the town, and to detain them for six or seven days, " so that it was an excessive detention indeed." Often, too, they used to appropriate a portion of the tax for themselves. The new law, therefore, was as follows :—

" If there be any place where the officials are tax-collecting and any one shall hear the report saying that they are tax-collecting to take the produce for themselves, and another shall come to report saying ' My man slave or my female slave has been taken away and detained many days at work by the officials,' the offender's nose shall be cut off, and he shall be sent to Tharu."

One more law may here be quoted. The police used often to steal the hides which the peasants had collected to hand over to the Government as their tax. Horemheb, having satisfied himself that a tale of this kind was not merely an excuse for not paying the tax, made this law :—

" As for any policeman concerning whom one shall hear it said that he goes about stealing hides, beginning with this day the law shall be executed against him, by beating him a hundred blows, opening five wounds, and taking from him by force the hides which he took."

To carry out these laws he appointed two chief judges of very high standing, who are said to have been " perfect in speech, excellent in good qualities, knowing how to judge the heart." Of these men the King writes : " I have directed them to the way of life, I have led them to the truth, I have taught them, saying, ' Do not receive the reward of another. How, then, shall those like you judge others, while there is one among you committing a crime against justice ? ' " Under these two officials Horemheb appointed many judges, who went on circuit around the country ; and the King took the wise step of arranging, on the one hand that their pay should be so good that they would not be tempted to take bribes, and, on the other hand, that the penalty for this crime should be most severe.

So many were the King's reforms that one is inclined to forget that he was primarily a soldier. He appears to have made some successful expeditions against the Syrians, but the fighting was probably near his own frontiers, for the empire lost by Akhnaton was not recovered for many years, and Horemheb seems to have felt that Egypt needed to learn to rule herself before she attempted to rule other nations. An expedition against some tribes in the Sudân was successfully carried through, and it is said that " his name was mighty in the land of Kush, his battle-cry was in their dwelling-places." Except for a semi-military expedition which was dispatched to the land of Punt, these are the only recorded foreign activities of the King ; but that he had spent much time in the organisation and improvement of the army is shown by the fact that three years after his death the Egyptian soldiers were swarming over the Lebanon and hammering at the doors of the cities of Jezreel.

Had he lived for another few years he might have been famous as a conqueror as well as an administrator, though old age might retard and tired bones refuse their office. As it is, however, his name is written sufficiently large in the book of the world's great men ; and, when he died, about B.C. 1315, after a reign of some thirty-five years, he had done more for Egypt than had almost any other Pharaoh.   He found the country in the wildest disorder, and he left it the master of itself, and ready to become once more the master of the empire which Akhnaton's doctrine of Peace and Goodwill had lost.   Under his direction the purged worship of the old gods, which for him meant but the maintenance of some time-proved customs, had gained the mastery over the chimerical worship of Aton ; without force or violence he had substituted the practical for the visionary ;   and to Amon and Order his grateful subjects were able to cry, " The sun of him who knew thee not has set, but he who knows thee shines ; the sanctuary of him who assailed thee is overwhelmed in darkness, but the whole earth is now in light."   In later years the names of Akhnaton, Smenkhkara, Tutankhamen, and Ay were all removed from the records as being tainted with the Aton-worship ;   and Horemheb was described as the immediate successor of Amenophis III, some thirty years thus being added to the actual length of his reign.

The tomb of this great Pharaoh was cut in the rocks on the west side of the Valley of the Tombs of the Kings, not far from the resting-place of Amenophis II.   In the days of the later Ramesside kings the tomb-plunderers entered the sepulchre, pulled the embalmed body of the king to pieces in the search for hidden jewels, scattered the bones of the three members of his family who were buried with him, and stole almost everything of value which they found.   There must have been other robberies after this, and finally the Government inspectors of about B.C. 1100 entered the tomb, and, seeing its condition, closed its mouth with a compact mass of stones.   The torrents of rain which sometimes fall in winter in Egypt percolated through this filling, and left it congealed and difficult to cut through ; and on the top of this hard mass tons of rubbish were tossed from other excavations, thus completely hiding the entrance.

In this condition, the tomb was found by us in February 1908.   We had been working on the side of the valley opposite to the tomb of Rameses III, where the accumulations of *débris* had entirely hidden the face of the rocks, and, as this was a central and likely spot for a "find", it was hoped that when the skin of rubbish had been cleared away the entrance of a royal tomb might be exposed. After a few weeks of digging, the mouth of a large shaft, cut into the limestone, was cleared. This proved to lead into a small chamber half-filled with rubbish, amongst which some fine jewellery, evidently hidden here, was found. This has been published by Mr. Davis in facsimile, and further mention of it here is unnecessary. Continuing the work it was not long before traces of another tomb became apparent, and in a few days' time we were able to look down from the surrounding mounds of rubbish upon the commencement of a rectangular cutting in the rock. The size and style of the entrance left no doubt that the work was to be dated to the end of the Eighteenth Dynasty, and the excavators were confident that the tomb of either Tutankhamon or Horemheb lay before them. Steps leading down to the entrance were presently uncovered, and finally the doorway itself was freed from *débris*.

On one of the door-posts an inscription was now seen, written in black ink by one of the Government inspectors of B.C. 1100. This stated that in the fourth year of an unknown king the tomb had been inspected, and had been found to be that of Horemheb.

We had hoped now to pass into the tomb without further difficulty, but in this we were disappointed, for the first corridor was quite choked with the rubbish placed there by the inspectors. This corridor led down at a steep angle through the limestone hillside, and, like all other parts of the tomb, it was carefully worked. It was not until two days later that enough clearing had been done to allow us to crawl in over the rubbish, which was still piled up so nearly to the roof that there was only just room to wriggle downwards over it with our backs pressing against the stone above. At the lower end of the corridor there was a flight of steps towards which the rubbish shelved, and, sliding down the slope, we were here able to stand once more. It was obvious that the tomb did not stop here, and work, therefore, had to be begun on the rubbish which choked the stairway in order to expose the entrance to further passages. A doorway soon became visible, and at last this was sufficiently cleared to permit of our crawling into the next corridor, though now we were even more closely squeezed between the roof and the *débris* than before.

The party which made the entrance consisted of Mr. Davis, Mr. Ayrton, Mr. Harold Jones, Mr. Max Dalison, formerly of the Egypt Exploration Fund, and myself. Wriggling and crawling, we pushed and pulled ourselves down the sloping rubbish, until, with a rattling avalanche of small stones, we arrived at the bottom of the passage, where we scrambled to our feet at the brink of a large rectangular well, or shaft. Holding the lamps aloft, the surrounding walls were seen to be covered with wonderfully preserved paintings, executed on slightly raised plaster. Here Horemheb was seen standing before Isis, Osiris, Horus, and other gods; and his cartouches stood out boldly from amidst the elaborate inscriptions. The colours were extremely rich, and, though there was so much to be seen ahead, we stood there for some minutes, looking at them with a feeling much akin to awe.

The shaft was partly filled with rubbish, and not being very deep, we were able to climb down it by means of a ladder, and up the other side to an entrance which formed a kind of window in the sheer wall. In entering a large tomb for the first time, there are one or two scenes which fix themselves upon the memory more forcefully than others, and one feels as though one might carry these impressions intact to the grave. In this tomb there was nothing so impressive as this view across the well and through the entrance in the opposite wall. At one's feet lay the dark pit; around one the gaudy paintings gleamed; and through the window-like aperture before one, a dim suggestion could be obtained of a white-pillared hall.   The intense eagerness to know what was beyond, and, at the same time, the feeling that it was almost desecration to climb into those halls which had stood silent for thousands of years, cast a spell over the scene and made it unforgetable.

This aperture had once been blocked up with stones, and the paintings had passed across it, thus hiding it from view, so that a robber entering the tomb might think that it ended here.   But the trick was an old one, and the plunderers had easily detected the entrance, had pulled away the blocks, and had climbed through. Following in their footsteps, we went up the ladder and passed through the entrance into the pillared hall.   Parts of the roof had fallen in, and other parts appeared to be likely to do so at any moment.   Clambering over the *débris* we descended another sloping corridor, which was entered through a cutting in the floor of the hall, originally blocked up and hidden.   This brought us into a chamber covered with paintings, like those around the well ; and again we were brought to a standstill by the amazingly fresh colours which arrested and held the attention.

We then passed on into the large burial-hall, the roof of which was supported by crumbling pillars.   Slabs of limestone had broken off here and there and had crashed down on to the floor, bringing with them portions of the ceiling painted with a design of yellow stars on a black ground.   On the walls were unfinished paintings, and it was interesting to notice that the north, south, east, and west were clearly marked upon the four walls for ceremonial purposes.

The main feature towards which our eyes were turned was the great pink granite sarcophagus which stood in the middle of the hall.   Its sides were covered with well-cut inscriptions of a religious nature ; and at the four corners there were figures of Isis and Nephthys, in relief, with their wings spread out as though in protection around the body.   Looking into the sarcophagus, the lid having been thrown off by the plunderers, we found it

The entrance of the Tomb of Horemheb in the Valley of the Tombs of the Kings

empty except for a skull and a few bones of more than one person. The sarcophagus stood upon the limestone floor, and under it small holes had been cut, in each of which a little wooden statue of a god had been placed. Thus the king's body was, so to speak, carried on the heads of the gods, and held aloft by their arms. This is a unique arrangement, and has never before been found in any burial.

In all directions broken figures of the gods were lying, and two defaced wooden statues of the king were over-thrown beside the sarcophagus. Dead flowers were found here and there amidst the *débris*, these being the remnant of the masses of garlands which were always heaped around and over the coffin.

Peering into a little side chamber on the right, we saw two skulls and some broken bones lying in the corner. These appeared to be female, and one of the skulls may have been that of Mutnezem, the queen. In another small chamber on the left there was a fine painting of Osiris on the back wall; and, crouching at the foot of this, a statuette of a god with upraised hands had been placed. As we turned the corner and came upon it in the full glare of the lamps, one felt that the arms were raised in horror at the sight of us, and that the god was gasping with surprise and indignation at our arrival. In the floor of another ante-chamber a square hole was cut, leading down to a small room. A block of stone had neatly fitted over the opening, thus hiding it from view; but the robbers had detected the crack, and had found the hiding place. Here there were a skull and a few bones, again of more than one person. Altogether there must have been four bodies buried in the tomb; and it seems that the inspectors, finding them strewn in all directions, had replaced one skull in the sarcophagus, two in the side room, and one in this hiding-place, dividing up the bones between these three places as they thought fit. It may be that the king himself was buried in the underground chamber, and that the sarcophagus was a sort of blind;

for he had seen the destruction caused by robbers in the tomb of Thutmosis IV, which he had restored, and he may have made this attempt to secure the safety of his own body. Whether this be so or not, Fate has not permitted the body of the great king to escape the hands of the destroyer, and it will now never be known with certainty whether one of these four heads wore the crown of the Pharaohs.

The temperature was very great in the tomb, and the perspiration streamed down our faces as we stood contemplating the devastation. Now the electric lamps would flash upon the gods supporting the ransacked sarcophagus, lighting for a moment their grotesque forms ; now the attention would concentrate upon some wooden figure of a hippopotamus-god or cow-headed deity ; and now the light would bring into prominence the great overthrown statue of the king. There is something peculiarly sensational in the examining of a tomb which has not been entered for such thousands of years, but it must be left to the imaginative reader to infuse a touch of that feeling of the dramatic into these words. It would be hopeless to attempt to put into writing those impressions which go to make the entering of a great Egyptian sepulchre so thrilling an experience : one cannot describe the silence, the echoing steps, the dark shadows, the hot breathless air ; nor tell of the sense of vast Time and the penetrating of it which stirs one so deeply.

The air was too bad to permit of our remaining long so deep in the bowels of the earth ; and the falling ceilings were a source of much danger. We therefore presently made our way through the halls and corridors back to the upper world, scrambling and crashing over the *débris*, and squeezing ourselves through the rabbit-hole by which we had entered. As we passed out of this hot, dark tomb into the brilliant sunshine and the bracing north wind, the gloomy wreck of the place was brought before the imagination with renewed force. The scattered bones, the broken statues, the dead flowers, grouped themselves in the mind into a picture of utter decay. In some of the tombs which have been opened the freshness of the objects has caused one to exclaim at the inaction of the years ; but here, where vivid and well-preserved wall-paintings looked down on a jumbled collection of smashed fragments of wood and bones, one felt how hardly the Powers deal with the dead. How far away seemed the great fight between Amon and Aton ; how futile the task which Horemheb accomplished so gloriously ! It was all over and forgotten, and one asked oneself what it mattered whether the way was difficult or the battle slow to win. In the fourth year of the reign of Horemheb a certain harper named Neferhotep partly composed a song which was peculiarly appropriate to the tune which ran in one's head at the opening of the tomb of this Pharaoh whom the harper served :—

" (1)Behold the dwelling of the dead. Their walls fall down ; their place is no more : they are as though they had never existed. (2) That which hath come into being must pass away again. The young man and the maidens go to their places ; the sun riseth at dawn, and setteth again in the hills of the west. Men beget and women conceive. The children, too, go to the places which are appointed for them. O, then, be happy ! Come, scents and perfumes are set before thee : *mahu*-flowers and lilies for the arms and neck of thy beloved. Come, songs and music are before thee. Set behind thee all cares ; think only upon gladness, until that day cometh whereon thou shalt go down to the land which loveth silence."

Horemheb must often have heard this song sung in his palace at Thebes by its composer ; but did he think, one wonders, that it would be the walls of his own tomb which would fall down, and his own bones which would be almost as though they had never existed ?

CHAPTER X

LOWER NUBIA AND THE GREAT RESERVOIR

When the great dam at Aswân on the frontier between Upper Egypt and Lower Nubia was built, the Nile valley for some eighty miles southwards was turned into a vast reservoir. The natives were handsomely compensated for the destruction of their houses and the submersion of their land, and their villages were rebuilt on the hillsides at a higher level. The reservoir is full each year from about January to June, while during the remaining months of the year the river resumes its natural level, and the people come down from their lofty dwelling-places to cultivate their small fields, like Mr. and Mrs. Noah from Ararat. Now, however, the dam, having proved so great a success, has been heightened ; and in recent years the level of the water in the reservoir has been so increased that the country is flooded for well over a hundred miles. Several ancient buildings and many cemeteries and other remains have gone under the water ; and for half the year the country is like a great lake with temples for islands. In order to decide what steps had to be taken to prevent any loss to Egyptology in this respect, the present writer made an elaborate report for the Government in 1906-7 ; and as a result of this a large sum of money—£60,000 or £70,000—was voted for archæological works. Not only was every temple repaired, strengthened, and thoroughly studied and photographed, but every single cemetery and ancient site was exhaustively excavated. Thus, not a scrap of information was lost to science, and every possible precaution was taken to safeguard the interest of the antiquary.

It was early in the summer of 1912 that I paid my last visit to Lower Nubia, on board a P.W.D. steamer ; and I should like to record here some unofficial impressions of this very interesting reach of the Nile.

Upon the first day of our journey we passed through the five great locks of the dam which mount to the higher level like some huge Brobdingnagian stairway, and steamed southwards over the wide stretch of the pent-up waters, past groves of palm-trees standing deep in the flood, past the rough points of submerged rocks which once formed the promontories of the mainland, past slopes of golden sand which had formerly descended to the edge of cultivated fields, but now slid straight into the water in the manner of a perilous chute. It was our plan to push through to Abu Simbel, which is some miles south of the area to be affected by the new flood-level, and then to examine the main ancient sites on the way down. At mid-morning we steamed through the magnificent Pass of Kalabsheh, where towering granite cliffs drop sheer into the water and rugged piles of that splendid stone form islands in the river ; and towards sunset we passed the temple of Dakkeh, whose lofty pylons can be seen for many a mile. About eight o'clock in the evening, when darkness had fallen and the sky was massed over with stars, we halted near the temple of Wady Sabu'a, and by the light of a lantern made our way to it over the soft sand.

The work in this temple is poor. The edges of the blocks of stone with which the walls are built are roughly trimmed, and the crevices are filled with plaster to hide the reproach of their bad workmanship. One wonders how much the dishonest contractor, or perhaps the Viceroy of Rameses II, in whose reign it was built, obtained out of the transaction ; for, knowing modern Egypt and the tortuous ways of the native architect, one has developed a sort of jocular misanthropy that is not bounded by the years. The friend who was with me, and who is a highly cultured barbarian, expressed unmitigated disapproval of the entire place, and begged to be conducted back to the steamer with all dispatch ; but to me the ruin, although undoubtedly a monument of slovenly work, has a rugged dignity. In the shifting light of the lantern which caused the shadows, like flibbertigibbets, to perform the most grotesque antics, and the decorated walls to stand out from them in a kind of luminous animation, one felt that there was still something to be learnt from it.

At dawn next day we steamed onwards, rounded the great bend of the Nile between Korôsko and Derr, and halted during the morning at the foot of the hill of Kasr Ibrîm, upon which the commanding ruins of an ancient fortress bask in the sunshine. One climbs up a winding path upon the north side of the hill, and mounts under impregnable walls to the narrow gateway, which it is almost surprising to find open. From inside this doorway a staircase rises to the higher levels of the hill ; and now the ruined walls of the barracks cluster in close array before one, while over to the right another and more elaborate doorway, flanked by massive pylons, stands almost on the edge of the cliffs. These two doorways date from about B.C. 25, when the Roman General Petronius placed a garrison here after he had defeated the one-eyed Ethiopian queen, Kandake, and her thirty thousand warriors and driven them into the Sudân. A few hundred years later a Byzantine garrison erected a Christian church on the hill-top a short way to the south ; and threading one's way through the narrow streets between the deserted houses, this building suddenly comes into view. The ruin has a peculiar charm. The masonry arches and the well-built apse have, at the first glance, almost a Norman appearance ; and here, as it were, at the top of the world, the scene is so foreign to Egypt that it holds all the charm of novelty to the Egyptologist, tired, as to some extent he must be, of the temples beside the Nile.

The cliffs on the west side of the ruins drop almost sheer to the river, and from the top one may throw down stones which strike the green water far out of earshot and only just within sight. Sitting here in the morning sunshine, after our hot climb up the hill, a silent content-ment possessed us which no words of mine can attempt to express. The river, the cultivation, and the desert were stretched out below us, all far away, and inviting only a mild quizzical contemplation. From this eminence we patronised Egypt, and smiled at all her petty troubles. What a place, we both declared, in which to build a little house ! We could sit at the door all day long, smoking a pipe and musing upon the world's worries at this safe distance from them. On second thoughts, however, my friend came to the conclusion that in a dreamer's life of this kind a very good piano would be necessary and a few reproductions of great pictures. A small library, too, would be essential, and perhaps a few congenial friends. I was about to discourse with some heat upon the oppress-iveness of culture and the intolerable demands it makes upon its devotees, chaining them to cities and communi-ties wherein alone its rites may be practised, when I was checked by a glance at my watch ; and forthwith we descended the hill down to the steamer and its sun-baked decks.

We reached Abu Simbel towards sunset, and at once went ashore. The temple is cut out of a bluff of rock which overlooks the Nile a few miles before the Sudân frontier is reached. It was dedicated to the hawk-god Harmachis, one of the forms of the sun-god ; and it was so designed that the rays of the rising sun strike right at the temple, illuminating the façade, and penetrating at certain times of the year into the innermost sanctuary, where the statue of Rameses the Great awaits it with the gods. The four enormous figures of Rameses which sit in such solemnity at the entrance, as though to greet the sun, will be familiar to the reader ; and those who have had the good fortune to visit this part of the world will remember that a great drift of sand had swept down the hillside at the north of the temple and had threatened

in a few years to engulf it entirely.   In 1909 this drift had
pushed almost to the doorway of the temple and had thus
covered the feet of the two colossi on that side of the
façade.   The terrace in front of the great statues had
here been hidden for thousands of years, and I suggested
that if the entire drift were removed some important
discoveries might be made.   These hopes were fully
realised when the work was undertaken in 1909-10 by the
Department of Antiquities under the direction of Monsieur
Barsanti.   When the drift had been attacked by some
hundreds of men and had been carted away in trucks to
form a large and level platform in front of the temple, the
buried terrace was exposed and was found to be ornamented with a series of statues : figures of the hawk, of
the sun, and of the king alternating at short intervals
along its whole length.   These figures, sculptured in pale-
coloured sandstone, now stand like sentinels at the feet
of the great deeper-toned colossi, and add very considerably to the sense of size and majesty which these huge
forms inspire.   At the north end of the terrace a small
open chapel was discovered, on the east side of which
were two miniature pylons.   In this chapel stood a high
altar, and upon this altar four sacred apes, sculptured in
stone, were found.   They crouched with their hands
raised in adoration to the rising sun, which, as it topped
the eastern hills, would strike right upon their faces
between the pylons.   Before them stood two small
obelisks, symbols of the sun ; and near by, upon another
altar, was a small shrine containing another ape and a
small scarab representing the re-creation of life at dawn.

The whole temple is built for the one hour of sunrise ;
and therefore the next morning we went ashore once more
before the sun had risen.   Sitting in front of the temple,
facing the colossi, we watched the light increase upon the
stone, the colour of which grew ever more warm and
golden.   It was as though the sandstone were illuminated
from within, like thin alabaster.   The serene faces of the
great statues became as nearly godlike as any work of man

can become. Their calm unmoved greeting to the sun, so different from that of us men, who must needs shade our eyes, being unable to look him in the face, had something sublime about it not convincingly to be explained away, and not to be diminished by the obvious fact that they were but masses of natural rock. I am not convinced that the mountains are dead, nor can I tell what gods of the western desert may not look out from this sacred hill through the eyes which the old men of Egypt have here made for them. Although I have seen this temple so many times, have watched the broken fragments of these colossi pinned back into position with iron bars, and have reckoned the tons of cement which have been shot into the cavities and cracks in their interior, yet still the spell of their monstrous dignity remains, they still seem to look to the eastern horizon with all the expectancy of living nature, and still speak with the voice of the winds of the dawn.

As the sun rose high and the first mystery of the daylight passed into a less suggestive glare, we entered the inner halls of the temple, which are excavated in the rock, and wandered from room to room. The light here was strong enough at this time of day to illuminate the whole interior, so that even the corners were not in darkness. Some of the reliefs are extremely well executed, and there is one scene in particular, upon the left wall, representing the Pharaoh in the act of slaying a foreign soldier in battle, which is one of the great masterpieces of Egyptian art, though I do not find it quoted in any of the textbooks. At length we passed out into the sunlight once more, and, after lingering a short while longer, the internal call for breakfast induced us to return to the steamer. We weighed anchor at once, and in a couple of hours or so reached the village of Toshkeh, on our return journey down stream.

On this occasion we paid no more than a rapid visit to the ancient cemeteries which lie a few hundred yards from the river at this point ; but when I was here in 1910, I went back some six miles into the western desert to visit the field of the battle of Toshkeh, where on August 3, 1889, Sir Francis (now Lord) Grenfell defeated an army of Dervishes under Wad er Nejumi. The Dervishes were invading Egypt along the desert route, which avoids the twisting course of the Nile, and at this point they were met by the opposing forces and practically annihilated. The battlefield is most interesting ; for many of the dead still lie upon the ground where they fell, and in all directions the marks of the conflict are apparent, even the tracks of the gun-carriages being still visible passing across the firm surface of the sand.   On a mound of rock, at the foot of which one may see the neat squares and circles of pebbles marking out the general's quarters on the eventful day, there is a monument under which the Egyptian soldiers who fell are buried ; and a commemorative inscription in marble proclaims to the unvisited and silent desert around how these men " gave their lives for their country ".   I trust that I shall not appear cynical if I record here the impression of surprise which one could not help feeling upon seeing these fine old British sentiments applied to Egyptian soldiery. The Egyptian Tommy, good fellow that he is, has not yet learnt to bother himself about patriotism, though in isolated cases he is beginning to read newspapers and to fill his head with sentiments to which it is difficult to put a name. It was cruel fate that caused him to be conscribed for the army, and something uncommonly like the black magic of an enemy that sent him in the month of August to fight in Nubia.   What the fuss was about hardly concerned him ; and, knowing the cheery, inconsequent *fellah*, it requires a considerable stretch of the imagination to suppose that he felt possessed of a country to defend or was prepared to give his life for it.

Behind some rocks we came across the skeleton of a sniper, still clad in a few rags of tattered blue. By his side were four used and three unused cartridges ; and a bullet-hole in his forehead explained the latter. Under another skeleton the soft sand was caked into a solid lump, where the blood had flowed from the fatal wound. A group of bodies in the open plain marked the site of a last stand ; and the bones of two jackals near by suggested the scene of savage feasting and quarrelling which took place under the moon for many nights after the slaughter. The battle was fiercely contested, and under the blazing summer sun it must have been a severe test of endurance to the Egyptian officers and men, most of whom were used to the more temperate climate of the north of Egypt. One portly officer told me that his tongue swelled in his mouth from thirst, and after the battle it was a good six hours before he could swallow more than a few drops of water at a time.

We spent the night at Derr, the capital of Lower Nubia, and early next morning steamed down to the temple of Amada, which stands on the left bank a few miles down stream.

Our next stop was at Korôsko, where the river bank is lined with the ruins of the barracks of the British troops stationed there during the troubled days of the 'eighties. We climbed up a hill behind these ruins, on the summit of which a guard-house is erected, where a view is to be obtained of the valley along which the road to the Sudân leads out. It was along this road that General Gordon made his way to Khartum in 1884. In this valley one may still see the tracks of the carts and gun-carriages of the ill-fated expedition which set out from here under Hicks Pasha and was utterly annihilated in the desert. The tracks pass down the valley and disappear amongst the hills ; and even so the expedition disappeared and was swallowed up. Some of the enemy, now good servants of the Government, will tell you how false guides misled the troops, and how they were shot down as they lay exhausted by thirst within a mile of the wells. At the mouth of this valley there is the cemetery, where some forty British officers and men lie buried. The tombstones, badly engraved by the regimental sculptor, and almost all bearing the one remembered text, " God is Love ", cut in shaky letters, are inclined, as my friend put it, to give one the hump ; and we walked back in silence to the steamer, leaving our fellow-countrymen to the complete stillness of this now deserted corner of the world, where, at all events, they must sleep sound.

From Korôsko we steamed all day down to Kubbân and Dakkeh, some seventy miles above Aswân. We spent the night at the latter place, and upon the following day visited the temples of Gerf Husên and Dendur, halting in the evening at Kalâbsheh, where the largest temple in Lower Nubia stands. This building is now deeply flooded when the reservoir is full, but it has been so thoroughly strengthened that there is no danger of it falling. Then, next morning, we steamed through the pass, under the granite cliffs, and halted at Tafeh, which lies on the west bank. The pent-up river has here inundated many acres of cultivable ground, and for a considerable distance we rowed in a small boat amidst palms and acacias standing in the flood. A little temple erected on what now is an island rises amidst the trees, and is reflected in the still water. There can be no doubt that the making of the reservoir has here converted mediocre scenery into a very paradise of beauty. The shadow of the trees upon the Nile, the sunlight that penetrates through the trees and illumines the grasses and plants below the surface, the granite cliffs that come down to the river and form a dark back-ground to the clear water, combine to form a picture of extraordinary charm. The temperature was over 110 in the shade ; and my companion who was not used to the climatic conditions of the upper country, said wistfully that he expected to have a fit at any moment. We reached the top, however, without accident ; and here the view was sufficiently magnificent to divert all thought from physical discomforts. Below us the Nile made its way through the pass, bordered at the entrance by the vivid green of the trees ; and beside us the picturesque ruins of a Roman pavilion made the scene work on the imagination as it did on the senses. " In this very pavilion," said I, " Juvenal may have sat to admire this self-same prospect ; for one of the garrisons under his command was to be found here." The thought set my friend quoting from the *Satires* ; and, as the perspiration ran like tears down his cheek, he had the hardihood to recite those lines from the *Fifteenth Satire* : " That nature gave the noble man a feeling heart she proves herself by giving him tears." After that we could but return to the steamer.

The temples of Kertassi and Dabôd were passed during the day, and at about sunset we moored against the walls of the temple of Philae, our journey at an end and the railway station of Shallal in sight. The temples rose from the water which flooded them, for the most part, to a depth of some ten feet or so ; and from the deck of the steamer we could step on to the roof of the Western Colonnade and could look down into the green depths from which the columns rose. As the day was hot, it was impossible to resist the inclination to bathe in this sacred area. We had had our swim each day, of course, but here there was the prospect of a bathe which should recall the fairy dreams of our youth and set us in mind of the forgotten tales of the palaces of the sea.

We dived into the water at a point where the roof of the colonnade was in ruins and the flood lay silently beneath us, lapping around the long rows of columns a few feet below their capitals ; and, coming to the surface in a shower of bubbles, we headed northwards, swimming along the covered colonnade, all the gods of Egypt sculptured upon the wall on our left, and on our right the columns between which the opposite colonnade was seen, separated from us by a canal-like stretch of open water. These two colonnades flank the great approach to the pylons of the Temple of Isis ; and when, therefore, we had reached their northern end, we turned to our right out of the shadows and swam towards the great doorway in the full radiance of the setting sun.   Here I recollected that there stood a high granite pedestal from which the statue of a seated lion had fallen ; and feeling our way carefully through the water, we found this submerged pedestal and came to rest upon it.   Deep below us lay the overthrown lion, and down to it we were constrained to descend, rising again with the blurred impression of a face that smiled hideously through a green veil.

We then swam onwards, and, turning on our backs, floated silently through the great doorway, the spread-winged vultures carved above us and the Pharaoh offering to the gods on either side.   Thus we passed into the forecourt of the Temple of Isis, and were completely shut in by the towering buildings.   The water here was so silent and unruffled, the reflections of the columns and walls were so clear, that the place seemed to have been hidden to the world for centuries ; and we had the feeling that we were exploring for the first time the mysterious sanctuaries of unknown gods.   We seemed to be intruders into some secret palace of the Nile, and we knew not what fairy adventure was before us.   Here was the silent green stretch of the water, in which our two heads moved about like floating gourds ; here were Hathor, and Isis, and many another goddess, furtively peeping at us from just below the surface, so that to satisfy ourselves we must needs sink under the flood and peer at them thus ; here were dark doorways leading to holy places wherein our voices echoed as though someone were calling us ; and here, too, were graceful columns whose elaborate capitals shimmered in the ripples which we made.

On our left was the temple known as the Birth House, where the celebrations took place in commemoration of the birth of Horus amidst the reeds and swamps of the Delta.   Into this temple we floated, turned upon our backs once more, passing from hall to hall.   The seven Hathors beat their tambourines to us in the sculptures upon the walls as though to encourage us to enter the mystery of the sanctuary ; and Taurt, the hippopotamus goddess, imprisoned for ever in stone, looked down upon us with envy as we moved so contentedly in her own element. The sanctuary was almost dark, and there was a cavernous silence in it that was not a little aweing. In the dim light we did obeisance to the figure of the hawk Horus, who stood in a clump of sculptured reeds, just above the surface of the flood ; and, diving once more, we laid sudden hands on that fair Isis who sat nursing her baby so tightly there under the waters. The light of the sunset glowed in our eyes as we swam out of these dark halls and turned again into the forecourt of Isis, making our way towards the main temple. The drab-coloured sandstone of the ruins became golden against the deep tone of the sky ; and the water spreading around us was made more green and mysterious by the contrast.

Looking down we could see the dim outlines of ruined walls traversing the paved court, and broad stairs descending into the darkness. Water-plants swayed beneath us, tangled themselves about the limbs of the submerged gods, and sinuously crept over the royal decrees of the Pharaohs. Beneath the water in this forecourt stands the great granite inscription which relates how the Pharaoh Ptolemy VII had given all the country from Philae southwards to the island of Derâr, near Dakkeh, to the great Isis to be her possession for ever ; and as we dived to look at the drowned face of the goddess the fear of her wrath was not altogether absent. The territory between these very points had been submerged and given over to Nilus ; and even here in her sanctuary the water-gods whispered, and only the spirits of the river ascended the steps of her altars.

The main temple, being built on a higher level, has no more than a foot of water in its halls, and through this we waded over to the stairway which ascends to the roof. A scramble over the top of the building ensued, and from its heights we looked down upon the whole panorama of the temples reflected in the lake of the reservoir like the palaces of a dream. Eastwards rose that famous

kiosk sometimes called " Pharaoh's Bed ", and somewhat nearer stood the little shrine of Hathor. South-
westwards the huge pylons reared themselves against the
sunset ; and northwards the top of the Roman gateway
made a solitary point on the face of the flood.

Seized with another impulse, we ran down the steps
once more, splashed through the halls of Isis, and slid into
the water down the broad stairway of the forecourt.
Bearing off to our left, we swam down a corridor, through
a dark chamber, and so out into an open avenue leading
between ruined walls to the temple of Hathor. Along
this we struck out, the rows of gods gliding by us, and
presently entered the temple, which caught much of the
last light of the day. Hathor being the Egyptian
Aphrodite, the walls of her shrine are covered with festive
scenes. Half submerged in the water, we could see in the
open court a figure standing beside some rushes, playing
a double pipe, other figures making music upon the harp,
an ape playing the guitar, the Pharaoh offering festal
coronets, flowers, and wine to the goddess of joy, and the
little dancing god Bes leaping about and beating a
tambourine. The water was not silent here, for the
evening breeze ruffled the surface and sent the ripples
whispering into the sanctuary ; and in answer to the
mood of the place we splashed through it, laughed at
little Bes, and sat whistling a tune upon a fallen
column. Then, as the early stars came out, we dived
through a small side-door, submerged almost to the lintel,
and, thus leaving the temple, swam across open water
towards the kiosk.

Looking beneath us as we went, we could sometimes dis-
cern the buildings below, and could catch glimpses of
strange shapes as we glided over the altars of forsaken
shrines and struck the bubbles down into the faces of gods
and Pharaohs. The half-seen ruins in the depths of the
water took hold of the imagination and suggested much
to the mind that would have been scorned in other circumstances. What spirits of the Nile dwelt in these sunken

The Nile at Philae, looking North

The island of Philae is seen in the middle of the picture. When the dam at Aswan is closed the water rises here, flooding Philae and the deserted villages in the foreground

chambers ?—what cities of the river were approached through these dusky halls ? If only one could have breath to dive down through that dark doorway below the water, down the wide stairs, and along the passage . . . . ! The reflections of the gathering stars suggested that there were little lamps to light the way below ; and presently, no doubt, we should swim into the illumination of fairy palaces, and come suddenly upon the enchanted maidens of the deep. They would take hold of us with their cool hands, glide over us with their soft limbs, and entangle us with their hair. The summons of their eyes would lead us onwards till their cold lips touched ours ; and thus down to fantastic depths they would beguile us, through chambers of silver lit by a thousand stars, to halls of gold illumined by many a sun. Their hands would hold our hands, feel the muscles of our arms, and touch our faces ; and ever they would lead us onwards, till of a sudden we should stand blinded at the doorway of that shining cavern wherein the old god Khnum dispensed the floods of the Nile and ordered their going.

The darkening water was replete with suggestions of this kind as we swam through it towards the kiosk. If only we could find the right doorway amidst all these ruins befow us ; if only the ghostly shadows of the water-plants, the pale forms of submerged altars, should be lit for a moment by the passing of some luminous spirit, so that we might dive below and follow . . ! But as the fancy thus drifted we had crossed the open space and had entered the shadow of the great kiosk, whose columns towered above our heads against the last-left light of the sky, and were reflected with the stars in the water beneath us. Seated here on a sunken wall, my companion asked me whether I had called to mind Shelley's *Ode to the West Wind* as we swam from the temple ; and therewith he repeated those haunting lines which tell of one who

Saw in sleep old palaces and towers . . .
All overgrown with azure moss and flowers
So sweet, the sense faints picturing them.

And as we swam back to the steamer at length, through the gate of Philadelphus and down the colonnade, I felt that the whole experience had given us a new point of view in regard to the reservoir.   One did not look forward only to the six months of each year when the water sinks and Philae is left once more high and dry : the portion of the year when it is inundated also makes it appeal. Philae clean and bare, as it must have been in ancient days, was good to look upon ; Philae overgrown with trees and grasses, as it was before the dam was built, was picturesque ; but Philae floating in the water, as it now does for half the year, has that indefinable charm of unreality which is the very essence of beauty.

CHAPTER XI

A NUBIAN HIGHWAY

OPPOSITE the town of Aswân, a short distance below the First Cataract of the Nile, there rises an island known to travellers by its Greek name of Elephantine. The river sweeps down from the cataract to east and west ; southwards one may watch it flowing around a dozen dark clumps of granite rocks, which thrust themselves as it were breathless above the water ; and northwards almost without hindrance it passes between the hills and palm-trees of the mainland. Nowadays should one stand upon the mounds which mark the site of the ancient city of Elephantine, and look east and north, one would feel that modern civilisation had hidden for ever the scenes of the past, and had prevented the imagination from re-picturing the place as it was in the older days. The huge Cataract Hotel overshadows the ruined city, and stares down from its pinnacle of granite on to the tumbled stones of ancient temples. On the island itself, opposite this hotel, the elaborate and ultra-modern rest-house of the Ministry of Public Works rises amidst its terraced gardens ; and farther to the north stands the imposing Savoy Hotel, surrounded by luxuriant trees and flowers unknown to the ancient Egyptians. Eastwards the long, neat promenade of Aswân edges the river, backed by the Grand Hotel, the Government offices, and other large buildings ; and at one end the noisy railway station tells the insistent tale of the Present. During the winter one may watch the busy launches and small craft plying to and fro, and may see the quality and fashion of Europe amusing itself at either end of the passage ; while at night the brilliant lights blaze into the waters of the Nile from a thousand electric lamps, and the sounds of the latest tune drift out through open windows. The place is modern : one sips one's whisky-and-soda above the crushed-down remains of Pharaonic splendours, plays tennis in a garden laid out above the libraries of the Ptolemies, and reads the *Daily Mail* where, maybe, melancholy Juvenal wrote his *Fifteenth Satire.*

But should one turn now to the west and south a different impression might be obtained. On the island still stands the imposing gateway of the rich temple destroyed for the sake of its building-stone in the days of Mohammed Ali ; and near it, not many years ago, an archæologist uncovered the intact burial vault of the sacred rams of the Nile-god Khnum. The rocky hills of the western mainland tower above the island, great drifts of golden sand carrying the eye from the summit to the water's edge ; and here, cut into the rocks, are the tombs of the ancient princes of Elephantine. In this direction there is hardly anything that is more modern than the ruined monastery of St. Simeon, built at the head of a sandy valley in the early days of Christianity, and destroyed by the fierce brother of Saladin in 1173 A.D. With one's back to the hotels, and one's face to the changeless hills, the history of the old city is able to be traced with something of the feeling of reality to aid the thoughts.

One period of that history stands out clearly and distinctly amidst the dim course of far-off events. From being a stronghold of a savage tribe the south end of the island had become covered by the houses and streets of a fine city, named *Abu* or " Elephant-city " (and hence Elephantine), no doubt after the elephant symbol of its chieftain. The feudal tendencies of the Vth and VIth Dynasties—about B.C. 2750 to 2475—had brought power and wealth to the local princes in many parts of Egypt ; and here the family of the chieftains of the island had begun to rise to a degree of some importance. This was largely due to the fact that to them was entrusted the office of " Keeper of the Door of the South ", and the protecting of the Egyptian frontier at the first Cataract from invasion by the negro tribes beyond.

The city rose amidst its trees and rocks at the foot of the cataract, at a point where in those days the river still ran swift, and where the distant roar of waters continuously drummed upon the ears. On the eastern mainland opposite the island stood the huts and hovels of the great *Swanu*, or market, which gave its name to the later town of Aswân ; and here the negroes, coming from the upper reaches of the river by the valley road which avoids the rocks of the cataract, met and traded with the inhabitants of Elephantine. At the far end of this road the barren islands of Philae, Bigeh, and others were regarded as neutral ground, and the rocks of the mainland were not yet forbidden territory to the Egyptians for some miles up-stream. But beyond this the country was little known, and those who penetrated into it took their lives in their hands.

First there came the land of the Kau tribes ; and then, farther to the south, the Wawat on the east bank and the Sethu on the west dwelt in barbaric independence. Still farther to the south lived the warlike Mazoi, who might sometimes be seen at the market, ostrich feathers in their hair and bows and clubs in their hands. The land of Arthet lay to the south again ; and lastly, not much below the Second Cataract and the modern Wady Hâlfa, there lived the almost unknown people of Aam.

Who dwelt to the south of this the Egyptians did not know. That territory was " The Land of the Ghosts " : the perilous borders of the world, and the misty ocean into which no man had penetrated, were there to be encountered. To the inhabitants of the brilliant little metropolis the peoples of the upper river appeared to be a hazy folk ; and the farther south their land the more mysterious were their surroundings and the ghostlier their ways. The negroes who came to the market no doubt told stories then, as they did in later times, of the great stature and the marvellous longevity of those distant races ; and though but a couple of hundred miles of winding river separated the Egyptian frontier from that of the land of Aam, that distance sufficed to twist the thoughts of the market-gossiper from the mortal to the immortal.

In archaic times an unknown Egyptian king had penetrated some sixty miles up the river, and had left a record on one of the rocks ; [1] and King Sneferu of the IIIrd Dynasty had devastated a part of the country. But from that time until the beginning of the Vth Dynasty the land and its people, left unmolested, had drifted once more into the pale regions of mystery. As the nobles of Elephantine grew in wealth and power, however, their attention began to be turned with some degree of fixidity towards the south ; and when the energetic King Sahura came to the throne, it was felt that the time had arrived for the probing of the mystery.

The roads which led to the south along the eastern bank of the river, and which were used by the negroes near the frontier when coming to the market, were not practicable for caravans bound for distant goals ; and the Egyptians turned their eyes, therefore, to the western hills, behind which the sorrowful lands of the Dead were somewhere situated. Almost exactly opposite the city lay a sand-covered valley, in which now stands the ruined monastery mentioned above. From the island a boat carried one across to the little reedy bay, from whence a trudge of half a mile or so over the soft sand brought one to the upper levels of the desert. Looking towards the north, the road which led eventually to Lower Egypt was to be seen ; to the west the eye wandered over the undulating wilderness to the far horizon, made awful by the presence

---

[1] The various rock-inscriptions of Lower Nubia mentioned in this chapter were found during a tour which I made in that country in the autumn of 1906, and are recorded in my *Antiquities of Lower Nubia and their Condition in* 1906-7, published for the Egyptian Government by the University Press, Oxford. The evidence for the locating of the various tribes is also given there.

of the Dead ; and to the south the sand-drifts and the rocky hillocks hid the untravelled paths to Aam and the Land of the Ghosts. Keeping the river on the left hand, it seemed to the Egyptians that they might here pass over the upper desert as far as the gods permitted man to penetrate ; and a descent to the Nile at any convenient point would bring them, like a bolt from heaven, upon the tribes there settled.

The army of Sahura—perhaps a thousand men with numerous baggage-donkeys—set out along this road, and after a march of a few days, as nearly straight ahead as possible, struck the river (which bends towards the west) at a point in the land of Arthet, now known as Tomâs. A tribute was no doubt collected from the rich fields which there border the Nile ; an inscription recording the name of one of the captains was cut upon a convenient face of rock ; and the army returned to Egypt to publish its heroism in the streets of Elephantine. Another expedition in the reign of King Asesa followed after a few years, the event being again recorded on the rocks. Farther than Arthet, however, these armed forces did not venture to go ; nor was this Nubian highroad used with great frequency during the following years.

About the year 2500 B.C. a prince of Elephantine named Herkhuf made up his mind to penetrate farther towards the mysterious lands of the south. It is forty-four centuries since he set out over the desert, with the wind whistling past his ears and a powerful sun warming his bones and his heart within him ; yet the story of his adventures may still be read, the path by which he travelled may still be discerned, and the names of his captains may still be seen on the rocks of the land of Arthet. Herkhuf, having obtained the necessary order from the Pharaoh, set out with his father Ata, " in order ", as he says, " to explore a road to the country of Aam." The road which he explored and opened up was probably a continuation of the route from Elephantine to Arthet,

passing not far back from the river, and descending to the
water between Abu Simbel and Wady Hâlfa in the heart
of the land of Aam.   The expedition was entirely successful, and Herkhuf states that he was " very greatly
praised for it ".   Emboldened by the fame which his
enterprise had brought him, he made a second expedition
to Aam, and was gone from Egypt eight months.   A
third excursion was more adventurous.   Herkhuf set
out upon the " Oasis-road ", which runs from a point
north of Aswan to Kurkur Oasis, and thence branches
to Tomâs or Arthet and to the Oasis of Khârgeh which
lies westward, and which in those days was inhabited by
Libyan tribes.   At the Kurkur junction Herkhuf met
with an army, under the leadership of the Prince of
Aam, which was on its way to chastise these Libyans ;
but how the wily Egyptian contrived to use it instead as
an escort to his own men back to Aam, and how he
returned to Egypt through the hostile territory of Sethu,
Arthet, and Wawat, with 300 asses laden with the presents
of his host, are tales too long to narrate here.

One story only may be recorded in this chapter.
During a fourth expedition to Aam, Herkhuf had managed
to obtain one of the dwarfs or pigmies who inhabited a
region of the Land of the Ghosts.   He at once informed
the king, now the boy Pepy II ; and in reply he received
the following letter, which is, perhaps, the earliest
example in the world's history of a private communication :—

" I have noted," writes the King, " the matter of your letter
which you have sent to me, in order that I might know that you
have returned in safety from Aam, with the army which was with
you . . .   You say in your letter that you have brought a
dancing pigmy of the god of the Land of the Ghosts, like the pigmy
which the Treasurer Baurded brought from the Land of Pount
in the time of Asesa.   You say to my majesty, ' Never before
has one like him been brought by anyone who has visited
Aam ' . . . . . .   Come northward, therefore, to the court
immediately, and bring this pigmy with you, which you must
bring living, prosperous, and healthy, from the Land of the
Ghosts, to dance for the King and to rejoice and gladden the heart
of the King.   When he goes down with you into the vessel,

The Nile at Aswan. On the hills to the left is the highroad to Nubia

appoint trustworthy people to be beside him at either side of the vessel : take care that he does not fall into the water. When he sleeps at night, appoint trustworthy people who shall sleep beside him in his cabin ; and make an inspection ten times each night. My majesty desires to see this pigmy more than the gifts of Sinai and of Pount. If you arrive in court, the pigmy being with you, alive, prosperous, and healthy, my majesty will do for you a greater thing than that which was done for the Treasurer Baurded in the time of Asesa, according to the heart's desire of my majesty to see this pigmy. Orders have been sent to the chief of the New Towns to arrange that food shall be taken from every store-city and every temple (on the road) without stinting.''

How easy it is to picture the excited boy awaiting the arrival of this wonder from the south, or to watch in the imagination the long caravan as it winds its way over the western hills from Aam to Elephantine, where Herkhuf and his prize will take ship to Memphis.

Later in the reign of Pepy II, the tribes of Arthet and Wawat revolted, and the Nubian highroad echoed with the songs of Egyptian soldiers. The commander of the expedition, named Pepynakht, slew a large number of the unfortunate negroes, took many prisoners, and collected a great quantity of plunder. It was perhaps during this disturbance that a certain prince of Elephantine, named Mekhu, was murdered in Arthet. News of his death was brought to his son Sabna by a ship's captain who had himself escaped. Sabna immediately collected a few soldiers and a hundred baggage-donkeys, bearing presents of honey, oil, ointment, and fine linen, and set out upon the same highroad towards Arthet. By judicious gifts of this oil and honey he was able to discover the body of his father ; and, loading it upon a donkey, he commenced the return journey. Before he was clear of Arthet, however, he found it necessary to avert an attack by presenting a southern negro chieftain with an elephant tusk three cubits in length, at the same time hinting that his best tusk was six cubits in length. But how the expedition arrived safely at Elephantine, and how Sabna buried his father there in the western hills behind the modern Savoy Hotel, and how he was rewarded

N

by the king for his really plucky undertaking, cannot here be related at length.

There was now no more mystery about the country on this side of the Second Cataract, and by the perseverance of these princes of Elephantine the way was made ready for the conquest of the Sudân, which the Egyptians commenced in the XIIth Dynasty and completed in the XVIIIth. We of the present day cannot, perhaps, appreciate how much pluck and obstinacy these nobles required in the undertaking of these expeditions. Not only were they penetrating into lands which were inhabited by the most savage tribes, but they believed these tribes to be endowed with superhuman powers. From childhood they had heard stories of their magical powers ; while in pushing their way into the distant land of Aam they assuredly expected to encounter those ghosts who hovered at the edge of the world. Their caravan routes over the western hills ran dangerously near the terrible territory of the Dead ; and, to their superstitious minds, their daily marches and their nightly camps were beset by monsters and by bogies compared to which the fierce Mazoi were as naught.

The reader who finds interest in the picture of Herkhuf exploring the roads of Aam, and of Sabna searching for his father's body in hostile Arthet, will ask whether any definite traces of the highroad still remain. One would have thought that after four thousand four hundred years it would have utterly disappeared ; but this is not the case. Let the visitor to Aswân step out some afternoon from the hall of his hotel, where the string band throbs in his ears and the latest Parisian gowns shimmer before his eyes, and let him take boat to the little western bay behind the ruins of Elephantine. Here in the late afternoon the long blue shadows fall, and he may walk in coolness over the sand towards the monastery which stands on the higher ground before him. At the top of the hill to his left he will presently see, some distance away, a large isolated boulder near the tomb of some old

Moslim saint ; and making his way up the hillside towards this boulder, he will suddenly come upon a paved causeway[1] which sweeps up over the sand to the rocky summit. Rough flat blocks of sandstone form the paving, and these are only here and there overwhelmed by the drifting sand, though it is evident that the road has been entirely buried at the point where it approaches the water.

Mounting to the hill-top, the causeway is seen to pass within a few yards of the great boulder, which one now finds to have been surrounded by a rough wall, as though to form a kind of sanctuary or chapel. On the sides of the rock there are several inscriptions recording the coming of various officials of the empire—tax-collectors, super-intendents of the Nubian gold mines, and so on. It is evident from this that the road was used for many a long year after Herkhuf and Sabna had done with it ; though it now possessed for the travellers no terrors, nor did it lead any more to the Land of the Ghosts.

At the point where the causeway passes the boulder the hard surface of the upper desert literally bristles with countless little heaps of stones, each consisting of a small upright slab of rock held in place by two or three others. Fragments of pottery indicate that a bowl, perhaps containing water, had been placed beside each pile. Here, then, are the memorials of the travellers who set out for distant Arthet from the fair city on the island, which may from this point be seen floating in the blue waters of the Nile below. These stones are the prayers of those who asked a prosperous journey from the gods of their city : from the old ram-headed Khnum who lived in the dark caverns below the Nile ; from Satet, the horned goddess whose bow and arrows were the terror of her enemies ; and from Anuket with the crown of lofty feathers. For a short distance one may follow the paved road, now, as it passes southwards and westwards amidst the blackened

---

[1] I can hardly suppose that I was the first to observe this road, and yet I can find no reference to it in any publication.

rocks and golden sand-drifts of this lifeless land ; but presently it tops a deeply shadowed ridge of rock and sand, and so descends into, and is lost amidst, the wide, undulating desert, ablaze with the light of the setting sun.

There are not many persons who will find themselves able to follow the road by camel, as I did, or to take ship up the Nile, to Arthet, in order to see the terminus of the first part of the highway. The road descends to the river behind the rich fields of the straggling village of Tomâs, near Derr, the present capital of Lower Nubia. The scenery here is beautiful in the extreme. A short distance down-stream a bluff of rock, projecting to the water's edge, and half covered with drift-sand, marks the probable boundary between Arthet and Sethu. One might slide here from the top of the bluff down the golden slopes to the verdant thorn-bushes which dip towards the river, and from either side of the track one's figure would be seen sharply against the deep blue of the sky. Sliding, one would see on the left the rocks and the sand of Sethu, and distantly the superb array of the mountains of Wawat ; while on the right the green bay into which the road descended would lie spread as a feast to the eye. Farther up-stream a wooded island rests upon the mirror of the Nile, whither the inhabitants must often have fled at the approach of the Egyptians from the desert.

On the low cliffs which form the backing of this bay many a captain of an expedition or master of a caravan has written his name, and sometimes a date has been added. " The Superintendent of all the caravan-conductors of the Land of the South : Sabna " : " the Captain of the Soldiers : Akab " ; " the Captain of the ships of Asesa : Khnumhotep " ; " the sixth year : written by the Captain of the soldiers . . ." : these are examples of the inscriptions which were here cut into the surface of the rock, and which to the archæologist are of the first importance. A caravan-conductor named Ara, who is probably to be identified with the father of Herkhuf, has left his name here ; and more than once

Sabna occurs. But perhaps the most interesting of these records are three short inscriptions which tell of an expedition to Arthet under the almost unknown Pharaoh Hornefersa, who probably reigned about B.C. 2400. It is in one of these inscriptions that the name of this country —Arthet—is given, thereby making it possible definitely to locate the territory of these people, and to identify this highway without any further question with the " Elephantine road " referred to in the inscriptions as leading from Elephantine to Arthet.

Above these rocks one steps on to the hard surface of the desert, and the eye may travel over the broken ground to the north for many a mile, and may follow the road by which Herkhuf carried home his pigmy, and Sabna his father's body, until the brown rocks meet the blue sky. To the south-west the second portion of the highway, leading on to Aam, may be followed ; but the point at which it descends again to the river has not been identified, though one may safely say that the terminus lay between Abu Simbel and the Second Cataract. Here the country has a different aspect. On the west bank of the Nile the sand lies thickly, and humps itself into low hillocks covered with scrub. Between these one may walk in the cool shade of groves of *sunt* and tamarisk, where flocks of goats stand dreaming on the pathway and birds sing overhead. On the east bank isolated hills of sandstone rise suddenly from the plain, and are reflected in the river as in a flawless mirror. The land of Aam is as beautiful as that of Arthet, though altogether different in character.

The later history of the highway cannot be traced in much detail. From the VIIth to the XIIth Dynasties the Egyptian Government was seldom strong enough at home to attempt to look after affairs abroad, and Lower Nubia relapsed into a state of independence. Amenemhat, the founder of the XIIth Dynasty, about 2000 B.C., was thus obliged to reconquer the country ; but his expedition seems to have travelled up the Nile and not across the desert. A few reigns later a fortress was built at the modern Anâybeh, in the land of Arthet, some miles above the terminus of the highway from Elephantine ; and the road must now have been used continuously as the express route from the city to the fortress. This stronghold is so much ruined and sand-covered that it has escaped observation until now, although its position has been ascertained from inscriptions. Mention is made of a fortress named Taray, and its distance from a certain known place is given, which exactly locates it at Anâybeh. At about the same date a large fortress was built on the west bank of the Second Cataract, and at the extreme north end of the highroad the walls of Elephantine were now strengthened.

Above the Second Cataract lay the land of Kush, and as civilisation advanced southwards the territory of the Ghosts had perforce to retreat before it. The Egyptians now knew that very human negroes inhabited the country beyond Aam ; but they could still ask themselves in whispers what manner of bogies dwelt to the south of Kush. While the immortals were falling back, however, the mortals from above the second Cataract were surely pushing forward. The people of Aam were slowly being displaced by them, and in consequence were hustling the tribes of Arethet. During the reign of Senusert III (1887 B.C.) the incursions of the negroes of Kush assumed the proportions of an invasion and the Egyptians were obliged to wage an expensive and lengthy war upon them. When at last they were driven back beyond the Second Cataract, the Pharaoh set up a boundary-stone ; and the words which he ordered to be inscribed upon it show plainly enough what a surpirse it was to him to find that his enemies had possessed none of those superhuman powers which his subjects had attributed to them.

" Why," he says, " they are not a mighty people after all ; they are poor and broken in heart. My majesty has seen them ; it is not an untruth. I captured their women, I carried off their subjects, went forth to their wells, smote their bulls. I reaped their grain, and set fire thereto. I swear as my father lived for me I speak in truth, without a lie therein coming out of my mouth."

The last sentence tells of the king's fear lest tradition should conquer proven fact, and his soldiers should endow the negroes of Kush with those mysterious powers of which their close proximity to the Land of Ghosts and the end of the world gave them the use.

During the XVIIIth Dynasty (1580-1350 B.C.) the highroad was used continuously both by the troops which were being launched against the Sudân, and by the officials who came to collect the taxes or to administer the laws. Great changes had taken place since the old days. The Land of the Ghosts had disappeared almost entirely from the geography, though still it might exist somewhere above Khartûm. The people of Aam, now more correctly called Emaam, had entirely absorbed Arthet, and Sethu had fallen to the share of Wawat. Persons travelling by the highroad, and descending to the river at Tomâs or near the Second Cataract, found themselves in the sphere of influence of Emaam at either place. One obtains some idea of the inhabitants of this once mysterious land from a painting in the tomb of Huy, the viceroy of the south, at Thebes. Here one sees a procession of negro princes who have come to do homage to the Pharaoh's representatives. They have evidently travelled by the highroad, for the Prince of Emaam rides in a heavy chariot drawn by two bulls, while his retinue walk behind him. A prince of Wawat is also shown ; while the chieftains of Kush are there in numbers, bringing with them the produce of their country. Their clothes are more or less Egyptian in style, and their wealth in gold is such as an Egyptian's eyes might stare at. In this sober, prosperous company, one looks in vain for a sign of that savage ferocity which made them the terror of Elephantine.

In the XIXth Dynasty (1350-1205 B.C.), when the armies of Rameses the Great and his successors passed up to the wars in the Sudân, the Elephantine road must have been one of the main routes of communication. The name of Rameses the Great is writ large upon the rocks of Tomâs, in contrast to the modest little records of those infinitely greater men of the early days. Not so long afterwards it was the people of the Sudân who were using the road to march on Egypt, and soon the Egyptians were obliged to bow the knee to a negro Pharaoh. Later when they were once more the masters of their own affairs, the tax-gatherers returned to Emaam, and the names of some have been left on the road.

At this time Elephantine had become a city of considerable wealth and importance. Splendid temples rose amidst the houses and the trees, and fortified walls around the south end of the island frowned down upon the swift river. Priests, soldiers, and nobles walked the streets amongst the throng of the townspeople, or sailed to and fro over the broken waters. At the foot of the western hills, the bay from which the Nubian highway ran must have often been the scene of the busy loading and unloading of pack-donkeys ; and at this time there may have been a masonry landing-stage at the river's edge to terminate worthily the paved causeway.

Then came the Greeks and the Romans, and one may picture perspiring legionaries hastening along the highroad to join Petronius in his chase of the one-eyed queen Kandake and her flying Ethiopians. One may see the agents of Shems-ed-Dulah, the brother of Saladin, passing along to rout out Christianity from Nubia ; and presently come the barbaric Mamelukes, driven before the armies of Ibrahim Pasha. The last great scene in the long history of this most ancient highroad was enacted not so many years ago. The Dervishes—the modern inhabitants of the Land of the Ghosts—marching on Egypt from the Sudân, picked up the road at the Second Cataract, at its earliest terminus, and headed towards Tomâs. An English and Egyptian force, travelling southwards, met and utterly defeated them some seven miles back from the river, behind the village of Toshkeh, not far from Abu Simbel. And if one journeys direct from the ancient land of Arthet to the land of Aam, the bones of the dead and the *débris* of their camp will be found strewn to right and left over the surface of the highway, as recorded in the last chapter.

Travelling in Egypt one sees so many remains of the solemn ceremonies of the ancient Egyptians, and reading at home one meets with so many representations of the sacred rites, that it is a real relief to come across some relic, such as this highroad, of human energy and toil. In the courts of the temples one has pictured the processions of the priests and the kneeling throng of the people. One has heard in the imagination the rhythmic chants, has smelt the heavy incense, and has seen the smoke of the sacrifice rising to the roof. Glum Pharaohs have stalked across the picture, raising their stiff hands to the dull gods, and rows of bedraggled prisoners have been led to the sanctuary, roped in impossible contortions. One has visited, or has read of a thousand tombs; and the slow funerals have passed in depressing array. But here on this highroad over the western hills, where the north wind blows free and the kites circle and call, where there comes vigour into the limbs and ambition into the heart, these relics of old adventures appeal with wonderful force. Here there are no mysteries except the mystery of the land to the south, and there are no prayers save the asking of a successful journey, and the piling of four stones to the honour of the gods. One does not pace through holy places whispering " How weird ! " but stick in hand, and whistling a tune down the wind, one follows in the footsteps of the bold caravan-masters of the past ; and one thanks them from the bottom of the heart for having played a man's part on their page of the world's history to serve for all time as an example. When the amusements of the luxurious hotels has given out, and the solemnity of the ancient ruins has begun to pall, the spirits of Herkhuf and of Sabna, of the captains and the caravan-conductors, are always to be found waiting on the breezy hill-tops behind the island of Elephantine, at the head of the Nubian highway.

CHAPTER XII

THE ALABASTER QUARRIES IN THE WADY ASSIOUT

A SHORT expedition into the desert is often successful in dispelling that slack boredom which an Egyptian summer produces in the mind of a lonely man ; and on one occasion, when my work carried me into a friend's district, we decided to try a tonic of this nature. We had come together in the police rest-house at Assiout, and we therefore arranged to visit some alabaster quarries which were said to exist in a desert valley known as the Wady Assiout, some five-and-twenty miles back from the Nile.

The rest-house was connected by telephone with the police outpost on the opposite side of the river ; and one sweltering noon we sent a sudden message across for camels to be saddled and to await us on that bank in an hour's time.

The journey across the swollen river in a rickety native boat took some considerable time ; and as the woodwork was too hot to sit upon, and the garments offered by the sailors in place of cushions too dangerously unclean, we were obliged to stand during the entire voyage, while the sun beat down mercilessly upon our helmets and the glare from the water beat up beneath them. The shade of the palms, therefore, where the camels awaited us, was a pleasant relief, and we were a little inclined to linger over the loading and saddling up.

However, by two o'clock we were trotting through the palm groves and along the rough country roads towards the desert. A smart little Bishari tracker, with his rifle at his side and his cartridge-belt across his shoulder, led the way on a lightly built camel ; and we followed, lumbering along on heavier mounts. One of these, known as *Abu Rasas*, " the Father of the Bullet," was a famous old veteran, so called because he was captured by the Dervishes during the war, escaped, and was shot in the stomach in the ensuing chase. A large growth over the region of the wound was then all that remained to tell of the time when he was a " prisoner of the Khalifa". This camel later, and in his old age, developed a marvellous propensity for jumping, and he used to be put over the fences with extraordinary success, to the delight of assembled crowds.

A ride of somewhat over an hour brought us to the edge of the desert, which here lies in an undulating expanse of sand leading back gradually to the low hills. In front of us opened the wide valley known as Wady Assiout, and it was along this that we intended to ride. Our objective was a disused alabaster quarry which lay in a rocky gauge leading off the left or north side of the valley ; and to this we directed our way, leaving on our right the little police outpost which here stands baking in the sun on the edge of the desert. We had not ridden far when my camel nearly trod upon a jackal which had evidently been fast asleep in a slight hollow of sand in the open plain. It sprang up, but went off at a very moderate pace, while we galloped our unwieldy camels after it, hallooing as we went. However, it soon outran us, and pulled up tamely to watch us when we turned back to our path.

I think our tracker believed us to be insane ; and if either of us broke into a song thereafter, or did any unusual thing as we jogged along, he eyed us suspiciously and perhaps a little pityingly. Mounted upon a trotting camel it is very difficult to refrain from doing eccentric things. The camel requires no attention, the saddle is comfortable ; and there is no chance of falling off. Thus, having nothing to do but jolt along contentedly, one is apt (for example) to begin to admire one's feet which are

crossed upon the camel's neck.   A rearrangement of the
bootlaces may ensue, and the consequent contortions are
uncommonly like those of a demented acrobat.   Or again,
one may take to hitting the flies off the camel with one's
stick ; and if the slaughter of a certain fly settled upon
the camel's nose is determined upon the necessary antics
may be truly amazing.   It may be discovered suddenly
that by opening one's mouth wide the tearing wind will
play a tune upon the teeth ; or again the natural exuber-
ance of physical motion will set one whistling or singing
in the noisiest manner.   All such actions, silently watched
by the native, give good cause for his inward comments ;
and when they are considered in relation to the hour of
the day at which we are given to moving abroad, the
tracker's point of view can be appreciated.   After all,
two Englishmen who ride out into the hell-hot wilderness
at midday in August, and who make wild noises at the
sight of a jackal, and whistle extraordinary snatches of
song with the perspiration running down their faces, are
not easily explicable to foreigners of any nationality or
colour.

As we rode over the broad expense of the desert, the
hills ahead formed themselves into groups of islands rising
from the wide waters of the mirage.   The pathway before
us melted into the great lake which stretched out to the
horizon, studded with these phantom islands always
changing shape as our view-point was altered.   It was
not until we had ridden for some time, and the afternoon
sun was passing down towards the hills behind us, that
the mirage disappeared and the rolling desert ahead became entirely clear.   Presently the pathway developed
into a road of some breadth which had evidently been
made for the purpose of the transport of the blocks of
alabaster from the quarry to which we were heading our
way.   The loose stones had been cleared to either side,
and the sudden dips had been filled in.   This road wound
away before us, lost here and there as it descended into an
old watercourse, and appearing once more as it climbed

an incline on the further side.   It was a long and rather
tedious business to set this twisting length of road behind
us, but at last, as the sun set, we reached the mouth of a
rocky gauge on our left, and riding along it for a short
distance, came in sight of our destination.

As we rode between the narrowing rocks the sun set,
and we walked our camels slowly that we might the better
appreciate the recurrent tragedy of the day and might
watch the sky in all the pity of its glory.   Before us there
clustered the alabaster rocks, and through a break in the
wall of the hills the whole expanse of the sunset could be
seen.   There were some undefined clouds gathered high
over the horizon, and these took the last glances of the
departed sun and displayed them against the darkening
sky.   Overhead three crows, black against the heavens,
flew home to their nests ; and presently a flight of cranes,
but now returned from Europe, passed from the north
towards the river, and faded into the red dusk of the
south, cleaving a path for the thoughts into the heart of
the haze.   In Egypt the death of the day is a sad business.
The red despair of the sky, the untold sorrow of the hills,
spreads a tone of melancholy over the mind ; and here in
this silent valley one's thoughts went away, sober, and
even mystical, into the haze, and there was no more
whistling of comic songs for awhile.

What man living in sedate Europe, even if he can understand the pathos of sunset, can feel the old peril of nightfall ?   I sometimes wonder how the Egyptologist in his
museum at home can hope, for example, to appreciate
the words of the " heretic " Pharaoh's Hymn to the Sun :

> "By thee men live, and their eyes look upon thy beauty,
>   But when thou settest they die."

Who that has not wandered in such a valley as this to
watch an Egyptian sunset can realise what death meant
to the old Egyptians ?   They joined the barque of the sun
and passed, like him, through the regions of the night :
their death was like his setting.   But it is only those who
have seen the launching of that barque, as now we saw

it, who can understand the meaning of those forgotten beliefs.

In western cities the sunset is usually unobserved. The light of day fades in a slow process, and the moment when the sun sinks behind the horizon passes unnoticed. But Egypt is dominated by the sun, and the moment of its setting is the affair of every man. It is a pregnant event ; and to us who now watched it here in the desert it was the occasion of the day. To us was made known at that hour much about ancient Egypt that can never be made known to the professor in his western study ; and in this respect the merest tourist in the land is a better scholar than he. In Europe there is a comfortable melancholy in the sunset ; but in Egypt there is a kind of foreboding also, an undefined feeling of anxiety which quite differentiates this time of day from the same hour in Europe. It is as though a man were abandoned to his own resources after being held in the protection of the light ; and it is only when the full darkness has fallen, and the comforting night closes around him that the mind is at peace once more.

Darkness falls rapidly in Egypt, and there was little light left by the time we reached the quarry. The hill of alabaster was outlined against the last-left glow of the western sky, but the valley in which we now stood was blurred and indistinct, and it was necessary to find quickly a sandy place amongst the boulders and gravel on which to lay our blankets. Such a spot was selected after a short search, and from it we scraped away all loose stones and pebbles, so that our rest should not be disturbed, in Nature's bed, by a bad mattress. The camels were then given their evening meal, without water ; and by starlight we fell upon our own frugal repast. That finished, there followed the happiest hour of these expeditions, when one reclines propped against a boulder and burns the evening sacrifice of tobacco to the gods of Contentment. The heat of the day had left the rocks by this time and the valley was fairly cool ; and now a quiet breeze whispered amongst the boulders and sighed over the hills. Overhead the Milky Way spread like a rainbow from horizon to horizon; and as I dropped into dreams my thoughts were of the old Egyptians who believed that this was the Nile of the Heavens, along which the dead floated in their ghostly boats. It must have been pleasant actually to *see* the place where one's fathers now amused themselves : the next world must have been made a very great reality thereby. I was thinking how strange it would be at night to glance up at the sky and exclaim " There goes grandpapa ! " when I fell asleep.

We were wakened once or twice in the night by the sharp, stinging bites of sandflies—one of the plagues of Egypt ; and the efforts of several bats to catch them within a few inches of one's face were met, I fear, with hard words. However, the night soon passed, and with the first light we were up and doing. An exploration of the place revealed much that was of interest, and, indeed, added one very valuable item to our stock of material for ancient Egyptian history.

Upon a face of cliff near the quarry I found a large inscription which showed that the alabaster had been worked in the reign of Queen Nefertari-Ahmosis, a name which means, by the way, " The Beautiful Companion of the Child of the Moon ". This queen was the wife of the Pharaoh Ahmosis I, who freed Egypt from the rule of the Hyksos in the sixteenth century B.C. Her monuments are not numerous, but it has been noticed that her name is given great prominence when it occurs beside that of her husband, although he was a popular hero. Here in this quarry no mention is made of the Pharaoh at all, and it would seem that the queen was paramount and that her name was sufficient upon public monuments.

As soon as the Hyksos had been driven from the land the temples were rebuilt, and there must have been a considerable demand for alabaster with which to ornament them. Inscriptions of this period describe the magnificent alabaster shrines which were constructed, and there are very numerous smaller objects of this material still extant. Most of the stone was procured from the famous Hatnub quarries, a few miles north of Assiout ; and it is an indication of the quantity required that this new quarry was opened.

There appears to be no other ancient inscription in this valley ; but there is abundant evidence that the stone was worked in modern times, perhaps in the days of Mohammed Ali or even later. The hill-side is covered with blocks of alabaster roughly hewn from the rock, and marked with numbers and short directions in Arabic writing. These magnificent white blocks, three or four feet square, abandoned here in the desert as though worthless, remind one very forcibly of the riches of this splendid country between the Nile and the Red Sea which has produced some of the finest ornamental stones ever used, some of the best gold of ancient times, and now is yielding a quantity of petroleum. In like manner one sees Imperial Porphyry lying abandoned at the quarries of Gebel Dukhân and Granito del Foro at those of Um Etgal, as though these materials were of no particular value. The Nile valley is rich enough, but the desert is prodigal.

At the foot of the hill several small huts are clustered, and a few yards away there is a well, now choked up. The large boulders have been rolled to one side in ancient days to form a roadway for the passage of the stone down this gauge and out to the open desert where the smoother road is picked up. In old times the stone was conveyed to the Nile on carts drawn by oxen and slaves, but in the more recent workings mules and horses were probably used ; and it is as well not to think of the cruelties inflicted on either as the carts sank in the soft gravel or jolted over the stones in this valley.

Researches were over in an hour's time, after which we made our breakfast upon the scraps left in the basket overnight. We then went for a stroll up a narrow valley leading off that in which we had camped, and here our attention was directed for the next quarter of an hour to the pursuit of a ten-inch grey lizard which we had found basking in the early blaze of the sun. Once or twice I have come across the same creature in desert places, and the natives have on each occasion expressed the greatest terror of it. They say that it will spring from the ground and fasten itself in the throat of a man on a camel or on any other elevation, whereupon he bursts into boils and blains and dies in horrible agonies. On one occasion the natives seized my camel's head when one of these lizards was observed in the distance, and turned us round, while others cautiously hurled stones at the monster. My friend and I were therefore most interested when we saw so terrific a little creature at our feet, and we did not cease the pursuit till we had run him to ground and had tweaked his tail to see what he could do. I have no doubt he is absolutely harmless.

The ride home now commenced, and continued until the blinding heat proclaimed it to be nearly one o'clock. At last, roasted to a turn, we reached the river and crossed the glaring water to Assiout. All the way home we had discussed the iced drinks which, by special arrangement, were to be waiting for us ; and I must admit that when tepid lemonade was brought to us with the remark that no ice was procurable the whole expedition seemed to have been a mistake.

CHAPTER XIII

A RIDE TO WADY SALAMÛNI

IT was at about noon in the month of August when my friend and I, perspiring in a rest-house at Sohag in Upper Egypt, conceived the idea of setting out at once for a sixty-mile ride into the Eastern Desert and back. The weather during the last few days had been unusually hot, and the thermometer had registered with regularity each afternoon its 115 degrees Fahrenheit in the shade. Looking now through the half-closed shutters towards the Nile, one saw the muddy river rushing past in full flood with the sun glaring down upon it from a leaden sky ; the parched fields and weakly coloured trees stirring in the baking hot wind ; and, in the distance across the water, the hazy hills of the Eastern Desert with no apparent vestige of shade upon them. In the sandy garden around the house the few flowers appeared to be scorched, and the despairing gardener could be seen lying asleep in the single patch of shadow. The sparrows, sitting upon the palings, held their beaks open and kept remarkably still. A dog, with its tongue lolling out of its mouth, crawled dejectedly past the sentry at the gate, who was too hot to kick it.

The morning's work being finished, we were seated in the long chairs, clad in pyjamas, drinking lukewarm lemonade, and talking about Scotch moors, when the idea came.

My friend had told me of a remarkable valley which he had visited some years ago, called the Wady Salamûni, wherein there were the ruins of a Coptic monastery still the object of a pilgrimage on certain occasions to pious Copts, and near by a well, known as Bir el Ain, charmingly situated amongst the rocks. It was to this well that we proposed to ride.

Speedily we arranged for horses to be sent round, and rapidly we filled our saddle-bags with the requirements for twenty-four hours : a small pillow and a blanket apiece, some hard-boiled eggs, cold meat, and biscuits, and two large bottles of water. That done, we dressed and ate a hasty luncheon, setting forth in the blaze of the sunshine at the infernal hour of one.

Mounting our horses at the gates of the rest-house, and accompanied by one policeman, we rode along the glaring river bank to the jimcrack landing-stage, where the little steam-ferry was waiting without a single passenger at this hottest hour of the day. The three horses were led into a clumsy native vessel which was then attached to the ferry and towed across the swollen river to the eastern bank, where it arrived with a bump that sent the horses staggering across the boat. We saddled up and were off well before two o'clock, cantering along the embanked road towards the town of Akhmîm. On either side of the road, and spreading around the town, the floods stretched in a glaring sheet of brown water, beaten into small waves on our left by the hot wind from the north, but smooth upon our right, and alive with millions of tadpoles swimming in the shelter of the embankment. Here and there villages formed islands in the sheet of water ; and a few palm-trees rose from the flood at various points like pin flags upon a large war map. Outside these villages the small boys splashed about in the water, having, it would seem, the time of their lives ; and as we rode along the straight unsheltered embankment, buffeted by the wind, roasted by the heat arising from the road, and baked by the sun above, our horses jumping about until the perspiration streamed from them and from us, we cast envious eyes at those happy children bathing in the shade of the palms, and omitted to realise for a while that we also were out for our pleasure.

At length we clattered over the bridge into the town of Akhmîm, and were swallowed up for a while in the narrow streets and winding alleys, where the sun beat down on us with renewed force, and the dust rose in clouds around us.

Akhmîm is one of the most ancient cities in Egypt, and in fact Leo Africanus says that it is *the* oldest, having been founded by Akhmîm, the son of Misraim, the off-spring of Cush, the son of Ham ! It is built upon the site of the ancient Panopolis, the main seat of the worship of Min—the Egyptian god who was identified in Greek days with Pan.   Herodotus tells us an extraordinary story which relates how Perseus came to this city while search-ing for the Gorgon's head, because he had been told by his mother that it was the place in which his ancestors had dwelt.   It is now much fallen from its ancient glory, but it is still a town of some 30,000 inhabitants.   It is a peculiarly picturesque place, unspoilt by the introduc-tion of debased European architecture, as are so many Egyptian towns.   It is now largely inhabited by Copts (*i.e.*, Christians)—a fact that is made apparent by the presence of very filthy pigs which run unchecked about the streets, and which are rather inclined to frighten one's horses.   The houses are well built, and in places pass across the street, so that one rides, as it were, through a tunnel, in the shadow of which the fruit-sellers spread their dates, pomegranates, and melons, upon richly coloured shawls, at the sides of the road.   Akhmîm, by the way, is famous for the manufacture of these shawls ; and Strabo tells us that in old days the inhabitants were notable manufacturers of linen.

There were few people about as we rode through the town, for the natives have a proverb which states that only dogs and Englishmen move abroad in the heat of the day.   Nevertheless, we had sudden encounters, round-ing sharp corners, with heavily laden camels or sleepy-eyed buffaloes ; and once or twice we had to ride with caution through groups of sleeping figures.   At the far side of the town we passed a very beautiful mosque, surrounded by a high wall, the doorway in which was ornamented with fine blue tiles.   Through it we could see the courtyard with its cool-looking sycamore and place of ablution, and the highly coloured mosque in the background ; but our horses were restive, and with this passing glimpse we were off once more along another embanked road leading towards the Eastern Desert, the hills of which now rose before us in the far distance. Again the hot wind beat upon us across the inundation, and once more the full glare of the open day surrounded us.

The afternoon was drawing in when at last we floundered through a half-flooded field on to the sandy slopes of the desert at the foot of the hills. Here there is a vast cemetery, dating from the days of the last Pharaohs, when the people of Panopolis laid their bones at the edge of the wilderness, the Eastern Desert being dedicated to Pan-of-the-Goodly-Way, the Egyptian Min, as so many ex-votos testify. The graves have all been dug out many years ago by robbers, and now the surface of the sand is littered with skulls and bones and portions of mummies. Dry, black faces grin at one, with set teeth and blind eyes, from the open tombs ; and mummified hands and arms supplicate the passer-by from the sand. My horse put his hoof through the brain-pan of some old subject of Pharaoh ; and, dismounting presently, I picked up the remains of a blue glazed drinking-vessel that had belonged to another. It is this plundering of ancient cemeteries that the Department of Antiquities has set itself to check ; but here the Government was thirty or forty years late in taking the matter up, and the watchman who now parades the cemetery, gun in hand, has little left him to protect.

These dead men's bones lie before the entrance of the Wady Salamûni, as though protecting the sacred place from the curiosity of modern eyes. No tourists have found their way here, and indeed but few white men of any kind. Sohag, the capital of the province, is not a convenient or interesting town at which to stop ; and to most persons it would seem unreasonable to suppose that anybody could wish to ride the long and tedious distance over the breadth of the Nile valley, and to penetrate amongst the forbidding hills of the desert, guarded by so many objectionable dead bodies. On the advice of my friend, the native Governor and his companions made the excursion ; but though marquees were erected and refreshments were lavishly displayed therein, I do not think that he made any pretence of enjoying himself.

Riding across the cemetery and picking our way amongst the open graves, we reached and entered at last the mouth of the valley, which cut into the solid range of hills like a great fissure, with walls of yellow limestone rising on either side to a height of some four hundred feet. Here we were sheltered from the wind, and at intervals there was the deep shadow of the rocks to give us comfort. Overhead, the strong blue of the sky formed an almost startling setting to the bold crest of the cliffs, where white-winged vultures circled above us or perched on ledges of rock to take stock of our cavalcade. In places the cliffs rose sheer to the sky ; sometimes the rock shelved back with tumbled *débris* of boulders and gravel sloping a third of the way up it ; or again, huge pinnacles of rock and cavernous ledges broke up the face of the cliff, as it were into grimaces. A prehistoric torrent had scooped out a deep recess in the base of the cliffs on either side, and had tumbled a mass of water-worn boulders into the bed of the valley, where they lay encased in gravel. This torrent at one time must have rushed and roared down from the desert, half filling the valley on its way to join the huge Nile ; but now it has sunk to a trickling subterranean stream, infiltrating through the gravel, its presence only indicated by the few bushes of scrub, and occasional stunted tamarisks and other trees which grow amidst the boulders in its old bed.

A path worn by Coptic pilgrims, and perhaps by others before them, wound in and out amidst the rocks, and upon this our horses picked their way. Now it would lead us over the soft gravel in the middle of the valley ; now it would rise high upon the sloping hillside to avoid a mass of boulders below ; and now it would pass over a level platform of rock, upon which the horses clattered and slipped. The pace was necessarily slow, and, as it was now past five o'clock, we were beginning to feel weary and uncommonly thirsty. The sun presently passed off the valley, and shone only upon the upper part of the cliffs, thus throwing a soft glow around us which gave a wonderfully rich tone to the browns and greys of the rocks. As we proceeded farther up the wady, the clumps of vegetation became less infrequent, and here and there one was surprised to see a small purple-flowered creeper winding amongst the stones. Protruding from small holes in the face of the rock another kind of creeper was growing. This is called by the natives by a word which we would translate as " capers ". It has a small round leaf of a silvery green, and it hangs down in thick clusters from the minute holes in the rock wherein, as by a miracle, it has taken root. I do not know its technical name, but I can testify to its beauty as we saw it, in the glow of the late afternoon, surrounded by the barren magnificence of the cliffs and rocks.

At one point, upon the right-hand side of the valley, the path led us past a large rock, upon the west face of which there were several Greek and Coptic inscriptions. One of the former is interesting, for it records the existence of a kind of sporting club whose members hunted wild animals in the desert. Two of the chief huntsmen, both Greeks, are mentioned by name : Messouēris and Alexikratēs. The old inhabitants of Panopolis seem to have prided themselves upon their sporting tendencies, and Herodotus says that they used to hold gymnastic games, comprising every sort of contest, in honour of Perseus.

In this connection I should like to record an incident which happened while we were at Sohag. Upholding the sporting traditions of the neighbourhood, the Deputy-Governor thought he would organise some shooting expeditions among the notables of the town, there being a few gazelle in the desert and plenty of duck in the pools at its edge. He therefore sent to Cairo for his three sporting-guns and some ammunition. These were forwarded to him by railway ; but some over-suspicious official examined the package, and immediately the rumour spread that a haul of contraband arms had been made. The Coptic papers next day published the astounding news, which was copied in the European press, that twenty guns and a large amount of ammunition had been seized, and that an anti-Coptic rising in Sohag, led by the Deputy-Governor, was imminent. Much excitement was caused thereby, and not a little trepidation amongst the Copts of Akhmîm and elsewhere, at which the kindly owner of the guns, with a twinkle in his eye, expressed his concern to us, as we sat with him one evening in the club which he and his friends had recently founded for the purpose of bringing Copts and Mussulmans together. Thus is the Unrest kept in the forefront of men's minds.

Proceeding slowly up the valley, we rode, slipping and scrambling, along the narrow pathway : the noise of our going echoed from cliff to cliff. Occasionally the shrill cry of a hawk rang through the wady, and its soaring flight would lead the eye up from the mellow tones of the rocks to the deep colour of the sky. Then a stumbling step would bring the attention down to the pathway once more, where a lizard, scuttling away over the stones, would direct one's glance into some shadowed cranny where the creepers flowered amongst the gravel. At intervals along the path small piles of stones had been placed upon the rocks at the wayside, either to mark the road or to act as the record of the passage of a pilgrim, this latter being the custom obtaining amongst desert people from remote times, though I have never been able to ascertain clearly whether it has a religious origin. Guiding ourselves by these little heaps when the path was obscure, at length we came, quite suddenly, upon the Coptic ruins to which the pilgrims were wont to journey ; and here we dismounted for a few minutes.

High upon a ledge of rock, a hundred feet from the valley, a small, ruined building of unburnt bricks clung

Two views in the Wady Salamûni: early morning

perilously to the cliff, and marked the site where a forgotten Coptic hermit had dwelt in the early centuries of
the Christian era.   A chimney in the rock appears to have
led up to it, for there is some more brickwork to be seen
here.   But probably a rope-ladder against the face of the
cliff was also used, for these anchorites were not uncommonly as agile as they were saintly, choosing to live, as
they so often did, in inaccessible caverns, or on the
perilous topes of ruined temples, or even upon the capital
of an ancient column.   Upon the shelving cliff-side ran
a ledge of rock, a continuation of that on which the
building was erected.   This had been made into a kind
of promenade about a hundred yards in length, blocked
at the far end by a stout wall.   A low fender of stone
passed along the brink of the ledge, thus preventing the
danger of a headlong fall into the valley below on the
part of the star-gazing hermit, who, presumably, took his
daily constitutional at this fine elevation.

In honour of the saint, as it would appear, a small
chapel had been built at the foot of the cliff ; and, though
this is now much ruined, two of its arches, constructed of
thin, red bricks, are still intact, and some of the white-
washed walls are yet standing.   Near this chapel there
are the much-destroyed ruins of what seems to have been
a small monastic settlement, perhaps founded in honour
of the hermit of the cliff dwelling ; but very little now
remains of the settlement.

A dramatic residence, indeed, for a man of God and for
his followers ! Here, in the splendid desolation of this
valley amongst the hills, one could well imagine an anchorite turning his thoughts to things beyond the ken of
the dweller in the cities.   There is an atmosphere of
expectancy in these desert cañons, a feeling that something lies waiting around the corner, a sense of elusiveness
inviting a search, a mysterious suggestion of an impending
event which I do not know how to describe, but which
might well be interpreted by a religious mystic as a
revelation of a higher power.   The feeling that one is

watched, and indeed watched benevolently, is experienced, I should think, by almost all travellers in the desert ; and there is no locality where one may lie down o' nights with a greater sense of security, nor any place where words may be whispered to the unknown, with better hope that they are heard. The people of the Greek age in Egypt, offering prayer to Pan in this desert, were wont to make their supplication to Pan who was " within hearing " ; and now, though the old gods are dead and the new God sometimes seems very far off, those who journey in the wilderness still may believe that there is Something listening and always " within hearing ".

Continuing our way up the valley a short distance farther, we came, just before sunset, to Bir el Ain, where we proposed to spend the night. As we approached the end of our journey we had noticed that the vegetation, such as there was, was fresher in colour, as though more fully watered ; and several birds were observed hereabouts. A black and white wheatear flew from rock to rock beside us ; two little pink-beaked finches rose from a tamarisk as we passed ; and, in a soft feathery tree of the acacia family, which grew solitary in the gravel bed, two very small birds—warblers of some kind—flitted silently from branch to branch, their little weight hardly stirring the twigs upon which they alighted. The nearness of the water thus was obvious ; but the charmed surroundings of the well were an extraordinary surprise. After the heat and exertion of the day, and the long ride through the almost sterile valley, the scene of our cool camping-ground beside the water possessed a charm which perhaps it would have held in lesser degree under other circumstances. To me it appeared as a kind of fairyland.

Under an overhanging cliff at one side of this magnificent cañon there was a small pool of clear water, on to which one looked down from the gravel surface of the old torrent bed. A few yards farther up the valley, amidst smooth, moss-covered boulders, there was a thick cluster of vivid green reeds and grasses. A gazelle-trodden path through these led to the brink of a second pool, which passed, in serpentine fashion, amongst the rocks, bordered by reeds swaying gently in the breeze. The water was clear and still, and, in the twilight, most mysterious. A few yards away three palm-trees spread their branches towards the enclosing walls of rock ; and near them a slow trickle of water passed out from a hole in the face of the cliff and ran tinkling down to feed the pool below. In all directions grasses and creepers, growing amidst the gravel and the boulders, made the valley alive with colour ; and yet this virility was enclosed in dead stone, like a jewel held in its case.

I must admit that I left my companion to superintend the policeman's work of watering and feeding the horses ; for the silent pool amidst the reeds kept me, as it were, enchanted by its side. How still it was in the gathering dusk, how far removed from the world of work ! Surely Pan was " within hearing " : Pan, whom the people of the nearest villages and towns had all worshipped in bygone days. If one kept quite still, moved not a muscle, perhaps he would suddenly appear, seated amongst the reeds over yonder, pipes in hand. The birds which had lately twittered and chirped in the valley were now silent, and one might have supposed them listening to music which the mortal ear could not distinguish. Perhaps of a sudden one's ears would be opened, one's eyes would see, and the god who, more than all other gods of his day, still holds the imagination, would be made manifest beside this desert pool. But the darkness increased and Pan did not come ; and soon the preparations for the night could wait no longer. When at last I arose from the cool and silent place, it was with the conviction firmly set in my mind that this pool and valley were not only sacred to the Copts, but had been holy ground, a sacred place of the god of Panopolis, or ever the Christian faith had been heard of.

It is not unusual in Egypt to find that the worship of a Coptic or Mussulman saint has been substituted for that

of an ancient Egyptian god.   At the head of the Nubian
highroad at Aswân the shrine of the ancient gods has been
made the site of a mediæval shêkh's tomb ;   and those
who now go there to make their prayers before and after
a journey are but carrying on a custom as old as history.
Amongst the ruins of Thebes there is a hill up which barren
women and as yet childless brides climb at dead of night
to lay their supplications before the shêkh whose tomb is
there erected.   They do not know that their ancestors
climbed the same hill in the days of the Pharaohs to offer
the same petitions to Meritseger, the serpent goddess who
had dwelt thereon since the beginning of things.   And so
in this valley I feel sure that the Coptic hermit who
resided here was of no great consequence as judged upon
his own merits, as indeed the fact that he is now forgotten
indicates, but that the inhabitants of Akhmîm, accustomed in the pagan days of Panopolis to regard this place
as holy ground, came gradually to ascribe to him the
origin of its sanctity and to forget that in reality its
sacredness dated from those days when Pan admired
himself in the reedy pool and danced upon the rounded
rocks.   *Sic transit gloria divini !*

The modern name of the place, Bir el Ain, is the Arabic
for " The Well of the Well-spring "—a somewhat uncomfortable sounding title, I am told, to native ears ;
and I am inclined to think that *ain* is derived from the
ancient Egyptian word of probably similar sound, meaning " a religious festival ".   The place might in that case
be so called because it was the well to which the yearly
processional festival of Pan made its journey.   We know
that the image of the god Amen was conducted in this
manner round the deserts over against Thebes, in a
festival which, Professor Sethe thinks, may have given its
name to the famous Wady Ain whither there is some
reason to suppose that the procession made its way.   It
does not require an undue stretch of the imagination,
therefore, to suppose that a similar religious ceremony
was performed over against Panopolis.

However, be this as it may, no one who has visited this pool, and who has sat at its edge in the cool of the twilight, will deny that Pan might be expected to have made an appearance here in the days of his power.

In the darkness my friend and I spread our blankets upon the gravel, and set to with relish upon our meal of cold meat and eggs, drinking deep from our water-bottles. Then, after a cigar smoked in the silence of contentment, and a last inspection of the horses, we settled down for sleep. The moon, rising behind the cliffs, threw a warm light upon the opposite crest of the rocks and cast the valley wherein we lay into deeper shadow. Not a sound was to be heard except the contented munching of the horses ; and long before the moonlight had waxed strong we had dropped quietly to sleep and to dreams of Pan.

At about midnight my friend started up from the ground of a sudden, and as he did so a dark creature bounded away up the valley to the pool, sending the gravel flying beneath its feet. In the light of the moon it appeared to be of great size, but its form was indistinct as it rushed past.

" It was *licking* my forehead ! " said my friend, not quite sure whether he had been dreaming or not.

" It was probably Pan," said I. And as it was too much bother to get up and find the policeman's rifle, my companion, rubbing his forehead, returned to the realms of sleep, whither I had preceded him ; and neither of us know whether our midnight visitor was a prowling hyena or something more uncanny.

An hour later he again sat up with a start, and away flew an enormous eagle-owl which had been contemplating him at a distance of a few inches from his face. I see, by the way, that Shelley, the great authority on Egyptian birds, states that this neighbourhood is much infested with this species of owl ; and I will testify that they are very formidable creatures. By this time the moon was sailing overhead, and it was difficult to sleep in the strong light, which turned the rocks to alabaster and the vegetation to wax. Moreover, there were things moving about in the valley : silent footfalls and deep breathings. And one of the horses became restive. However, sleep at last claimed us, and we did not wake again until the first light of dawn was apparent in the sky.

Speedily we arose and washed in the cool water of the spring, thereafter making a breakfast from the remains of the evening's meal, washed down with water. At five o'clock we set off to walk a further distance of three or four miles up the valley, to a place where my companion, on his last visit, had found another hollow full of clear water which passed into a passage between the over-hanging cliffs and thence opened out into a cavernous pool. He had dived in and had swum into this further pool, where the daylight penetrated in subdued power through an opening in the rocks above ; and we now were desirous of repeating the performance. A rough path, probably made by the people of the desert who watered their flocks in this valley, led us with some interruptions, up the narrowing wady, as yet untouched by the sun's rays. Now we clambered up the hillside, now down into the river-bed ; now we jumped from boulder to boulder, and now trudged through soft shingle. At length we came to a place where the valley forked, and here a dark cleft in the rocks on our left front marked the spot where the pool should have been. But, alas ! the water had dried up, and even the mud at the bottom, stamped by the hoofs of gazelle, was hard and firm. Along the narrow passage where my friend had swum in deep water we walked dry-shod, and so entered the cavern hollowed out by the downward rush of long-forgotten torrents. Nevertheless the place was not without its attractions, and its romantic situation amidst pinnacles of rock and gigantic boulders made it well worth seeing.

Returning to the valley outside, we became the object of hostility of two grey hawks, who made a spirited attack upon us, swooping down to within a few feet of our heads and screeching at us in a truly brave manner. Their nest must have been close at hand, but we had no time to make a search for it. Walking back to the Bir el Ain with the sun now blazing upon us, we reached once more the shadow of the palms and the cool sight of the water, somewhat before eight o'clock.

I should mention, perhaps, that I found in the pool a curious creature, swimming near the bottom. It was shaped almost precisely like a scorpion, having the long tail and claws of that objectionable creature ; but it was of a dark olive-green colour, and appeared to be both helpless and harmless. I have no idea what it is called technically, nor how it comes to be found in isolated desert-pools.

Lying down at the edge of the pool with my back against a comfortably sloping stone, and a water-bottle by my side, half an hour of profound comfort slipped by. The cool breeze of early morning rustled amongst the reeds and swayed the branches of the palms ; dragon-flies hovered over the quiet water ; finches uttered their strange note from the tamarisk near by ; and overhead the hawks circled and cried above the majestic cliffs. It was enchanting here to lie, remote from the worries of work, and to let the mind wander in a kind of inconsequent contemplation of things in general. But soon it was time to be moving out into the sun once more, and we had to bid adieu to this holy place of Pan, where life was cool and shadowed, and where there was water for the thirsty and the soothing sound of the wind in the reeds for the weary. The blazing ride down the valley and along the embanked road to Akhmîm was accomplished at a tolerable pace, but from Akhmîm to the river bank we went at full gallop, arriving in a cloud of dust just in time to catch the steam ferry ; and half an hour later the rest-house at Sohag was echoing with the impatient shouts for drinks, baths, shaving-water, luncheon, and all the rest of the urgent and unordered requirements of two very hot, very dirty, and very hungry mortals.

CHAPTER XIV

THE CHILDREN OF EGYPT

" Now remember," said a sun-burnt British sergeant
to a new arrival in Egypt, " in dealing with these 'ere
natives—severity always ; justice when possible." The
British officer or civilian, however, is seldom inclined to be
severe with the native villagers, soldiers, and workmen
with whom he comes into contact ; for, after a short
residence on the banks of the Nile, it becomes clear to
him that he has to deal with a pack of good-natured
youths who merit severe treatment not more frequently
than do our English schoolboys, and who, like them, are
most amenable to a line of conduct which is kindly,
consistent, and strongly maintained.

The Egyptian peasant seems to have failed to grow up.
It is as though he were a relic of the days when the world
was young, preserved to this present age together with
the Sphinx and the Pyramids. The mind of the lower-
class Egyptian has not expanded since the time of the
Pharaohs, and when one looks at the modern inhabitants
of the country one sees in them the people of five thousand
years ago, the tenants of the world's youth. Thus it
comes about that the British official in Egypt has to teach
as well as take up his share of the burden of government.
He has to act as tutor to a most engaging, though sometimes provoking, rabble of children.

How can you be severe with a native who sends you a
beautiful letter, written in purple ink, upon pink paper,
addressed to " Sir Excellency Mister Chief Inspector " ;
and beginning, " Honoured Enormity " ; or how can you
apply the booted toe to the petitioner who commences
his appeal with the words, " Sire, prithee goggle not at my

Modern Egyptian peasants beside a water-wheel

beseech " ? I have from time to time collected some of these letters received from natives, and in reading them over it is impossible to overcome the feeling that one has inadvertently slipped through a rent in the veil of Time and become a denizen of the land of childhood. To make my meaning clear, I will here quote some of these documents ; and the reader will thus understand how difficult it is to regard the writers as responsible men of our sober twentieth century.

Little children, before they are taught their manners, are wont to tell tales against one another to their mothers or nurses ; and the English official in Egypt is continuously besieged by complaints of this kind, most of which are quite unable to be substantiated. Here, for example, is a typical specimen :

" Mohammed Aly, the watchman of the Rest-house, states that while he was watching his spot the Head Watchman came and asked him to go and buy two pigeons. Having the watchman went, the Head Watchman entered the house and began to drink kind of intoxications. On his return found him drinking. He annoyed and became too angry. He said it was not right. Thereupon they quarrelled and he insulted him with his foot. This watchman prays you to peep through this matter."

A native who had had words with one of our employees attempted to revenge himself by writing to me to accuse his enemy of taking bribes.

" I have the honour to inform your kindness," says the letter, " that Ahmed Hassan the Chief Porter under your noble direction is taking bibes (sic) like hens, eggs, veg., and some other things, and he takes also one pound from every porter. So I beg from your kindness to examine him in this manufacture and to accept my request and highly obliged."

Revenge is also the motive of another complaint, reading as follows :

" I lay this matter before you, as I know you are very fond to know all what your men do. The Inspector at . . . became so proud of himself thinking he was the only chief one there who can do as he likes. He is always willing to mischief the poor in order that he can do what he likes. Also he is a gallant and tries to lead the good women a fast life. That is because he is not willing to be watched by the faithful men of occupation. He is always interfering with some other man's affairs, and he is hard trying to gather money so much for himself."

P

Here is another effort :

" Sir, with heart full of deep sympathy and eyes full of hot tears, I am Ahmed Hassan who was dismissed last week, have the honour to inform you :—I am a poor man have crowded children and a wife without state cannot find any way by which I live, that is case deserving kindness upon justice. What shall I do ? Kindly I beg you sir for the sake of by God to remain me in my job."

A request for employment was worded in the following confident manner :

" Petitioner, Mohammed Ahmed, your slave, begs to state that he has served the Government in Cairo twenty years, and thanks God his has done his duties most energetically. Born in a tropical country and having spent thirty years in Egypt my body has become damp and now I am very anxious to return to my own place. As you have done me so many kindnesses in the past I shall be obliged if you will recommend me for employment there, as I am poor and am well convinced that the most beloved thing to you is my welfare."

The correct address on the envelope often puzzles the native greatly. Lord Cromer once received a letter addressed simply to " The Lord, Cairo ". Sir Eldon Gorst was on one occasion addressed as " His Majesty Gorst ". Lord Edward Cecil was once the recipient of a letter addressed to " Sessel the Substitute ", he being then an Under-Secretary of State, an office which is called in Arabic " El Wakil "—i.e. " Deputy ".

The native stable-boy in charge of our hospital for sick animals desired a rise in his wages, and wrote me the following petition :

" We respectfully beg to lay before your kind notice. I am Abdullah Ahmed of the animals. I beg to acquainted your Excellency I had been appointed to that place according to your noble order. I beg to inform you Sir from the time in which I worked I got a great tired because I feed buffaloes, camels, she goats, cows, he horses, asses, all these animals with out sickness neither wounds. Although I say to the police officer increase my wages he say No, fool. I beg you to increase my wages and I implore God to grant you a happy life."

The above letters have been written either by the professional scribes who are generally to be found seated outside the government offices in any provincial town, or by friends of the petitioners who had learnt to write while employed as dragomans or servants in European households. Sometimes, too, a minor clerk in a Government office will not be above writing such a letter in return for a basket of vegetables, let us say, or a couple of pigeons. Such people pride themselves on their knowledge of English, and often display a keen desire to converse or correspond with one another in our language however slight their acquaintance with its intricacies may be.

An example of the ludicrous results of this affectation is shown upon a sheet of paper which I have before me. At the head of the paper is my Egyptian secretary's note to a certain station-master, reading, " Kindly reserve three sleeping baths (berths) on the train to-night." The station-master sent the note on to the *wagon-lit* inspector with the words, " Please make the needful and write and obliged." The inspector forwarded the note to the superintendent with the endorsement, " Please command " ; and that official returned it after adding the words, " Yours truly, are reserved." The station-master then received the note and forwarded it to my secretary, with the message : " Dear. You find your require and oblige " ; and my secretary sent it on to me with the final endorsement : " Sir, the baths are ready."

There is another class of correspondence of which a few specimens lie before me. These are letters, petitions, and reports of minor native officials, who, although belonging to the lower classes by birth, have received a good education and speak English with some fluency. Writers of this class generally use language which is somewhat Biblical in character, as will be seen in the following petition :

" Sir, one, only one Kind word from you will go a great way off and do a great deal of good, therefore, I write these lines in the hope of getting that good word. I have already been tried in the furnace. Poverty, mortification, and disappointment have done their work upon me, and my soul and body are now sufficiently sick. Will you therefore, have compassion upon me and approve my reinstatement in the office from which I was dismissed as a last chance ? "

Here are two short letters of a different type. The first was written by a sporting Egyptian employed in my department, whose pony I had ridden with enjoyment on two occasions. It reads :

" As I believe you will be pleased to hear that my horse whom you have loved has gained the first prize in the first course of our Sporting Club races yesterday, therefore I have written these words to you for pleasure."

The second letter was left at my house on Christmas Day by another employee, and reads :

" With the greatest pleasure and most gaiety I have come to say Happy Christmas to you."

Both these are typical specimens of a naïve and childlike, but quite charming, class of letter which an English official in Egypt constantly receives.

The following official note was received by me from an Egyptian of a somewhat nervous temperament :

"The Inspector of . . . begs to inform you that he is quite sure that the robbers will be found in their hiding. When he received your word saying that you would attack them at this midnight his hand shivered with gladness and his heart was full of joy. He will be at the place of meeting with the horses at the time you say, but owing to his mother is about to die he hopes you will not need him to accompany you."

I must now be permitted to relate a few anecdotes concerning the children of Egypt, which will further display that quality of youthful simplicity which is usually so very engaging, and which leads more often to an internal convulsion than to an outburst of wrath.

A curious fact in regard to the Egyptian peasant is that, in a manner of the little child, he seldom knows his own age. A lad with a budding moustache will tell you in all seriousness that he is forty, and a wizened old man will, with many gestures indicating his uncertainty, declare himself to be " perhaps about thirty." A true story is told of an old native who was taken before the magistrate on a charge of stealing six buns from a pastrycook's shop. Asked what his age was, he replied that he thought he was about 112. The magistrate turned to the clerk and inquired whether any previous offence was recorded against the prisoner. The clerk replied that there seemed to be nothing against him—at any rate not for the last hundred years. The magistrate then addressed the old man once more, and asked him whether he had no grandchildren or other descendants with whom he could live and who could keep him out of mischief. " Oh," replied the prisoner, " I am well enough looked after, thank you. I live with mother."

A somewhat similar tale comes from the upper reaches of the Nile. In the Sudân there are always a large number of camp followers who do odd jobs for the troops stationed in outlying places, and these men receive daily rations from the War Office, the amount varying according to the age of the individual. A short time ago a grey-haired native sergeant of many years' service asked his commanding officer whether the rations of one of these hangers-on might be increased from those of a boy to those of an adult. " Why ? " asked the officer. " Is the man more than eighteen years old ? " " Oh yes, I think he *must* be," said the sergeant, after some hesitation. " He is my father."

The Egyptian is generally inclined to be very literal in the interpretation of his instructions, and several amusing anecdotes are told in this regard. An English official died suddenly at a lonely outpost in the Sudân, and the Egyptian officer on whom the charge of affairs had devolved wired acquainting the authorities with the sad news. Very wisely the Englishman at headquarters, who had heard stories of persons being buried alive, telegraphed back saying : " Make certain that he is really dead before burial." The reply of the Egyptian official was received a few hours later. It reads : " Have made certain with revolver."

Another story is told of an Egyptian clerk at a railway station in the far south who was much disinclined to act on any occasion without precise instructions. One day the officer at the depot received a telegram from him which read : " Station-master is being devoured by lion on platform. Please wire instructions." On another occasion this same clerk telegraphed down the line to the nearest English official the following startling message. " Station attacked by lions, tigers, bears, and wolves." The Englishman replied : " Your message ridiculous. Wire precisely what you mean." To this the clerk, after some hesitation, humbly answered, " Delete tigers and bears."

When the great dam at Aswân was being built, the Egyptian government gave notice to all Nile boatmen that the river would be closed to traffic at this point for the period of one year. In spite of ample warning, however, several vessels arrived from Lower Nubia after the date fixed for the closing of the waterway, and were therefore held up on the south side of the works. After waiting a month or two one of the skippers came to the engineer in charge and asked him how long he would have to wait before he could continue his journey down stream, as he was somewhat in a hurry.

" Well," said the official, " I expect you will have to stay where you are for about ten months more."

" Thank you, sir," the boatman answered, quite unmoved. " Would you be so kind as to lend me a bit of rope ? I suppose I shall have to tie up."

There are times when the simplicity of the Egyptian becomes annoying. Indeed there are occasions when these irresponsible ways lead to terrible crimes, for which the hangman's rope is none too severe a punishment. A tragic story of this kind was told me a year or two ago in Upper Egypt. Three young peasants wished to play a practical joke on an unpopular villager, who was for the moment believed to be absent from home ; and they decided that the most amusing plan would be to enter his house and make hay with his goods and chattels. They therefore went at dead of night to the place, and made an examination to ascertain the easiest manner of forcing an entrance. In the back wall they discovered that several bricks were loose, and by removing these a hole was made of a size sufficient to permit of a child crawling through. With many suppressed giggles they returned to their own dwelling place and secured the services of a little girl about nine years old who was related to one of their number. They then hurried back to their victim's house, and telling the girl that she must open one of the doors or windows from the inside, they pushed her through the hole. Now it so happened that the unpopular gentleman had returned from his travels and was asleep within the front chamber ; and very soon the little girl appeared at the hole in the wall, calling to her companions to pull her back again as quickly as possible. At that moment the owner of the house awoke, and, hearing the noise, rushed into the back room. There he saw in the semi-darkness the figure of the girl struggling to escape through the hole, and promptly he seized her by the legs and began to pull. The practical jokers on the other side of the wall, realising what was happening, grabbed the girl's head and also began to pull.

" Allah ! " said one of them. " He'll drag her in and recognise who she is, and then he'll have us up for burglary."

" Pull ! " gasped another ; " he'll get her ! "

" You'll pull her head off if you're not careful," said the third.

" O well, she's only a girl," answered his companion. They now each had a hand upon the unfortunate child's head and throat, and with a mighty tug they pulled her through the hole. They then picked up the limp body and raced back to their own home.

" Well, well," panted one, as they sat once more in safety, " that was a narrow squeak ! "

" Poor little girl ! " said the second. " She was a comely lass ! "

" Ah me ! " sighed the third. " But we'll give her a good funeral to-morrow."

Their alternate laughter and tears presently attracted

the attention of other members of the family, and soon their crime was out.

During an epidemic of cholera some years ago orders were sent to the native authorities in the villages to "isolate" any cases of the illness which might be detected. An English official, happening to visit one of these villages a short time after this order had been issued, asked the head man whether any cases of cholera had occurred among his people.

"Only one," replied the old Egyptian—" a girl. We 'isolated' her."

"Good!" said the Englishman. "How did you do it?"

The native smiled and drew his finger across his throat. "With a knife," he said.

The Egyptian's idea of justice is peculiar; and although the better class native judges are usually excellent exponents of the law, instances are often to be noticed of an absurdly childish reasoning. A short time ago two natives were had up before the courts on the charge of having carried firearms without licenses. In passing sentence the native judge fined one of the offenders one hundred piastres and the other fifty piastres. An English official asked the Judge why he had not given the same punishment to both men.

"Well, you see," said the Egyptian, "one of the guns was longer than the other."

So much has been written in regard to native superstitions that little need here be said upon the subject. I cannot refrain, however, from recording one story dealing with this phase of Egyptian life. A native *effendi*, a man of the educated classes, found himself in trouble one morning at the Zoological Gardens at Cairo owing to the fact that he had been observed by one of the keepers to climb the railings surrounding the giraffes' compound and to open and shut an umbrella several times, apparently for the purpose of frightening one of the animals. When he was closely questioned as to his actions he stated that he had wished to shade the giraffe's neck from the sun, in order that he might have the pleasure of watching the creature shrink to the size of a mouse, a phenomenon which he had been told would be observed if a shadow were cast upon that part of its anatomy at noon.

Another native, who had been watching a chimpanzee with awful interest for some time, asked the keeper what manner of diet was provided for animals of that kind. The keeper having told him, the visitor smiled, and, taking his arm, drew him aside. " Now that nobody can hear what we are saying," he whispered, " tell me truly : do you not feed them on the flesh of criminals who die in the city prisons ? " As a deterrent to crime it might have been as well had the keeper admitted that such was the case.

Egyptians will believe stories of the wildest kind, which in Europe only a child would accept. For example, when the Aswân Dam was built, many natives declared that the English had only undertaken the work in order to convey the water of the Nile in pipes to England for the benefit of the British farmer. Many of the peasants believe that England is inhabited solely by men who spend one half of the year in digging through perpetual ice and snow for the gold which lies below, and the other half of the year in spending the proceeds in Egypt, which is obviously the hub of the universe.

This credulity is so general that the native peasant, believing the English official to be similarly minded, often invents, and even acts out, the most absurd story by which to conceal the actual facts of a case. It recently happened that two brothers were followed home one night through the streets of their village by a watchman who regarded them as suspicious characters. Entering their house and shutting the door, the two men observed through the crack that the watchman took up his stand outside. One therefore suggested to the other that they should get him into trouble by accusing him of some unjustified act of violence against themselves ; and it was finally agreed that the elder brother should shoot the younger in the leg, and that they should then declare that the officious watchman was the aggressor. The family gun was procured, the younger brother held out his leg, and the elder fired at him. Unfortunately, however, he was not a good shot, and the wretched victim, receiving the whole charge in his stomach, promptly died. The watchman was at once accused of the crime, and was sent to prison on a charge of man-slaughter. He also had a brother; and this man, thirsting for revenge, went to the enemy's house, and there shot himself in the leg, declaring to the people who rushed in that he had been the victim of a murderous assault. His story, however, was not believed, and at length the whole tale came out.

A year or two ago some natives who were harvesting in their fields sent one of their women down to the river for water. As she was returning with the water-jar upon her head, a boy of about fifteen years of age belonging to another family asked her to let him drink from the jar. This she refused to do, there was a quarrel, and the woman received a knife-wound from which she died. The boy's family at once handed him over to the relatives of the victim, and made no attempt to shield him from the consequences of his act. The aggrieved party, however, were by no means satisfied. " This is all very well," they said, " but you have killed one of our finest women, and you offer us a miserable little boy as the murderer. That will not do at all." They therefore accused the headman of the offending family, and concocted their story so well that he was found guilty and sent to penal servitude.

In conclusion I must relate one more story in order to illustrate the peculiar manner in which tragedy and comedy go hand in hand amongst the children of Egypt. A well-known robber was arrested at a small station in the Sudân during the time when martial law was still in force; and he was promptly sentenced to death. The solitary English officer in charge of the post refrained from attending the execution, the arrangements for which were left to the discretion of his Egyptian colleagues. A gibbet was erected, and about nine o'clock on the next morning the condemned man was driven up to it in a mule-cart. The rope was passed round his neck, the mule was whipped up, and the cart passed from under the feet of the victim, who was left swinging in mid-air. The officer, however, had forgotten to tie the man's hands ; and he promptly swarmed up the rope to the cross-beam, there seating himself comfortably in the piping hot sunshine, while the troops stood gaping around him, the officer mopping his forehead in an ecstasy of heat and vexation. Nobody knew what to do. They could not shoot the man, for their orders were to hang him ; and, on the barren sandy ground, no stones could be found to throw at him in order to dislodge him. The Egyptian officer therefore entered into friendly conversation with him, begging him to come down and be hanged like a man, instead of sitting up there swinging his legs like a monkey. This the robber totally refused to do, and he declared that nothing short of a free pardon would induce him to descend. The officer therefore endeavoured to appeal to the man's better feelings, " Look here," he said, " it is all very nice for you, sitting up there in the breeze, but down here it is dreadfully hot ; and, you know, none of us have yet had our breakfasts, and we are feeling extraordinarily faint and uncomfortable. Please do come down and be hanged properly, or I, for my part, will most certainly be sick."

The robber, however, refused to move ; and at last the English officer was sent for, who, acting in accordance with an unwritten law, pardoned him there and then, thereby enlisting the faithful services of a scout who has since done very valuable work.

CHAPTER XV

AN ANCIENT EGYPTIAN POEM

A CENTURY ago, when the hieroglyphical script of the Ancient Egyptians first began to be deciphered, it would hardly have been believed possible that scholars would one day find themselves possessed of such a vast literature as is now at the disposal of Egyptologists ; nor would it have been dreamed that the subtilties of the language, the idioms, or even the grammatical structure, would ever be so fully understood as they are at the present day. Thanks mainly to the diligent work of a group of painstaking German Jews, and to the brilliant labours of a handful of European and American scholars, we can now translate the many hieroglyphic or hieratic texts which have come down to us, with a degree of accuracy almost equal to that obtained in our renderings of Greek and Latin. Poems, prayers, tales serious and comic, historical narratives, satires, and letters, are now able to be put into modern language with the full certainty that the meaning has been grasped ; and the wealth and variety of the material thus presented to us is astonishing.

One of the most remarkable documents of all those which have come down from Pharaonic times is that which records the dialogue between a man about to commit suicide and his own soul, composed somewhere about the year B.C. 2000. The papyrus upon which it is written is now preserved in Berlin ; and the text has been translated by Professor Erman and Professor Breasted, whose renderings I have, in the main, here followed. The man is supposed to be weary of his mortal life, owing, it would seem, to the fact that his body has been disfigured by some dreadful mutilation, perhaps inflicted by his enemies ; and the burden of the flesh has

become intolerable to him. His soul, however, enjoys
its sojourn upon earth, and has no desire to be launched
into another sphere. The distinction between soul and
body is somewhat difficult for us to understand, but
actually it may be supposed that the dialogue represents
the battle in the unfortunate man's mind between the
desire for freedom from bodily pain on the one hand, and
the dread of death on the other.

"Recollect," says the life-loving soul, "that burial is
lamentation and a bringer of tears, causing a man to be
full of sorrow. It is taking a man from his home and
casting him out upon the heights (of the desert). But
you will not be going up there that you may see the sun,
There are those who build (their tombs) in red granite.
who construct their sepulchres within a pyramid; there are
those who (lie) splendidly in splendid structures . . .
But their memorial altars are as forsaken as are (the
bodies of) those weary-ones who, without a surviving
relative, die on the pathway across the inundation, the
flood taking hold of them on the one side, the heat (of
the sun) on the other, and to whom (alone) the fish along
the brink of the water speak. Hearken to me !—pursue
the gladness of the day and forget sorrow."

But the man does not fear death so greatly as he dreads
life now that his body has become hideous and an object
to be shunned by others. "My name," he cries in the
bitterness of his distress, "is more horrible than the
stench of a (dead) bird on a summer day when the sun is
hot. . . . Yea, my name is more abhorrent than a
woman against whom gossip is told to her husband."
He then burst into a tirade against humanity in general.
"The quiet man perishes," he declares ; "the bold-faced
walk abroad. Hearts are full of thieving ; the (only)
man in whom one can trust is he of no understanding
. . . I am burdened with misery, and have no faithful
friend . . ."

Then, in the anguish of his mind, he utters a welcome to
Death which will stand for all time amongst the greatest

poems in existence. The brevity of his metaphors, which are yet amply descriptive, are reminiscent of the best Japanese poetry, and show the same masterly handling of the structure of imagination, the same ability in the selection of the essential materials for the formation of a mind-picture.

" Death is before me to-day
Like the recovery of a sick man ;
Like going out into the garden after an illness.
Death is before me to-day
Like the fragrance of myrrh ;
Like sitting under a (ship's) sail on a windy day.
Death is before me to-day
Like the scent of lotus flowers ;
Like resting on the roadside to drink deep.
Death is before me to-day
Like the course of the overflowing water-channel,
Like the return of a man from a ship of war to his house.
Death is before me to-day
Like the clearing of (mist from) the sky ;
Like a man fowling therein toward that of which he was not aware.
Death is before me to-day
As a man craves to see his home
When he has spent years in captivity."

I doubt whether, in the whole world's literature, Death has ever been portrayed in more alluring fashion or so sweetly sung. Could one but think of the experience of life's termination as being like that of going out from the monotony of the sick-room into the vivid freshness of the garden, when one's senses are all quickened by long absence from growing things, truly Death would be a sensation which would make all the distress of life worth while. Or does the reader know the enchantment of sitting upon the deck of a Nile-vessel when the steady north wind fills out the great sail above him, white against the deep blue of the sky, and drives the prow through the waters with the insistency of nature itself ? Does he know that indefinable sense of reliability which is conveyed to a sailor by the straining sail spread above him in the sunlight ?   Has he felt the confident exultation of that passage through the waters, when the mind, aware of the destination, is absorbed by the majesty of the journey? Even so, says our poet, is Death; the triumphant rush forward to a sure harbour. The picture of the over-flowing water-channel is one that will best be appreciated by those who have lived amongst the fields of Egypt. The farmer digs a rough channel through the soil with his hoe, and into this he suddenly releases the water which has been held back awhile by a little bank of earth, so that it rushes forward on to the rich ground, travelling along its appointed way in the sunlight. And to the joyful overflow of the cool water upon the prepared earth the poet tells us that Death is to be likened.

The metaphor in regard to the clearing of the mist requires to be explained before its extreme beauty can be appreciated by those unfamiliar with Egypt. Upon a reed-covered lake of the Delta a hunter's canoe is silently propelled through the dense, white mist of early morning, as yet undissolved by the risen sun. Presently the little craft comes to rest amidst the tall stems of the papyrus-plants; and in the stillness of the morning the clearing of the air is awaited, in order that the hunter may learn in which direction to move towards his quarry. Then, of a sudden, the sun breaks through the vapour, the white volume of the mist rolls aside, and he finds himself already in full, close view of the flock of duck and wild-fowl which he is seeking but of whose presence he was not aware. Even so is Death: the rending of the mist, and the sudden, proximate vision of that which stirs a hunter's heart.

As the lines of this poem are read and their sense is received by the brain, the series of pictures spring into life in the imagination with a clarity which is evidence of the author's mastery in the selection of words. Each sentence is expressed with such lucidity, such poignancy, and such convincing brevity, that the brain responds almost automatically. The meaning of the words leaps to the mind, the curtain swings up, the picture is seen in its perfection; and so clear is the vision that one is almost loath to read on and thus to change the scene. But not only is a series of pictures called before the imagination : there is also their application to the poet's imagery of Death ; and, line by line, the reader is introduced to mankind's ultimate tragedy in a new and wondrous aspect.

In spite of this laudation of Death, the soul still protests against the destruction of its earthly home ; and there-upon the man describes the great privileges enjoyed by " those who are yonder ", that is to say, the dead. They shall sit, he declares, in the barque of the sun and shall traverse the sky like the stars ; they shall converse face to face with the solar gods and shall not be repelled by them ; and they shall at last be able to inflict punish-ment for evil-doing where punishment is due, and shall seize hold of the wicked in the manner of the living gods. The idea of an ultimate Justice, and of the ability of the dead to sit in judgment upon those who had wronged them in life, at length overcome the scruples of the soul ; and the embittered man is thus left free to put an end to his existence.

CHAPTER XVI

THE STORY OF THE SHIPWRECKED SAILOR

WHEN the early Spanish explorers led their expeditions to Florida, it was their intention to find the Fountain of Perpetual Youth, tales of its potent waters having reached Peter Martyr as early as 1511. This desire to discover the things pertaining to Fairyland has been, throughout history, one of the most fertile sources of adventure. From the days when the archaic Egyptians penetrated into the regions south of the Cataracts, where they believed that the inhabitants were other than human, and into Pount, the " land of the Gods," the hope of Fairyland has led men to search the face of the earth and to penetrate into its unknown places. It has been the theme of countless stories : it has supplied material for innumerable songs.

And in spite of the circumambulations of science about us, in spite of the hardening of all the tissues of our imagination, in spite of the phenomenal development of the commonplace, this desire for a glimpse of the miraculous is still set deeply in our hearts. The old quest of Fairyland is as active now as ever it was. We still presume, in our unworthiness, to pass the barriers, and to walk upon those paths which lead to the enchanted forests and through them to the city of the Moon. At any moment we are ready to set forth, like Arthur's knights, in search of the Holy Grail.

The explorer who penetrates into Central Africa in quest of King Solomon's mines is impelled by a hope closely akin to that of the Spaniards. The excavator who digs for the buried treasures of the Incas or of the

Egyptians is often led by a desire for the fabulous. Search was recently made in the western desert of Egypt for a lost city of burnished copper ; and the Anglo-Egyptian official is constantly urged by credulous natives to take camels across the wilderness in quest of a town whose houses and temples are of pure gold. What archæologist has not at some time given ear to the whispers that tell of long-lost treasures, of forgotten cities, of Atlantis swallowed by the sea ? It is not only the children who love the tales of Fairyland. How happily we have read Kipling's *Puck of Pook's Hill*, De la Motte Fouqué's *Undine*, Kenneth Graham's *Wind in the Willows*, or F. W. Bain's *Indian Stories*. Fairy plays, such as Barrie's *Peter Pan*, and Maeterlinck's *Blue Bird* have been enormously successful. Say what we will, fairy tales still hold their old power over us, and still we turn to them as a relief from the commonplace.

Some of us, failing to find Fairyland upon earth, have transferred it to the kingdom of Death ; and it has become the hope for the future. Each Sunday in church the congregation of business men and hard-worked women set aside the things of their monotonous life, and sing the songs of the endless search. To the rolling notes of the organ they tell the tale of the Elysian Fields : they take their unfulfilled desire for Fairyland and adjust it to their deathless hope of Heaven. They sing of crystal fountains, of streets paved with gold, of meadows dressed with living green where they shall dwell as children who now as exiles mourn. There everlasting spring abides and never-withering flowers ; there ten thousand times ten thousand clad in sparkling raiment throng up the steeps of light. Here in the church the most unimaginative people cry aloud upon their God for Fairyland.

> " The roseate hues of early dawn,
>   The brightness of the day,
>   The crimson of the sunset sky,
>   How fast they fade away !
>   Oh, for the pearly gates of Heaven,
>   Oh, for the golden floor . . ."

They know no way of picturing the incomprehensible state of the future, and they interpret it, therefore, in the terms of the fairy tale.

I am inclined to think that this sovereignty of the fairies is beneficial. Fairy tales fill the minds of the young with knowledge of the kindly people who will reward with many gifts those who are charitable to the old ; they teach a code of chivalry that brings as its reward the love of the beautiful princess in the tower ; they tell of dangers overcome by courage and perseverance ; they suggest a contact with nature which otherwise might never be developed. Where angels and archangels overawe by their omnipotence, the microscopic fairies who can sit singing upon a mushroom and dangle from the swaying stem of a bluebell, carry the thoughts down the scale of life to the little and really important things. A sleepy child will rather believe that the Queen of the Fairies is acting sentry upon the knob of the bedpost than that an angel stands at the head of the cot with great wings spread in protection—wings which suggest the probability of claws and a beak to match.

The dragons which can only be slain by the noble knight, the enchantments which can only be broken by the outwitting of the evil witch, the lady who can only be won by perils bravely endured, form the material of moral lessons which no other method of teaching could so impress upon the youthful mind.

And when mature years are attained the atmosphere of Fairyland remains with us. The lost songs of the little people drift through the brain, recalling the infinite possibilities of beauty and goodness which are so slightly out of reach; the forgotten wonder of elves and brownies suggests itself to us from the heart of flowers and amidst the leaves of trees. The clear depths of the sea take half their charm from the memory of the mermaid's palace ; the silence of forests is rich with the expectancy of the Knight of the Golden Plume ; the large spaces of kitchens and corridors are hushed for the concealment of Robin Goodfellow.

It is the elusiveness, the enchantment of Fairyland which, for the mature mind, constitutes its greatest value and charm ; it is a man's desire for the realms of Midsummer-night that makes the building of those realms in our childhood so valuable. We are constantly endeavouring to recapture the grace of that intangible kingdom, and the hope of ultimate success retains the elasticity of the mind. Held fast by the stiffened joints of reason and closeted with the gout of science, we are fettered prisoners in the world unless there be the knowledge that something eludes us to lead us on. We know quite well that the fairies do not exist, but at the same time we cannot deny that the elusive atmosphere of Fairyland is one with that of our fondest dreams.

Who has not, upon a grey morning, awakened from sleep with the knowledge that he has passed out from a kingdom of dream more dear than all the realms of real life ? Vainly we endeavour to recall the lost details, but only the impression remains. That impression, however, warms the tone of our whole day, and frames our thoughts as it were with precious stones. Thus also it is with the memory of our childhood's idea of Fairyland : the impression is recalled, the brain peers forward, the thoughts go on tiptoe, and we feel that we have caught a glimpse of Beauty. Indeed, the recollection of the atmosphere created in our youthful minds by means of fairy tales is perhaps the most abundant of the sources of our knowledge of Beauty in mature years.

I do not suppose that I am alone in declaring that some of the most tender feelings of childhood are inspired by the misfortunes of the Beast in the story of " Beauty and the Beast " ; and the Sleeping Beauty is the first love of many a small boy. Man, from his youth up, craves enchantment ; and though the business of life gives him no opportunity for indulging in day-dreams, there are few of us indeed who have not at some time sought the phantom isles and sought in vain. There is no stormy night, when the wind moans through the trees, and the

moon-rack flies overhead, but takes something of its
mystery from the recollection of the enchantments of the
dark ages.   The sun does not sink into the sea amidst the
low-lying clouds but some vague thought is brought to
mind of the uncharted isle whereon that maiden lies
sleeping whose hair is dark as heaven's wrath, and whose
breast is white like alabaster in the pathway of the moon.
There she lies in the charmed circle under the trees, where
none may enter until that hour when some pale, lost
mariner shall surprise the secret of the pathway, and,
coming suddenly upon her, shall kiss her shadowed lips.
Vague, elusive, undefined, as such fancies must be, they
yet tinge the thoughts of almost every man at certain
moments of his life, and set him searching for the enchantment of bygone days.   Eagerly he looks for those

> " .   .   .   Magic casements opening on the foam
> Of perilous seas, in faery lands forlorn " ;

and it is the fact of their unreality that gives them their
haunting value.

The following story, preserved in a papyrus now believed to be at Petrograd, describes a mysterious
island whereon there dwelt a monster most lovable and
most forlorn : a creature so tenderly drawn, indeed, that
the reader will not fail to enthrone him in the little company of the nobility of the kingdom of the fairy tale.
Translations of the story by two or three *savants* have
appeared ; but the present version, which I give in its
literal form, has been prepared especially for me by
Dr. Alan Gardiner ; and, coming from him, it may be
said to be the last word of the science upon the subject
of this difficult text, which, after much study, I had to
confess was beyond my powers as a student of the
Ancient Egyptian language.

The scene with which the story opens is clearly indicated
by the introductory sentences, though actually it is not
described.   A large war-galley had come swinging down
the Nile from the land of Wawat in the south, the oars
flashing in the Nubian sunlight.   On the left the granite

rocks of the island of Bigeh towered above the vessel ; on the right the island of Philae, as yet devoid of buildings, rested placidly on the blue waters.   Ahead were the docks of Shallal, where the clustered boats lay darkly against the yellow of the desert, and busy groups of figures, loading and unloading cargoes, moved to and fro over the sand.   Away to the left, behind Bigeh, the distant roar of the First Cataract could be heard as the waters went rushing down from Nubia across the frontier into Egypt.

The great vessel had just returned from the little-known country of Ethiopia, which bordered the Land of Ghosts, having its frontiers upon the shores of the sea that encircled the world ; and the sailors were all straining their eyes towards these docks which formed the southernmost outpost of Egypt, their home.   The greatest excitement prevailed on deck ; but in the cabin, erected of vari-coloured cloth in the stern of the vessel, the noble leader of the expedition which was now at its conclusion lay in a troubled sleep, tossing nervously upon his bed. His dreams were all of the terrible ordeal which was before him.   He could take no pleasure in his home-coming, for he was driven nigh crazy by the thought of entering the presence of the great Pharaoh himself in order to make his report.

It is almost impossible to realise nowadays the agonies of mind that a man had to suffer who was obliged to approach the incarnation of the sun upon earth, and to crave the indulgence of this god in regard to any short-comings in the conduct of the affairs entrusted to him. Of all the kings of the earth the Pharaoh was the most terrible, the most thoroughly frightening.   Not only did he hold the lives of his subjects in his hand to do with them as he chose, but he also controlled the welfare of their immortal souls ; for, being a god, he had dominion over the realms of the dead.   To be censured by the Pharaoh was to be excommunicated from the pleasures of this earth and outlawed from the fair estate of heaven. A well-known Egyptian noble named Sinuhe, the hero of a fine tale of adventure, describes himself as petrified with terror when he entered the audience chamber. " I stretched myself on my stomach," he writes, " and became unconscious before him (the Pharaoh). This god addressed me kindly, but I was as a man overtaken by the twilight : my soul departed, my flesh trembled ; my heart was no more in my body that I should know life from death."[1] Similarly another personage writes : " Remember the day of bringing the tribute, when thou passest into the Presence under the window, the nobles on each side before his Majesty, the nobles and ambassadors (?) of all countries. They stand and gaze at the tribute, while thou fearest and shrinkest back, and thy hand is weak, and thou knowest not whether it is life or death that is before thee ; and thou art brave (only) in praying to thy gods : ' Save me, prosper me this one time.' "[2]

Of the Pharaoh it is written—

" Thine eye is clearer than the stars of heaven ;
Thou seest farther than the sun.
If I speak afar off, thine ear hears ;
If I do a hidden deed, thine eye sees it."[3]

Or again—

" The god of taste is in thy mouth,
The god of knowledge is in thy heart ;
Thy tongue is enthroned in the temple of truth ;
God is seated upon thy lips."[4]

To meet face to face this all-knowing, all-seeing, celestial creature, from whom there could be no secrets hid nor any guilt concealed, was an ordeal to which a man might well look forward with utter horror. It was this terrible dread that, in the tale with which we are now concerned, held the captain of this Nubian vessel in agony upon his couch.

As he lay there, biting his finger-nails, one of the ship's officers, himself a former leader of expeditions, entered the cabin to announce their arrival at the Shallal docks.

[1] Sinuhe, 254-256.　　　　　[2] Papyrus Koller, 5, 1-4.
[3] Anastasi Papyri, **4, 5,** 5ff.　　[4] Kubban stela.

" Good news, prince," he said cheerfully to his writhing master. " Look, we have reached home. They have taken the mallet and driven in the mooring-post ; the ship's cable has been put on land. There is merrymaking and thanksgiving, and every man is embracing his fellow. Our crew has returned unscathed, without loss to our soldiers. We have reached the end of Wawat, we have passed Bigeh. Yes, indeed, we have returned safely ; we have reached our own land."

At this the prince seems to have groaned anew, much to the distress of his friend, who could but urge him to pull himself together and to play the man.

" Listen to me, prince," he begged," for I am one void of exaggeration. Wash yourself, pour water on your fingers."

The wretched man replied, it would seem, with a repetition of his fears ; whereupon the old sailor seems to have sat down by his side and to have given him a word of advice as to how he should behave in the king's presence. " Make answer when you are addressed," he said ; " speak to the king with a heart in you ; answer without restraint. For it is a man's mouth that saves him . . . But do as you will : to talk to you is weari- some (to you)."

Presently the old sailor was seized with an idea. He would tell a story, no matter whether it were strictly true or not, in which his own adventures should be set forth. He would describe how he was wrecked upon an unknown island, how he was saved from death, and how, on his return, he was conducted into the Pharaoh's presence. A narrative of his own experiences before his sovereign might give heart to his captain, and might effectually lift the intolerable burden of dread from the princely shoulders.

" I will relate to you," he began, " a similar thing which befell me my very self. I was making a journey to the mines of the sovereign . . ."

The prince may here be supposed to have sat up and given gloomy attention to his friend's words, for Egyptians

The Pharaoh Rameses II, B.C. 1292–1225. From his statue now at Turin

of all ages have loved a good story, and tales of adventure in the south were, in early times, most acceptable. The royal gold-mines referred to were probably situated at the southernmost end of the eastern Egyptian desert. To reach them one would take ship from Kossair or some other Red Sea port, sail down the coast to the frontiers of Pount, the modern Somaliland, and then travel inland by caravan. It was a perilous undertaking, and, at the time when this story was written, the journey must have furnished material for amazing yarns.

" I went down on the Great Green Sea," continued the speaker, " in a ship one hundred and fifty cubits[1] in length and forty cubits in breadth, and in it were a hundred and fifty sailors, picked men of Egypt. They scanned the heavens and they scanned the earth, and their hearts were stouter than lions. They foretold the storm or ever it came, and the tempest when as yet it was not."

A storm arose while they were out of sight of land, and rapidly increased in violence, until the waves, according to the very restrained estimate of the narrator, were eight cubits high—that is to say, about thirteen or fourteen feet. To one who was accustomed to the waves of the Nile, and was not familiar with those of the Red Sea, this would be a great height ; and the passage thus suggests that the scribe was an untravelled man. A vessel of 150 cubits, or about 250 feet, in length might have been expected to ride out a storm of this magnitude ; but, according to the story, she went to pieces, and the whole ship's company, with the single exception of the teller of the tale, were drowned. The survivor managed to cling to a plank of wood, which was driven by the wind towards the shores of an uncharted island, and here at length he was cast up by the waves.

Not far from the beach there was a small thicket, and to this the castaway hastened, sheltering therein from the fury of the storm. For three days in deep despair he lay hidden, " without a companion," as he said, " save

---

[1] The average cubit was about 20½ inches.

my heart " ; but at last the tempest subsided, the sun shone in the heavens once again, and the famished mariner was able to go in search of food, which, to his delight, he found in abundance.

The scene upon which he gazed as he plucked the fruit of the laden trees was most mysterious, and all that he saw around him must have had an appearance not altogether consistent with reality, for, indeed, the island was not real. It had been called into existence, perhaps, at the bidding of some god to relieve the tedium of an eternal afternoon, and suddenly it had appeared, floating upon the blue waters of the ocean. How long it had remained there, how long it would still remain, none could tell, for at any moment the mind of the god might be diverted, and instantly it would dissolve and vanish as would a dream. Beneath the isle the seas moved, and there in the darkness the fishes of the deep, with luminous, round eyes, passed to and fro, nibbling the roots of the trees above them. Overhead the heavens stretched, and around about spread the expanse of the sea upon which no living thing might be seen, save only the dolphins as they leapt in the sunshine and sank again amidst the gleaming spray.

There was abundant vegetation upon the island, but it does not appear to have looked quite real. The fig-trees were heavy with fruit, the vines were festooned from bough to bough, hung with clusters of grapes, and pomegranates were ripe for the plucking. But there seems to have been an unearthliness about them, as though a deep enchantment were upon them. In the tangled undergrowth through which the bewildered sailor walked there lay great melons and pumpkins. The breeze wafted to his nostrils the smell of the incense-trees ; and the scent of the flowers, after the storm, must have made every breath he breathed a pleasure of Paradise to him. Moving over the luxuriant ground, he put up flights of wonderful birds which sped towards the interior, red, green, and golden, against the sky. Monkeys chattered at him from the trees, and sprang from branch to branch amidst the dancing flowers. In shadowed pools of clear water fishes were to be seen, gliding amidst the reeds ; and amongst the rocks beside the sea the castaway could look down upon the creatures of the deep imprisoned between the tides.

Food in all forms was to hand, and he had but to fill his arms with the good things which Fate had provided. " I found there," he said, " figs, grapes, and all manner of goodly onions ; melons and pomegranates were there, and pumpkins of every kind. Fishes were there and fowls ; there was nought that was lacking in it. I satisfied myself, and set upon the ground the abundance of that with which my arms were filled. I took the fire-borer and kindled a fire, and made a burnt-offering to the gods."

Seated in the warm sunshine amidst the trees, eating a roast fowl seasoned with onions or some equally palatable concoction, he seems to have found the life of a shipwrecked mariner by no means as distressing as he had anticipated ; and the wording of the narrative appears to be so arranged that an impression of comfortable ease and security may surround his sunlit figure. Suddenly, however, all was changed. " I heard," said he, " a sound as of thunder, and I thought it was the waves of the sea." Then " the trees creaked and the earth trembled " ; and, like the Egyptian that he was, he went down on his shaking hands and knees, and buried his face in the ground.

At length " I uncovered my face," he declared, " and I found it was a serpent that came, of the length of thirty cubits "--about fifty feet—" and his tail was more than two cubits " in diameter. " His skin was overlaid with gold, and his eyebrows were of real lapis lazuli, and he was exceeding perfect."

" He opened his mouth to me," he continued, " as I lay on my stomach before him, and said to me : ' Who brought thee, who brought thee, little one ?—who brought thee ? If thou delayest to tell me who brought thee to this island I will cause thee to know thyself (again only) when thou art ashes and art become that which is not seen ' "—that is to say, a ghost.

" Thus you spoke to me," whispered the old sailor, as though again addressing the serpent, who, in the narration of these adventures, had become once more a very present reality to him, " but I heard it not. I lay before thee, and was unconscious."

Continuing his story, he told how the great serpent lifted him tenderly in his golden mouth, and carried him to his dwelling-place, setting him down there without hurt, amongst the fruit-trees and the flowers. The Egyptian at once flung himself upon his stomach before him, and lay there in a stupor of terror. The serpent, however, meant him no harm, and indeed looked down on him with tender pity as he questioned him once more.

" Who brought thee, who brought thee, little one ? " he asked again. " Who brought thee to this island of the Great Green Sea, whereof the (under) half is waves ? "

On his hands and knees before the kindly monster the shipwrecked Egyptian managed to regain possession of his faculties sufficiently to give an account of himself.

" I was going down to the mines," he faltered, " on a mission of the sovereign, in a ship one hundred and fifty cubits in length and forty in breadth, and in it were one hundred and fifty sailors, picked men of Egypt. They scanned the heavens and they scanned the earth, and their hearts were stouter than lions. They foretold the storm or ever it came, and the tempest when as yet it was not. Every one of them his heart was stout and his arm strong beyond his fellow. There was none unproven amongst them. The storm arose while we were on the Great Green Sea, before we touched land ; and as we sailed it redoubled (its strength), and the waves thereof were eight cubits. There was a plank of wood to which I clung. The ship perished, and of them that were in her not one was left saving me alone, who now am at your side. And I was brought to this island by the waves of the Great Green Sea."

At this point the man seems to have been overcome once more with terror, and the serpent, therefore, hastened to reassure him.

" Fear not, little one," he said in his gentle voice ; " fear not. Let not thy face be dismayed. If thou hast come to me it is God who has let thee live, who has brought thee to this phantom isle in which there is naught that is lacking, but it is full of all good things. Behold, thou shall pass month for month until thou accomplish four months upon this island. And a ship shall come from home, and sailors in it whom thou knowest, and thou shalt go home with them, and shalt die in thine own city."

" How glad is he," exclaimed the old mariner as he related his adventures to the prince, " how glad is he that recounts what he has experienced when the calamity is passed ! " The prince, no doubt, replied with a melancholy grunt, and the thread of the story was once more taken up.

There was a particular reason why the serpent should be touched and interested to hear how Providence had saved the Egyptian from death, for he himself had survived a great calamity, and had been saved from an equally terrible fate, as he now proceeded to relate.

" I will tell thee the like thereof," he said, " which happened in this island. I dwelt herein with my brothers, and my children were among them. Seventy-two serpents we were, all told, with my offspring and my brothers ; nor have I yet mentioned to thee a little girl brought to me by fortune. A star came down, and all these went up in flames. And it happened so that I was not together with them when they were consumed ; I was not in their midst. I could have died (of grief) for them when I found them as a single pile of corpses."

It is clear from the story that this great serpent was intended to be pictured as a sad and lonely, but most lovable, character. All alone upon this ghostly isle, the last of his race, one is to imagine him dreaming of the little girl who was taken from him, together with all his family. Although fabulous himself, and half divine, he was yet the victim of the gods, and was made to suffer real sorrows in his unreal existence. Day by day he wandered over his limited domain, twisting his golden body amidst the pumpkins, and rearing himself above the fig-trees, thundering down to the beach to salute the passing dolphins, or sunning himself, a golden blaze, upon the rocks. There remained naught for him to do but to await the cessation of the phantasy of his life ; and yet, though his lot was hard, he was ready at once to subordinate his sorrows to those of the shipwrecked sailor before him. No more is said of his distress, but with his next words he seems to have dismissed his own misfortunes, and to have attempted to comfort the Egyptian.

" If thou art brave," he said, " and restrainest thy longing, thou shalt press thy children to thy bosom and kiss thy wife, and behold thy house—that is the best of all things. Thou shalt reach home, and shalt dwell there amongst thy brothers."

" Thereat," said the mariner, " I cast me upon my stomach and touched the ground before him, and I said to him : ' I will tell of thy might to the Sovereign, I will cause him to be acquainted with thy greatness. I will let bring to thee the perfume and spices, myrrh and sweet-scented woods, and incense of the sanctuaries where-withal every god is propitiated. I will recount all that has befallen me, and that which I have seen by his might ; and they shall praise thee in that city before the magistrates of the entire land. I will slaughter to thee oxen as a burnt-offering, geese will I pluck for thee, and I will let bring to thee vessels laden with all the goodly things of Egypt, as may be (fitly) done to a god who loves men in a distant land, a land unknown to me '."

At these words the serpent opened his golden mouth and fell to laughing. The thought that this little mortal, grovelling before him, could believe himself able to repay the kindnesses received tickled him immensely.

" Hast thou not much incense (here, then) ? " he laughed. " Art not become a lord of frankincense ?

And I, behold I am prince of Pount," the land of perfumes,
" and the incense, *that* is my very own.   As for the spices
which thou sayest shall be brought, they are the wealth
of this island.   But it shall happen when thou hast left
this place, never shalt thou see this island more, for it
shall be changed to waves."

The teller of the story does not relate in what manner
he received this well-merited reproof.   The gentle monster, no doubt, was tolerant of his presumptuousness, and
soon put him at his ease again.   During the whole period
of the Egyptian's residence on the island, in fact, the
golden serpent seems to have been invariably kind to him.
The days passed by like a happy dream, and the spell of
the island's enchantment possessed him so that, in after
times, the details of the events of every day were lost in
the single illusion of the whole adventure.

At last the ship arrived, as it had been foretold, and the
sailor watched her passing over the hazy sea towards the
mysterious shore.   " I went and got me up into a tall
tree," he said, " and I recognised those that were in it.
And I went to report the matter (to the serpent), and
I found that he knew it."

Very tenderly the great monster addressed him.   " Fare
thee well, little one," he said.   " Fare thee well to thy
house.   Mayest thou see thy children and raise up a good
name in thy city.   Behold, such are my wishes for thee."

" Then," continued the sailor, " I laid me on my
stomach, my arms were bended before him.   And he gave
me a freight of frankincense, perfume and myrrh, sweet-
scented woods and antimony, giraffe's tails, great heaps
of incense, elephant tusks, dogs, apes and baboons, and
all manner of valuable things.   And I loaded them in
that ship, and I laid myself on my stomach to make
thanksgiving to him.   Then he said to me : " Behold,
thou shalt come home in two months, and shalt press thy
children to thy bosom, and shalt flourish in their midst ;
and there thou shalt be buried."

To appreciate the significance of these last words it is

necessary to remember what an important matter it was to an Egyptian that he should be buried in his native city. In our own case the position upon the map of the place where we lay down our discarded bones is generally not of first-rate importance and the thought of being buried in foreign lands does not frighten us. Whether our body is to be packed away in the necropolis of our city, or shovelled into a hole on the outskirts of Timbuctoo, is not a matter of vital interest. There is a certain sentiment that leads us to desire interment amidst familiar scenes, but it is subordinated with ease to other considerations. To the Egyptian, however, it was a matter of paramount importance. " What is a greater thing," says Sinuhe in the tale of his adventures in Asia, " than that I should be buried in the land in which I was born ? " " Thou shalt not die in a foreign land ; Asiatics shall not conduct thee to the tomb," says the Pharaoh to him ; and again, " It is no little thing that thou shalt be buried without Asiatics conducting thee." There is a stela now preserved in Stuttgart, in which the deceased man asks those who pass his tomb to say a prayer for his soul ; and he adjures them in these words : " So truly as ye wish that your native gods should praise you, and that ye should be established in your seats, and that ye should hand down your offices to your children : that ye should reach your homes in safety, and recount your travels to your wives ;— then say a prayer," &c.

The serpent was thus giving the castaway a promise which meant more to him than all the other blessings, and it was with a light heart indeed that he ran down to the beach to greet his countrymen. " I went down to the shore where the ship was," he continued, " and I called to the soldiers which were in that ship, and I gave praises upon the shore to the lord of this island, and likewise did they which were in the ship."

Then he stepped on board, the gangway was drawn up, and, with a great sweep of the oars, the ship passed out into the open sea. Standing on deck amongst the new cargo, the officers and their rescued friend bowed low to the great serpent who towered above the trees at the water's edge, gleaming in the sunshine. " Fare thee well, little one," his deep voice rolled across the water ; and again they bowed in obeisance to him.   The main-sail was unfurled to the wind, and the vessel scudded bravely across the Great Green Sea ; but for some time yet they must have kept their eyes upon the fair shape of the phantom island, as the trees blended into the hills and the hills at last into the haze ; and their vision must have been focussed upon that one gleaming point where the golden serpent, alone once more with his memories, watched the ship moving over the fairy seas.

" So sailed we northwards," said the sailor, " to the place of the Sovereign, and we reached home in two months, in accordance with all that he had said.   And I entered in before the Sovereign, and I brought to him this tribute which I had taken away from within this island.   Then gave he thanksgivings for me before the magistrates of the entire land.   And I was made a ' Follower ', and was rewarded with the serfs of such an one."

The old sailor turned to the gloomy prince as he brought his story to an end.   " Look at me," he exclaimed, " now that I have reached land, now that I have seen (again in memory) what I have experienced.   Hearken thou to me, for behold, to hearken is good for men."

But the prince only sighed the more deeply, and, with a despairing gesture, replied : " Be not (so) superior, my friend ! Doth one give water to a bird on the eve, when it is to be slain on the morrow ? " With these words the manuscript abruptly ends, and we are supposed to leave the prince still disconsolate in his cabin, while his friend, unable to cheer him, returns to his duties on deck.

CHAPTER XVII

THEBAN THIEVES

THEBES was the ancient capital of Egypt, and its ruins are the most extensive in the Nile Valley. On the east bank of the river, at the modern towns of Luxor and Karnak, there are the remains of mighty temples; and on the west bank, in the neighbourhood of the village of Gurneh, tombs, mortuary chapels, and temples literally cover the ground. The inhabitants of these three places have for generations augmented their incomes by a traffic in antiquities, and the peasants of Gurneh have, more especially, become famous as the most hardy pilferers of the tombs of their ancestors in all Egypt. In conducting this lucrative business they have lately had the misfortune to be recognised as thieves and robbers by the Government, and it used to be one of my duties to point this out to them. As a matter of fact they are no more thieves than you or I. It is as natural for them to scratch in the sand for antiquities as it is for us to pick flowers by the roadside; antiquities, like flowers, are the product of soil, and it is largely because the one is more rare than the other that its promiscuous appropriation has been constituted an offence. The native who is sometimes child enough to put his eyes out rather than serve in the army, who will often suffer all manner of wrongs rather than carry his case to the local courts, and who will hide his money under his bed rather than trust it to the safest bank, is not likely to be intelligent enough to realise that, on scientific grounds, he is committing a crime in digging for scarabs. He is beginning to understand that in the eyes of the law he is a criminal, but he has not yet learnt so to regard himself. I here name him thief, for officially that is his designation ; but there is no sting in the word, nor is any insult intended. By all cultured persons the robbery of antiquities must be regarded as a grave offence, and one which has to be checked. But the point is ethical ; and what has the Theban to do with ethics ?

The robbery of antiquities is carried out in many different ways and from many different motives. Sometimes it is romantic treasure hunting that the official has to deal with ; sometimes it is adventurous robbery with violence ; sometimes it is the taking advantage of chance discoveries ; sometimes it is the pilfering of objects found in authorised excavations ; and sometimes it is the stealing of fragments smashed from the walls of ancient monuments. All these forms of robbery, except the last, may call for the sympathy of every reader of these lines who happens not to have cultivated that vaguely defined " archæological sense " which is, practically, the product of this present generation alone ; and in the instances which are here to be given the point of view of the " Theban thief " will be readily appreciated.

Treasure hunting is a relic of childhood that remains, like all other forms of romance and adventure, a permanently youthful feature in our worn old hearts. It has been drilled into us by the tales of our boyhood, and, in later life, it has become part of that universal desire to get something for nothing which lies behind our most honest efforts to obtain the goods of this world. Who has not desired the hidden wealth of the late Captain Kidd, or coveted the lost treasure of the Incas ? I once wrote an article which was entitled *Excavations in Egypt*, but the editor of the magazine in which it appeared hastily altered these words to *Treasure Hunting in Egypt*, and thereby commanded the attention of twice the number of readers. Can we wonder, then, that this form of adventure is so often met with in Egypt, the land of hidden treasure ? The Department of Antiquities has published a collection of mediæval traditions with regard to this subject, which is known as the Book of the Pearl.

In it one is told the exact places where excavations should be made in order to lay bare the wealth of the ancients. " Go to such and such a spot," says this curious book, " and dig to the depth of so many cubits, and you will find a trapdoor ; descend through this and you will find a chamber wherein are forty jars filled with gold.   Take what you want, and give thanks to God."   Many of the sites referred to have been literally hacked out of all recognition by the picks and spades of thousands of gold-seekers ; and it may be that sometimes their efforts have been rewarded, since a certain amount of genuine infor-mation is embodied in the traditions.   The late Sir Gaston Maspero, Director-General of the Cairo Museum, used to tell a story of how a native came to him asking permission to excavate at a certain spot where he believed treasure to be hidden.   Sir Gaston accompanied him to the place, and a tunnel was bored into what appeared to be virgin sand and rock.   At the end of the first day's work the futility of his labours was pointed out to the man, but he was not to be daunted.   For two more days he stood watching the work from morn to nightfall with hope burning in his eyes, and on the following morning his reward came.   Suddenly the ground gave way before the picks of the workmen, and a hole was seen leading into a forgotten cave.   In this cave the implements of some mediæval coiners were discovered, and an amount of metal, false and true, was found which had been used by them in the process of their business.

A short time ago a man applied for permission to per-form a similar kind of excavation at a place called Nag Hamadi, and in my absence permission was given him. On my return the following report was submitted : "   . . . Having reached up the spot indicated the man started to blow the stones by means of the Denamits. Also he slaught a lamb, thinking that there is a treasure, and that when the lamb being slaught he will discover it at once."   In plainer English, the man had blown up the rocks with dynamite, and had attempted to further his efforts by sacrificing a lamb to the *djin* who guarded the treasure. The *djin*, however, was not thus to be propitiated, and the gold of the Pharaohs was never found. More recently the watchmen of the famous temple of Der el Bahri found themselves in trouble owing to the discovery that part of the ancient pavement showed signs of having been raised, stone by stone, in order that the ground below might be searched for the treasure which a tradition, such as those in the Book of the Pearl, had reported as lying hid there.

Almost as romantic and entertaining as treasure hunting is robbery with violence. We all remember our boyhood's fascination for piracy, smuggling, and the profession of Dick Turpin ; and to the Theban peasant, who is essentially youthful in his ideas, this form of fortune hunting has irresistible attractions. When a new tomb is discovered by authorised archæologists, especially when it is situated in some remote spot such as the Valley of the Kings, there is always some fear of an armed raid ; and the police guard the spot night and day until the antiquities have been removed to Cairo. The workmen who have been employed in the excavation return to their homes with wonderful tales of the wealth which the tomb contains, and in the evening the discovery is discussed by the women at the well where the water is drawn for the village, with the result that it very soon assumes prodigious proportions, inflaming the minds of all men with the greed of gold. Visitors often ask why it is that the mummies of the Pharaohs are not left to lie each in its own tomb ; and it is argued that they look neither congruous nor dignified in the glass cases of the museum. The answer is obvious to all who know the country : put them back in their tombs, and, without continuous police protection, they will be broken into fragments by robbers, bolts and bars notwithstanding. The experiment of leaving the mummy and some of the antiquities *in situ* has only once been tried, and it has not been a complete success. It was done in the case of the tomb of

Amenophis II at Thebes, the mummy being laid in its original sarcophagus'; and a model boat, used in one of the funeral ceremonies, was also left in the tomb.   One night the six watchmen who were in charge of the royal tombs stated that they had been attacked by an armed force ; and the tomb in question was seen to have been entered, the iron doors having been forced.   The mummy of the Pharaoh was found lying on the floor of the burial-hall, its chest smashed in ; and the boat had disappeared, nor has it since been recovered.   The watchman showed signs of having put up something of a fight, their clothes being riddled with bullet-holes ; but here and there the cloth looked much as though it had been singed, which suggested, as did other evidence, that they themselves had fired the guns and had acted the struggle.   The truth of the matter will never be known, but its lesson is obvious. The mummy was put back into its sarcophagus, and there it has remained secure ever since ; but one never knows how soon it will be dragged forth once more to be searched for the gold with which every native thinks it is stuffed.

Some years ago an armed gang walked off with a complete series of mortuary reliefs belonging to a tomb at Sakkârah.   They came by night, overpowered the watchmen, loaded the blocks of stone on to camels, and disappeared into the darkness.   Sometimes it is an entire cemetery that is attacked ; and, if it happens to be situated some miles from the nearest police-station, a good deal of work can be done before the authorities get wind of the affair.   One winter six hundred men set to work upon a patch of desert ground where a tomb had been accidentally found, and ere I received the news, they had robbed a score of little graves, many of which must have contained objects purchasable by the dealers in antiquities for quite large sums of money.   At Abydos a tomb which we had just discovered was raided by the villagers, and we only regained possession of it after a rapid exchange of shots, one of which came near ending my own gay career. But how amusing the adventure must have been for the raiders !

The appropriation of treasure-trove come upon by chance, or the digging out of graves accidentally discovered, is a very natural form of robbery for the natives to indulge in, and one which commends itself to the sympathies of all those not actively concerned in its suppression. There are very few persons even in western countries who would be willing to hand over to the Government a hoard of gold discovered in their own back garden. In Egypt the law used to be that the treasure-trove thus discovered belonged to the owner of the property ; and thus there was always a certain amount of excavation going on behind the walls of the houses. It is still the law that the peasants may carry away the accumulated rubbish on the upper layers of ancient town sites, in order to use it as a fertiliser for their crops, since it contains valuable phosphates. The work is supervised by watchmen, but this does not prevent the stealing of almost all the antiquities which are found. As illegal excavators, these sebakhîn, or manure-diggers, are the worst offenders for they search for the phosphates in all manner of places, and are constantly coming upon tombs or ruins which they promptly clear of their contents. One sees them driving their donkeys along the roads, each laden with a sack of manure, and it is certain that some of these sacks contain antiquities.

In Thebes many of the natives live inside the tombs of the ancient nobles, these generally consisting of two or three rock-hewn halls from which a tunnel leads down to the burial chamber. Generally this tunnel is choked with *débris*, and the owner of the house will perhaps come upon it by chance, and will dig it out, in the vain hope that earlier plunderers have left some of the antiquities undisturbed. It recently happened that an entire family was asphyxiated while attempting to penetrate into a newly-discovered tunnel, each member entering to ascertain the fate of the previous explorer, and each being overcome by the gases.   On one occasion I was asked by a native to accompany him down a tunnel, the entrance of which was in his stable, in order to view a sarcophagus which lay at the bottom.   We each took a candle, and crouching down to avoid the low roof, we descended the narrow, winding rabbit-hole of a passage, the loose stones sliding beneath our feet.   The air was very foul ; and below us there was a thunderous roar of thousands of wings beating through the echoing passage—the winds of evil-smelling bats.   Presently we reached this uncomfortable zone.   So thickly did the bats hang from the ceiling that the rock itself seemed to be black ; but as we advanced, and the creatures took to their wings, this black covering seemed to peel off the grey rock.   During the entire descent this curious spectacle of regularly receding blackness and advancing grey was to be seen a yard or so in front of us.   The roar of wings was now deafening, for the space into which we were driving the bats was very confined.   My guide shouted to me that we must let them pass out of the tomb over our heads.   We therefore crouched down, and a few stones were flung into the darkness ahead.   Then, with a roar and a rush of air, they came, bumping into us, entangling themselves in our clothes, slapping our faces and hands with their unwholesome wings, and clinging to our fingers.   At last the thunder died away in the passage behind us, and we were able to advance more easily, though the ground was alive with the bats maimed in the frantic flight which had taken place, floundering out of our way and squeaking shrilly.   The sarcophagus proved to be of no interest, so the encounter with the bats was to no purpose.

The pilfering of antiquities found during the course of authorised excavations is one of the most common forms of robbery.   The overseer cannot always watch the workmen sufficiently closely to prevent them pocketing the small objects which they find, and it is an easy matter to carry off the stolen goods even though the men are searched at the end of the day.   A little girl minding her father's sheep and goats in the neighbourhood of the excavations, and apparently occupying her hands with the spinning of flax, is perhaps the receiver of the objects. Thus it is more profitable to dig for antiquities even in authorised excavations than to work the water-hoist, which is one of the usual occupations of the peasant. Pulling the hoisting-pole down, and swinging it up again with its load of water many thousands of times in a day, is monotonous work ; whereas digging in the ground, with the eyes keenly watching for the appearance of antiquities, is always interesting and exciting. And why should the digger refrain from appropriating the objects which his pick reveals ? If he do not make use of his opportunities and carry off the antiquities, the western director of the works will take them to his own country and sell them for his own profit. All natives believe that the archæologists work for the purpose of making money. Speaking of Professor Flinders Petrie, a peasant said to me once : " He has worked five-and-twenty years now ; he must be *very* rich." He would never believe that the antiquities were given to museums without any payment being made to the finder.

The stealing of fragments broken out of the walls of " show " monuments is almost the only form of robbery which will receive general condemnation. That this vandalism is also distasteful to the natives themselves is shown by the fact that several better-class Egyptians living in the neighbourhood of Thebes subscribed, at my invitation, the sum of £50 for the protection of certain beautiful tombs. When they were shown the works undertaken with their money, they expressed themselves in a letter to me as being " pleased with the delicate inscriptions in the tombs, but very awfully angry at the damage which the devils of ignorant people had made." A native of moderate intelligence can quite appreciate the argument that whereas the continuous warfare between the agents of the Department of Antiquities and the illegal excavators of small graves is what might be called an honourable game, the smashing of public monuments cannot be called fair-play from whatever point of view the matter is approached.   Often revenge or spite is the cause of this damage.   It is sometimes necessary to act with severity to the peasants who infringe the rules of the Department, but a serious danger lies in such action, for it is the nature of the Thebans to revenge themselves not on the official directly but on the monuments which he is known to love.   Two years ago a native illegally built himself a house on Government ground, and I was obliged to go through the formality of pulling it down, which I did by obliging him to remove a few layers of brickwork around the walls.   A short time afterwards a famous tomb was broken into and a part of the paintings destroyed ; and there was enough evidence to show that the owner of this house was the culprit, though unfortunately he could not be convicted.   One man actually had the audacity to warn me that any severity on my part would be met by destruction of monuments.   Under these circumstances an official finds himself in a dilemma.   If he mantains the dignity and prestige of his Department by punishing any offences against it, he endangers the very objects for the care of which he is responsible ; and it is hard to say whether under a lax or a severe administration the more damage would be done.

The produce of these various forms of robbery is easily disposed of.   When once the antiquities have passed into the hands of the dealers there is little chance of further trouble.   The dealer can always say that he came into possession of an object years ago, before the antiquity laws were made, and it is almost impossible to prove that he did not.   You may have the body of a statue and he the head : he can always damage the line of breakage, and say that the head does not belong to that statue, or, if the connection is too obvious, he can say that he found the head while excavating twenty years ago on the site where now you have found the body.   Nor is it desirable to bring an action against the man in a case of this kind, for it might go against the official. Dealing in antiquities is regarded as a perfectly honourable business. The official, crawling about the desert on his stomach in the bitter cold of a winter's night in order to hold up a convoy of stolen antiquities, may use hard language in regard to the trade, but he can see that in the eyes of the natives there is not much against it. One of the Theban dealers led so holy a life that he will assuredly be regarded as a saint by future generations.

The sale of small antiquities to tourists was prohibited by me on the public roads, except at certain places ; but of course it could be done with impunity by the exercise of a little care. Men and boys and even little girls as they pass will stare at you with studying eyes, and if you seem to be a likely purchaser, they will draw from the folds of their garments some little object which they will offer for sale. Along the road in the glory of the setting sun there will come as fine a young man as you will see on a day's march. Surely he is bent on some noble mission : what lofty thoughts are occupying his mind, you wonder. But, as you pass, out comes the scarab from his pocket, and he shouts, " Wanty scarab, mister ?—two shillin'," while you ride on your way a greater cynic than before.

Some years ago a large inscribed stone was stolen from a certain temple, and was promptly sold to a man who sometimes traded in such objects. This man carried the stone, hidden in a sack of grain, to the house of a friend, and having deposited it in a place of hiding, tramped home, with his stick across his shoulders, in an attitude of deep unconcern. An enemy of his, however, had watched him, and promptly gave information. Acting on this the police set out to search the house. When we reached the entrance we were met by the owner, and a warrant was shown to him. A heated argument followed, at the end of which the infuriated man waved us in with a magnificent and most dramatic gesture. There were some twenty rooms in the house, and the stifling heat of

a July noon made the task none too enjoyable. The
police inspector was extremely thorough in his work, and
an hour had passed before three rooms had been searched.
He looked into the cupboards, went down on his knees
to peer into the ovens, stood on tiptoe to search the
fragile wooden shelves (it was a heavy stone which we
were looking for), hunted under the mats, and even peeped
into a little tobacco-tin.   In one of the rooms there were
three or four beds arranged along the middle of the floor.
The inspector pulled off the mattresses, and out from
under each there leapt a dozen rats, which, if I may be
believed, made for the walls and ran straight up them,
disappearing in the rafter-holes at the top.   The sight of
countless rats hurrying up perpendicular walls may be
familiar to some people, but, being abstemious, I venture
to call it an amazing spectacle, worthy of record.   Then
came the opening of one or two travelling-trunks.   The
inspector ran his hand through the clothes which lay
therein, and out jumped a few more rats, which likewise
went up the walls.   The searching of the remaining rooms
carried us well through the afternoon ; and at last, hot
and weary, we decided to abandon the hunt.   Two nights
later a man was seen walking away from the house with
a heavy sack on his back ; and the stone is now, no doubt,
in the Western hemisphere.

I must here relate the story of a very remarkable "deal"
in which I became involved, and which caused quite a
sensation in Cairo in the winter of 1912-13.

One of my native inspectors came to me in Cairo one
day, and reported that strange events were taking place
by night at a certain point upon the Suez Canal.   Some
Bedouin were camped in the desert upon the far side of
the Canal, and were said to be in possession of some fine
antique bronzes which were believed to have come from
Turkey or Syria ; and a certain Bulgarian dealer, named
Nikola Yamani, was endeavouring to purchase these and
to bring them secretly into Egypt for sale.   I therefore
gave the inspector the necessary instructions, with the

result that as soon as Nikola had made his purchase he was asked to bring the objects to the nearest office of the Department of Antiquities, which happened to be at the town of Zagazig, and there to give me the opportunity of buying them from him for the Cairo museum. Now it so happened that one of the Diplomatic Secretaries at the British Agency was anxious to finance some excavations amongst the ruins of the ancient Bubastis, near Zagazig ; and when I went down by train a few days later to look at these bronzes, he came with me to look at the site of his proposed excavations.

This simple fact caused all the trouble which I am about to relate ; for destiny moved in the following manner. The coming of the Diplomatic Secretary, shining in the reflected glory of his chief, Lord Kitchener, was tele-graphed to the Egyptian provincial Governor, who lived at Zagazig ; the Governor met us and took us in semi-state to lunch with him ; Nikola Yamani saw the procession, thought the whole might of the British Empire had come to seize his antiquities, dashed off to the Inspector's office, bribed the native clerk in charge to hide the one and only fine piece in the collection, and then sat down to await our arrival, satisfied that, even if we seized all the pieces, he would still be in possession of the important bronze statuette which now was hidden under a couch in an adjoining room.

Later, when we came to the office, I decided at once that the bronzes which were shown to me were not worth purchasing for the nation ; and, when we returned to Cairo, I described them to the head of the Museum, Sir Gaston Maspero, and we officially rejected them. Their owner, therefore, went to the office to claim them ; and his rage may be imagined when the rogue of a clerk, whom he had bribed to hide the best piece, looked him in the face and told him that he must have been bewitched, for no bronze had ever been hidden at all. A lie of this kind, which sounds so blatant to our ears, can easily pass muster in Egypt by the introduction of this suggestion that the victim has been bewitched ; for it is common knowledge there that persons who have fallen into the power of the *djins* often believe themselves possessed of imaginary wealth.

Nikola, angry and perplexed, at length decided to come to me in Cairo and to confess the truth ; and he arrived, a very tragic figure, with tears pouring from his eyes. " I listened to that wicked clerk," he said, " who told me that Lord Kitchener's Secretary would certainly seize the one good bronze for England, or you would seize it for Cairo ; and now my deceit has turned upon myself." He paced about the room, wringing his hands, as he spoke ; and I could but forgive him his deception, which had been due to a very natural fear, and promise to do my best to recover the bronze for him, since he had lost it while it had been at the office of my Department.

As a result of the steps which I took, the clerk was arrested, but denied all knowledge of the stolen antiquity ; Nikola, meanwhile, more or less burgled the house of the clerk, and was chased out by the inmates at the point of a revolver ; and at length, after strange adventures in the native underworld, we traced the bronze to a well-known Arab dealer, who, of course, declared that he knew nothing of the matter.

I then invited the above-mentioned Diplomatic Secretary, and a well-known colleague of his at the British Agency to help me, my idea being that the fear of the redoubtable Lord Kitchener, which had been the cause of the trouble, might now be employed to some purpose ; and these two good friends readily joined in the hunt. Space will not allow me to describe the exciting events which followed, and which might have formed the plot of a Sherlock Holmes adventure—our trapping the Arab dealer and holding him prisoner while a certain hiding-place of his was searched ; the false scents which he caused us to follow up ; our final exasperation with him, and the giving of a time-limit in which he was to confess if he wished to save himself from the deepest and darkest

dungeon in Cairo. Suffice it to say that, one minute
before the time-limit expired, the man confessed that he
had bought the missing bronze from the Zagazig clerk,
and had sold it to a well-known Italian dealer.

We then approached this latter dealer, telling him that
the object which he had bought had been stolen from
Nikola, and must be returned ; and, after further adventures, the bronze was at last handed back to its owner,
who came to me and, with tears of gratitude, blessed me
and my posterity unto the end of the world.

Up to this point I had not seen the object in question ;
but now my two friends saw it and described it to me,
and again I discussed with Sir Gaston Maspero the desira-
bility of purchasing it for the Museum. He objected,
however, to spend public money on an antiquity found
outside Egypt ; and he therefore gave Nikola permission
to dispose of it as he pleased. The man promptly offered
it to one of these two friends of mine, who as promptly
bought it ; and I then saw it for the first time. It represented a boy dressed in the ancient costume of Armenia
or Media, and wearing the royal crown of Armenia such
as that seen on the coins of Tigranes ; and it evidently
dated from Roman times. It was more interesting than
beautiful ; but it was certainly immensely valuable ; and,
having suggested to its new owner that he should give
some big museum the opportunity of purchasing it, I
introduced him to the representative of the Metropolitan
Museum of New York, who, however, did not take the
matter up.

My friend later explained to his colleague and myself
that he could not think of claiming sole possession of this
statuette, since we three together had rescued it and
brought it back to its original owner, and that, if it were
sold, he would wish us to have a share of the profits.
He then placed the figure in the hands of a well-known
dealer, and at length it was sold for a rather dis-
appointing sum.

Such was my only personal adventure into commerce ;

and even this, accidental as it was, would not have been permissible had the bronze been Egyptian, or found in Egypt, or had it been an object which the Cairo Museum ought to have acquired.

The attempt to regain a lost antiquity is seldom crowned with success. It is so extremely difficult to obtain reliable information; and as soon as a man is suspected his enemies will rush in with false accusations. Thirty-eight separate accusations were sent in against a certain head watchman during the first days after the fact had leaked out that he was under suspicion. Not one of them could be shown to be true. Sometimes one man will bring a charge against another for the better ment of his own interests. Here is a letter from a watch man who had resigned, but wished to rejoin. " To his Exec. Chief Director of the tembels. I have honour to inform that I am your servant X, watchman on the tembels before this time. Sir from one year ago I work in the Santruple (?) as a watchman about four years ago. And I not make anything wrong and your Exec. know me. Now I want to work in my place in the tembel, because the man which in it be not attintive to His, but always in the coffee . . . He also steal the scribed stones. Please give your order to point me again. Your servant, X." " The coffee " is, of course, the *café* which adjoins the temple.

Once a young man came to me with an accusation against his own father, who, he said, had stolen a statu-ette. The tale which he told was circumstantial, but it was hotly denied by his infuriated parent. He looked, however, a trifle more honest than his father, and when a younger brother was brought in as witness, one felt that the guilt of the old man would be the probable finding. The boy stared steadfastly at the ground for some moments, however, and then launched out into an elaborate explanation of the whole affair. He said that he asked his father to lend him four pounds, but the father had refused. The son insisted that that sum was

Gold cups and armlet of about B.C. 1000, found accidentally by a native in a mound by a roadside in Lower Egypt. Now in Cairo Museum

due to him as his share in some transaction, and pointed out that though he only asked for it as a loan, he had in reality a claim to it. The old man refused to hand it over, and the son therefore, waited his opportunity and stole it from his house, carrying it off triumphantly to his own establishment. Here he gave it into the charge of his young wife, and went about his business. The father, however, guessed where the money had gone ; and while his son was out, invaded his house, beat his daughter-in-law on the soles of her feet until she confessed where the money was hidden, and then, having obtained it, returned to his home. When the son came back to his house he learnt what had happened, and, out of spite, at once prepared the accusation which he had brought to me. The story appeared to be true in so far as the quarrel over the money was concerned, but that the accusation was invented proved to be untrue.

Sometimes the peasants have such honest faces that it is difficult to believe that they are guilty of deceit. A lady came to the camp of a certain party of excavators at Thebes, holding in her hand a scarab. " Do tell me," she said to one of the archæologists, " whether this scarab is genuine. I am sure it must be for I bought it from a boy who assured me that he had stolen it from your excavations, and he looked such an honest little fellow that I am sure he was speaking the truth."

In order to check pilfering in a certain excavation in which I was assisting we made a rule that the selected workmen should not be allowed to put unselected substitutes in their place. One day I came upon a man whose appearance did not seem familiar, although his back was turned to me. I asked him who he was, whereupon he turned upon me a countenance which might have served for the model of a painting of St. John, and in a low sweet voice he told me of the illness of the real workman, and of how he had taken over the work in order to obtain money for the purchase of medicine for him, they being friends from their youth up. I sent him away and told

s

him to call for any medicine he might want that evening. I did not see him again until about a week later, when I happened to meet him in the village with a policeman on either side of him, from one of whom I learned that he was a well-known thief. Thus is one deceived even in the case of real criminals : how then can one expect to get at the truth when the crime committed is so light an affair as the stealing of an antiquity ?

The following is a letter received from one of the greatest thieves in Thebes, who, when I last heard of him, was serving a term of imprisonment in the provincial gaol :—

" Sir General Inspector,—I offer this application stating that I am from the natives of Gurneh, saying the following :—

On Saturday last I came to your office and have been told that my family using the sate to strengthen against the Department. The result of this talking that all these things which somebody pretends are not the fact. In fact I am taking great care of the antiquities for the purpose of my living matter. Accordingly, I wish to be appointed in the vacant of watching to the antiquities in my village and promise myself that if anything happens I do hold myself responsible."

I have no idea what " using the sate to strengthen " means.

It is sometimes said that the European excavators are committing an offence against the sensibilities of the peasants by digging up the bodies of their ancestors. Nobody will repeat this remark who has walked over a cemetery plundered by the natives themselves. Here bodies may be seen lying in all directions, torn limb from limb by the gold-seekers ; here beautiful vases may be smashed to atoms in order to make more rare the specimens preserved. The peasant has no respect whatsoever for the sanctity of the ancient dead, nor does any superstition in this regard deter him in his work of destruction. Fortunately superstition sometimes checks other forms of robbery. *Djins* are believed to guard the hoards of ancient wealth which some of the tombs are thought to contain, as, for example, in the case of the tomb in which the family was asphyxiated, where a fiend of this kind was thought to have throttled the unfortunate explorers. Twin brothers are thought to have the power of changing themselves into cats at will ; and a certain Huseyn Osman, a harmless individual enough, and a most expert digger, would often turn himself into a cat at night-time, not only for the purpose of stealing his brother Mohammed Osman's dinner, but also in order to protect the tombs which his patron was occupied in excavating. One of the overseers in some recent excavations was said to have the power of detecting all robberies on his works. The archæologist, however, is unfortunately unable to rely upon this form of protection, and many are the schemes for the prevention of pilfering which are tried.

In some excavations a sum of money is given to the workman for every antiquity found by him, and these sums are sufficiently high to prevent any outbidding by the dealers. Work thus becomes very expensive for the archæologist, who is sometimes called upon to pay £10 or £20 in a day. The system has also another disadvantage, namely, that the workmen are apt to bring antiquities from far and near to " discover " in their diggings in order to obtain a good price for them. Nevertheless, it would appear to be the most successful of the systems. In the Government excavations it is usual to employ a number of overseers to watch for the small finds, while for only the really valuable discoveries is a reward given.

For finding the famous gold hawk's head at Hieraconopolis a workman received £14, and with this princely sum in his pocket he went to a certain Englishman to ask advice as to the spending of it. He was troubled, he said, to decide whether to buy a wife or a cow. He admitted that he had already one wife, and that two of them would be sure to introduce some friction into what was now a peaceful household ; and he quite realised that a cow would be less apt to quarrel with his first wife. The Englishman, very properly, voted for the cow, and the peasant returned home deep in thought. While pondering over the matter during the next few weeks, he entertained his friends with some freedom, and soon he found to his dismay that he had not enough money left to buy either a wife or a cow. Thereupon he set to with a will, and soon spent the remaining guineas in riotous living. When he was next seen by the Englishman he was a beggar, and, what was worse, his taste for evil living had had several weeks of cultivation.

The case of the fortunate finder of a certain great *cache* of mummies was different. He received a reward of £400, and this he buried in a very secret place. When he died his possessions descended to his sons. After the funeral they sat round the grave of the old man, and very rightly discussed his virtues until the sun set. Then they returned to the house and began to dig for the hidden money. For some days they turned the sand of the floor over; but failing to find what they sought, they commenced operations on a patch of desert under the shade of some tamarisks where their father was wont to sit of an afternoon. It is said that for twelve hours they worked like persons possessed, the men hacking at the ground, and the boys carrying away the sand in baskets to a convenient distance. But the money was never found.

It is not often that the finders of antiquities inform the authorities of their good fortune, but when they do so an attempt is made to give them a good reward. A letter from the finder of an inscribed statue, who wished to claim his reward, read as follows : " With all delight I please inform you that on 8th Jan. was found a headless temple of granite sitting on a chair and printed on it."

I will end this chapter as I began it, in the defence of the Theban thieves. In a place where every yard of ground contains antiquities, and where those antiquities may be so readily converted into golden guineas, can one wonder that every man, woman, and child makes use of his opportunities in this respect to better his fortune? The peasant does not take any interest in the history of mankind, and he cannot be expected to know that in digging out a grave and scattering its contents, through the agency of dealers, over the face of the globe, he loses for ever the facts which the archæologist is striving so hard to obtain. The scientific excavator does not think the antiquities themselves so valuable as the record of the exact arrangement in which they were found. From such data alone can he obtain his knowledge of the manners and customs of this wonderful people. When two objects are found together, the date of one being known and that of the other unknown, the archæological value of the find lies in the fact that the former will place the latter in its correct chronological position. But if these two objects are sold separately, the find may perhaps lose its entire significance. The trained archæologist records every atom of information with which he meets; the native records nothing. And hence, if there is any value at all in the study of the history of mankind, illegal excavation must be stopped.

CHAPTER XVIII

THE ERROR OF POMPOUS HISTORY

" REASON will tell you," wrote George Hakewill in 1627, " that old age or antiquity is to be accounted by the farther distance from the beginning and the nearer approach to the end, the times wherein we now live being in propriety of speech the most ancient since the world's creation." The same thought was expressed by Giordano Bruno in 1564, and by Pascal in his *Treatise on Vacuum*. " For as old age," the latter writes, " is that period of life most remote from infancy, who does not see that old age in this universal man ought not to be sought in the times nearest his birth, but in those most remote from it ? " " These present times," says Bacon, " are the ancient times, when the world is ancient, and not those which we account ancient, *ordine retrogrado* by a computation backward from ourselves."

It is curious to notice how completely we have all fallen into the error which these writers expose. We speak naturally of " the elder days," and we attribute to any period of the " olden times " an age which is in reality the sum of all the ages since. We seem to forget that antiquity, viewed as a period, is only old when we falsely add to it our own weight of years ; and that antiquities, as objects, are only hoary when they have taken upon them the marks of their slow attainment, century by century, to the venerable age in which we now live. It is the Present that is old and hoary, not the Past. It is To-day that is burdened with the cares of advanced life ; and, as compared with its heavy accountability, the bygone ages are light-hearted, irresponsible and unsubdued : for it is our own epoch, not theirs, that is encrusted with the corrosion of time.

When we essay to study history we are accustomed to take the Present as our standpoint, and, looking back to some remote period, we find it old with the years we have crossed to reach it. But the historian should rather take the Past as his natural standpoint, and should forget To-day ; for in dealing with bygone events it is surely obvious that we have no right to make the circumstances of our present existence our criterion. We must project ourselves into the youthful ages which we are studying, and must cast aside the cumbrous habits of thought which have been built up within us by the experiences of our ripe maturity. There is only one right way to examine the past years of mankind : we must look at them as, individually, we look at our own childhood, remembering the sensations and emotions of those times and contemplating life with those eyes. We cannot hope to comprehend the outlook of the Past unless we divest our minds of a large part of the world's subsequent experience ; for the Past is simply the nursery of the Present, and differs from it in just that degree in which a boy differs from a man.

The regarding of former ages as being ancient and hoary has led the historian to introduce them to the reader in an unnecessarily sober and heavy manner. It has long been the habit to write history as though the story of the Past were a solemn subject calling for a grave and even melancholy treatment. The writing of an historical treatise is usually regarded as a legitimate opportunity for the display of the author's turn for rhythmic prose or knowledge of punctuation and grammar. Rolling, dignified words, sentences which frown in their tremendousness, periods staid and smooth, are employed as the means whereby the picture of the Past, as he sees it, may be conveyed to the imagination of his readers. Macaulay even speaks of a certain subject as being " beneath the dignity of history." The historian fails to see that it is not the giving out of the facts, but only their discovery, which requires ponderous study.

The men and women who walked the earth in the days of its youth are not antiquated : the up-to-date young men and the modern young women are the real old fogies, for they are the tenants of the world's old age, the products of the most ancient phase of the human story. To the Past we must go as a relief from To-day's harshness ; for the Past is spread out before us as a children's garden, where jolly laughter and sudden, quick-ended tears are to be experienced ; where the waters are alive with mermen and the woods are filled with brownies ; where nymphs and fairies dwell among the flowers, and enchanted castles crown the hilltops ; where heroes die for fame, and the victors marry kings' daughters. There in that garden we may forget the mature cruelty and the sins of the present time ; for if there be wickedness in the Past, we may usually name it the thoughtless mischief of childhood.

One contemplates with positive relief the tortures and massacres of the distant ages, for they are child's play as compared with the reasoned brutality of these wicked olden days in which we now live. How pleasant it is to turn from the organised beastliness of our own times to the irresponsible slaughter of the early Christians in Rome or to the wholesale impalings and flayings which followed an Assyrian battle ! In the last-named cases we are but shocked at the suffering inflicted by the inhabitants of the world's nursery upon one another ; but in the other we are appalled by the spectacle of humanity's old men gleefully slaughtering one another.

The historian should always remember that by rights it is to the days of long ago that he and his readers ought to turn for those scenes which make their special appeal to the ardent eyes of youth. It is into the early times that we must all wander when, sick of life's conformity and weary of the cramped stiffness of the conventions amongst which we move, we would breathe the unen-closed air of a freer order of things. He must not, there-fore, amidst the stately forest of his phrases hide the gateway of this joyous domain both from himself and his followers. It should stand open and unconcealed at the end of the highroad which leads from the Present to the Past ; so that all those who make the great adventure and set out in search of the forgotten years shall, by his direction, find that gateway and pass through it into the land where the burden of To-day's old age drops from the shoulders and the buoyancy of the early times stimulates and enlivens.

There, in those enchanted regions, men are heroes and women are beautiful, and all that the heart desires is to be found. There, and perhaps only there, grow " the flower of peace, and the rose that cannot wither." Beyond that gateway stand the gorgeous palaces wherein sit the queens of the young world, of whose beauty the fairest women of our own age have but a semblance. There they rest upon their marble thrones, their loveliness causing the brain to reel and the heart to faint ; and into their presence the initiate may penetrate, unchecked and unannounced. Here in this garden a man may at will become one with burly Antony ; and with pleasant arrogance may mount the dais steps to Cleopatra's side, and put his arm about her bewildering shoulders. He may merge himself into splendid Lucullus, and watch with mild amusement the amazement of his self-invited guests, Cicero and Pompey, served at a moment's notice with a fifty-thousand drachmae dinner in the sumptuous apartment called " Apollo ".

In the twinkling of an eye, for so mighty is the magic of the garden, he may turn from Lucullus to become that Roman's enemy, the swift-footed royal athlete Mithradates, wooing the reluctant Monime in the palace of Miletus on the banks of Meander. Now he is young Cimon, intoxicated by the beauty of Asteria of Salamis ; and now he is Demetrius in the happy toils of the fair Lamia. Mounting the magic carpet he may leap over the seas and deserts to Babylon, where, with a gesture, he may become one with Sargon, and may parade the hanging gardens in the light of the tremendous moon. Away he may fly once more to the valley of the Nile, whence, in the guise of King Unis, he may ascend the " ladder of the sun ", burst open the " double gates of the sky ", and play with " the imperishable stars ".

There is no end to the entertainment which he may enjoy in the Garden of the Past ; and, coming back, happy and breathless, to his home in the Present, is it to be supposed that he, who is bursting with what he has seen and done, will desire to record in heavy and stately language the adventures he has experienced in that irresponsible playground ? He who writes the history of the Past in pompous phrases has never left the Present.

If, in revolt against his urban inaction, a man desires to kick his heels in the freedom of other lands, he need not travel to Monte Carlo or to Paris, there to shock the astonished natives by behaving himself in a manner not permitted in the city of his birth : he may, instead, seat himself by his fireside and, book in hand, may transport his cumbrous form to countries and periods which will view his eccentricities without amazement. Who will there question his sanity if he dress himself in seaweed and flounder about the floor, pretending to be a fish ? Did not the Society of Inimitable Livers thus amuse themselves in the royal palace at Alexandria ? Or who will accuse him of intemperance if he take his place amongst the guests at a feast in Memphis, and dance a jig for the applause of Pharaoh ? Has not Pharaoh himself said, as Herkhuf tells us, " My Majesty desires to see this man dance more than the treasure of Sinai, more than the gifts of Pount " ?

If he be in search of joke and jest, can he do better than read the tales of mankind's youth ? By his fireside, and exerting no muscle in the search for a merry atmosphere, he may see the worthy Antigonus, now grown old, walking the paved street of his city to pay a visit to his son Demetrius who lies ill in yonder house. He may watch the stern old man, as he is about to enter the door, met by a beautiful damsel who is coming out through it. Antigonus passes her without a sign, and entering the sickroom sits himself down by his son's bed and feels his pulse. "The fever has just left me," he may hear the young man say. "Yes," replies his father, looking straight before him, "I met it going out at the door." Or again, with no effort of the ears or eyes, he may see Marcus Appius rise in his place in a court at Rome and open his final speech for the defence with the words "I have been desired by my client to employ on his behalf industry, eloquence and fidelity . . ."; and he may hear the caustic Cicero respond in an undertone "And how have you had the heart not to accede to any one of his requests?"

If he be in search of love, there in the Past he will find it; for the bygone ages contain in themselves all the love of every man and woman who has ever lived. If he be concerned in the pursuit of beauty, there will he behold it; for all the loveliness that the sun and moon have looked upon are now become part of the Past. But, above all, if he be in quest of his childhood, of the high hopes and the beating pulse of youth, there in the playground of the Past he will find them.

In recent years there has been a very considerable tendency amongst jaded people to revive within themselves the pleasures of their childhood by an ardent, though often somewhat forced, emulation of the habits of infancy. The charm of the grown man or woman who can play joyously with children, and can enter enthusiastically into their amusements, has been perceived, and an attempt has been made to acquire this faculty. To play with children, however, requires the employment of a rare talent, of a difficult art; and there are many who, though loving the society of the young, feel aware after a while of the loss of a real interest in their pretences. It is no longer a pleasure, nay it is an agony, to fall head-long upon the lawn in the manner of a slain warrior; it is with a distressing effort of body and mind that we may now crawl under the bed and believe ourselves thus to have penetrated into an Oriental castle.

To those who desire to retain their childhood's atmosphere yet are conscious of these difficulties: a study of the days when the world was young comes as the supplying of a long-felt want. We who in our individual lives realise with sorrow how very far we have travelled from the schoolroom and the nursery, need not struggle vainly to revive interest in our own forgotten games; we may hasten instead to the world's childhood, there wholeheartedly to romp and wrestle, laugh and cry, make-believe and frolic, with the men and women of the Past. We shall not find ourselves too clumsy to play with *their* toys, nor too big to crawl into *their* houses, for their toys are real armies and kingdoms, and their houses real palaces of marble.

The writing of the history of the Past—I do not mean the collection of the data upon which the narrative is based—must no longer be regarded as the particular field of the very serious: rather let the deeds of To-day claim the dignified treatment of weighty men; for the Present and not the Past is the antiquated age, the age hung with cobwebs, the age that is as old as the hills. The story which the historian has to tell should be made to glow in the imagination, to be young and virile and full of the element of life; for of all men the student of the Past is the most closely in touch with Youth.

INDEX

Printed by
PURNELL AND SONS
PAULTON, ENGLAND